GENDER AND ARCHITECTURE

GENDER AND ARCHITECTURE

Edited by

Louise Durning
and
Richard Wrigley

JOHN WILEY & SONS, LTD

Chichester • New York • Weinheim • Brisbane • Singapore • Toronto

OTHER WILEY EDITORIAL OFFICES

John Wiley & Sons, Inc., 605 Third Avenue, New York, NY 10158-0012, USA

WILEY-VCH Verlag GmbH, Pappelallee 3, D-69469 Weinheim, Germany

Jacaranda Wiley Ltd, 33 Park Road, Milton, Queensland 4064, Australia

John Wiley & Sons (Asia) Pte Ltd, 2 Clementi Loop #02-01, Jin Xing Distripark, Singapore 129809

John Wiley & Sons (Canada) Ltd, 22 Worcester Road, Rexdale, Ontario M9W 1L1, Canada

LIBRARY OF CONGRESS CATALOGING-IN-PUBLICATION DATA

Gender and architecture / edited by Louise Durning and Richard
Wrigley.
    p. cm.
  Includes bibliographical references and index.
  ISBN 0-471-98532-5 — ISBN 0-471-98533-3 (pbk.)
  1. Architecture and women. 2. Feminism and architecture, 3. Space
(Architecture) I. Durning, Louise. II. Wrigley, Richard.

NA2543.W65 G455 2000
720'82—dc21
                                                            99–045847

BRITISH LIBRARY CATALOGUING IN PUBLICATION DATA

A catalogue record for this book is available from the British Library

ISBN 0-471-98532-5 (hardback)
ISBN 0-471-98533-3 (paperback)

Typeset in 9/12pt Caslon 224 by Mayhew Typesetting, Rhayader, Powys
Printed and bound in Great Britain by Bookcraft (Bath) Ltd, Midsomer Norton, Somerset
This book is printed on acid-free paper responsibly manufactured from sustainable forestry,
in which at least two trees are planted for each one used for paper production.

CONTENTS

INTRODUCTION

Louise Durning and Richard Wrigley

Architectural history has for too long been identified with a rather conservative refusal of methodological reflection, and remained at one remove from the willingness to embrace disciplinary and theoretical innovation and diversity that has informed art history during at least the last generation. Indicative of this retention of a predominantly formalist *modus operandi* has been the slowness with which architectural history has shown signs of taking on board any of the implications of work in gender studies, and the general problematics of the politics of sexuality. Consideration of visual art has been particularly fruitful in the exploration of different patterns of gendered identities because of the ways in which it depends on the constructed and contested nature of representation. Given its inherently social presence, it is therefore all the more surprising that the history of architecture has been called on so little in this avenue of investigation. Elaborate analysis of architecture's physicality and structure could be said to distract from, or be a substitute for, investigation of the production of meanings on and in its confines, spaces, thresholds, sight lines, arenas and stages. Yet architecture structures and defines many of the social spaces in which different gendered identities are rehearsed, performed and made visible as a form of shared private and public spectacle. Architecture and the spaces it creates are continuous; thus architectural space is not the container of identities, but a constitutive element in them.

Architectural history's priorities are beginning to change, but it is probably true to say that manifestations of critical, theoretically aware, gender-conscious architectural history are mostly to be found in relation to modern phenomena, above all the generic issue of urban space, and the role of gender politics in the contemporary architectural profession.[1] By contrast, the essays in this collection have deliberately been chosen because they address topics from the Renaissance to the early twentieth century. The topics' variety also serves to open up a complementary range of ways of thinking about the significance of gender in the production, use and representation of architecture, and within the historiography of architectural history. This latter issue is one addressed by many of the papers, in so far as their authors seek to situate their work in the context of earlier studies; that is, not merely as regards matters of empirical novelty, but rather in terms of the attention that has been given or not to gender politics. The present volume is intended as a contribution to the opening up of this important area of cultural history.

Of all the components in architectural history which have resisted properly historical analysis, the most unavoidable must be the assumed centrality of classicism in European architecture. The myth of classicism has flourished because it has been assumed to be synonymous with the inevitable progress of humanistic values. Christy Anderson analyses a key moment in English architectural history, one, indeed, which has been presumed to be foundational in the assimilation of Continental values and practices. She shows that the 'heroic' role conventionally ascribed to Inigo Jones in this process needs to be replaced by a contextualized understanding of the close connection between architecture and a specific configuration of masculinity. Jones's own remarks on this have tended to be taken for granted as part and parcel of the onward march of classicism in English architecture. However, as Anderson argues, architecture gave a public and physical form to a changing ideal of masculinity just at the time when those ideas were taking shape. Thus, what emerges is a historicized alignment between a specific mode of masculinity, and a new architectural idiom – also involving a significant shift in the cultural status of the architectural profession. The visual style (or at least the style to which Jones *et al.* aspired) inscribed certain conventions and values which were also to be found in other significant sites for the display of culturally distinguished masculinity, notably the highly conventionalized phenomenon of men's vestimentary identity.

Joanne Mosley explores the nature of literary architecture in the sixteenth century in the work of four important authors, two male – Rabelais and Montaigne – and two female – Marguerite de Navarre and St Teresa of Avila. Each of these authors uses an evocation of an edifice to convey his or her central ideas, which are in each case aspects of the theme of freedom and captivity – ideas with strongly gendered associations. Literary architecture is inherently symbolic; different forms of spiritual and intellectual struggle and liberation are narrated using metaphors of solidity and durability, enclosure and elevation. In his narrative of the exploits of Gargantua, Rabelais describes at length the elaborate architectural complex of the Abbey of Thélème, a utopian realm, where, amongst other enlightened freedoms, equality of the sexes reigns. Despite the detailed description of the edifice, Rabelais leaves the reader in no doubt that the benign order which prevails in the Abbey is an elaborate figment of his imagination. For Montaigne, his tower was a place of retreat – one feasible because his role as owner and head of family allowed him to resort to this mode of self-elected confinement (which in practice meant one where women were excluded). This was for Montaigne a symbolic space for reflection and composition. Yet the attainment of this condition of authorial independence was dependent on his prerogative as paterfamilias to disengage from domestic life. Marguerite de Navarre's poem *The Prisons* encapsulates a journey from secular, worldly captivity to spiritual freedom, initially articulated through the voice of a male protagonist. This reduces the text's autobiographical character, but extends its signification. Successive prisons are evoked in language which blurs the distinction between fantasy and reality. Constructions are ideal – as in the building dedicated to the acquisition of knowledge for its own sake whose pillars consist of books. Only when united with the Godhead does the narrator's identity (including the ambiguous voice of the female author writing as a man), and the confining space of the prisons, evaporate. Most metaphoric of all is Teresa of Avila's *Interior Castle*, made of crystal, at the heart of which is God, in the form of a king. Teresa presents this imagined castle – representing the soul – as a means of escape from a real, concrete prison, which in worldly terms corresponds to the convent. The castle's structure corresponds to the path towards spiritual revelation, notionally measured by spatial proximity to Christ, along which souls (untrammelled by gender) may proceed. Mosley notes that, of all these examples of literary architecture, only Montaigne directly echoes the social constraints applying to men and women. But the predilection for captivity, in the edifices elaborated by Marguerite de Navarre, can be understood to be less a social issue (given the author's royal status) than one of gender.

That elite women had some say in their public representation is also evident in the case of Lady Margaret Beaufort, mother of Henry VII, and founder of Christ's College, Cambridge. As Louise Durning notes, the architectural history of these colleges has rather taken for granted their single-sex status, and focused on a typological reading of the institutions' component parts. Against this view she proposes a reading of this particular college complex which emphasizes its representational functions, accommodating an anomalous female presence, both spatially and in the articulation of its surfaces. In part, this is seen in the creation of a hierarchical sequence of rooms at the heart of the college, designed for her own use. More spectacularly, the visibility of her authority was echoed through the elaborate sculptural displays of her heraldic identity and externally visible elements such as a prominent oriel window. These innovations within the collegiate plan are shown to inscribe the potent ambiguities of her status – as a woman at the centre of a masculine community, and as mother to the king.

The convent provides an opportunity to investigate the architectural, spatial and representational issues that arise in the creation, maintenance and regulation of a single sex institution. In Helen Hills' account of the convents and convent churches of early modern, particularly southern, Italy, relations of secular and sacred, decoration and plainness, access and confinement, vision and visibility, are shown to be complexly interwoven. Questions of the ways in which urban space shapes varieties of gendered identity are shown to be no less pertinent to the apparently closed domain of female religious communities. Though elaborately screened from the gaze of the outside world, nuns were able to partake of the spectacle of the congregation and in certain cases the city. Convents also participated in hierarchies of wealth, status and power through their links to leading families, and also, in architectural terms, through the lavish decoration that existed in church interiors. Regulation of the exceptional moments of contact with priests (at Communion – when the disembodied but for all that emphatically gendered body of Christ also symbolically crossed the threshold) and other special visitors had to deal with the fact that convents were elaborately screened and layered. Hills works with a metaphoric reading of an equivalence between the architectural entity of the convent and the nuns' bodies to draw out parallels and projections. She places her study in the context of developing literature on convents and their architecture, putting forward a reading of these institutions which emphatically aims to integrate both aspects of their history. The architecture of convents and their churches is shown to play an active and elaborate role in the symbolic structuring and regulation of conventual life, under the aegis of theocratic authority, and also in its external perception, habitually informed by the clichés of secular licentiousness.

Faced with the undeniably predominant maleness of the architectural profession in eighteenth-century France, Tanis Hinchcliffe's search for the presence
of women in the architecture of the period led her to women as clients of
architects. The limits of female education meant that the kind of actively
consultative participation which architecturally informed men might aspire to was
far less likely. In some cases, as with certain members of the royal family,
architects were passed from one client to the next, along a linear patronage
network. Architecture commissioned by and lived in by independent women was
judged in terms of conventions of stylistic decorum intimately linked to awareness
of its inhabitants' social status. Accusations of a discrepancy between the dignity
of the architecture and the moral condition of the patron was heightened in the
case of women, who, when judged against the sharply hierarchical yardstick of
architecture's symbolic language, were more liable to be found wanting – to be out
of place and out of order. One building type which recurs in these examples is
the 'pavillon' – a detached house in its own garden – a building type which
corresponded to late eighteenth-century forms of élite informal sociability. In
fact, in the examples discussed in this chapter, relations between this hetero-
geneous class of clients varied considerably, counter to retrospective stereotypes
of female cultural patrons as frivolous, vain and essentially concerned with
excessive decoration.

The urban spaces of central London in the early nineteenth century were
evolving as rapidly as the flux of commerce and the circulation of transport and
sociability which constituted and sustained them. New species of club, gambling
haunt and brothel were inserted into these larger zones. The arcade engendered a
particular form of promenading – fitted to the inspection of promenaders and of
commodities visible in shop windows. Above all the bow window was a place to
look out from, but which also allowed external spectators to see the gathering
within. Fashion played the role of distinguishing these self-possessed promenaders.
Jane Rendell focuses on the gendered modes of personal display and spectatorship
which were adapted to such spaces in the form of male corinthians, ramblers,
dandies and female cyprians. The existence of an insidious subculture of prostitution was embodied in the visible, mobile presence of cyprians, whose bodies
were a focus for anxious scrutiny. Drawing on Luce Irigaray, she sees this as a
parody of the commodity status conferred on women in modern Western urban
society. In rejecting the simplistically binary public/private polarity, Rendell seeks
to map a more complex situation in which a culture of heightened intervisibility
was articulated around the new spaces of the modern city.

Esther da Costa Meyer investigates the appearance of agoraphobia at the end of
the nineteenth century, and theoretical attempts then and subsequently to explain
this pathological phenomenon. At the heart of this analysis is a critical examination of the ways in which certain assumptions about women and urban space are
construed as being essentially interconnected. As with Jane Rendell's paper,
simplistic notions of public and private are shown to be inadequate to the complex
nature of lived and imagined experience. Agoraphobia is often assumed to have
been exclusively confined to women, but empirically this is not the case. Although
the phenomenon has been understood in different ways, agoraphobia was

symptomatic of the profoundly problematic nature of urban public space. Da Costa Meyer reviews the different modes of analysis which have sought to explain the condition – psychoanalytic, sociological, behaviourist, feminist, New Historicist. Amongst the variety of ideas which the study points towards, we might note the way that the status of architecture is thrown into question: 'Are the buildings and urban space just empty husks to which repressed pathologic behaviour attaches itself? Are they, in other words, simply neutral signifiers? Or is there not some underlying reason that leads victims of agoraphobia to cast their scenarios of fear and foreboding in architectural terms?'

Reina Lewis explores the harem and its representations across a group of early twentieth-century texts which collectively narrate a series of displacements and identifications, written, as she puts it 'from West to East, from East to West, and back again'. This cross-over is inscribed in texts by Oriental women, who write about the harem in the context of the 'newly desegregating spaces of the modernising Ottoman empire', and also about their reactions to Europe (for example, Zeyneb Hanum's astonished encounter with a Western 'harem' – the Ladies' Gallery in the Houses of Parliament). Books published in the West which presented themselves as authentic accounts of harem life faced considerable editorial pressure to conform to established stereotypes (the harem as the locus of excess, tyranny, perversion), thereby seeking not to disappoint the Occidental audience's expectations. Narratives based on first-hand experience in Turkey stress the contrast between the opulent rituals and structures specific to the imperial harem, and the more familiar, domestic ethos of ordinary harems. Analysis of the dynamics of these interior spaces is complemented by accounts of encounters between Western and Turkish women in Istanbul's public spaces – such as hotels and omnibuses – which produce conflicts of identity and identification. Just as Turkish women's descriptions of women's spaces in American and European texts registers a dissatisfaction when compared to the *modus vivendi* of the harem which they had left behind, so Western women found themselves disconcertingly excluded from the prerogatives claimed by newly independent Turkish women.

The artist's studio has attained the status of a mythic site for creativity. Colin Rhodes shows how Kirchner's studio – a focus for the Brücke group – was a space as artfully constructed as their images, and that this applies especially to images of the studio itself. This studio was not a neutral, dedicated working space for concentrated art-working, nor merely a place for the disinterested posing of pictorial motifs, but rather a space within which the ethos of the Brücke imagery was symbiotically lived out – domestic and aesthetic were redefined. Sculptures and decorations were not secondary backdrops, akin to the paraphernalia of the bohemian studio, but metonymic elements of an alternative lifestyle. Its situation in the heart of the city heightened the sense of redemptive transgression; the studio was a primitivizing oasis, as it were, of aesthetic, social and sexual enfranchisement. This synthetic mode of activity, and the nature of the urban studio space, is quite different from other Brücke outdoor scenes inspired by the naturism practised by the Moritzburg lakes near Dresden. Nor should these Brücke images of the studio-living space be relegated to the imprecise status of essays in escapism. Representations of the studio conflated the search for an alternative

6
—

pictorial language with the powerful sense of 'otherness' created by non-Western carving and decoration, and in the exercise of sexual freedom.

* * *

Each of these studies presents original research, and investigates the links between the theoretical understanding of architecture and its concrete experience – both in terms of internal spaces, and the presence and effects of buildings within an urban environment. The role of the architect in producing architecture's gendered identities is examined in several contributions, as is the intervention of patrons who sought to define the buildings which they were commissioning or using in terms of the articulation of particular configurations of gender relations. The essays seek to understand how and why architecture has articulated widely varying formations of gender, and relates these to specific historical situations and contexts. Amongst all its other social, political and ideological functions, and in a way that is inseparable from them, architecture is shown to play a powerful and multifarious role in the constitution of the subject from early modern to recent times.

NOTE

1. This is not the place to attempt a bibliographical survey, but certain important recent texts need to be signalled. On modernism and urban space, see Mary Macleod, 'Everyday and "Other" Spaces' in Debra Coleman, Elizabeth Danze and Carol Henderson (eds), *Architecture and Feminism* (New York: Princeton Architectural Press, 1996), pp. 1–37; Elizabeth Wilson, *The Sphinx in the City: Urban Life, Disorder, and Women* (London: Virago, 1991); Joel Snyder (ed.), *Stud: Architectures of Masculinity* (New York: Princeton Architectural Press, 1996); Mark Wigley, *White Walls, Designer Dresses: the Fashioning of Modern Architecture* (Cambridge, MA and London: MIT Press, 1995); Leslie Kanes Weisman, *Discrimination by Design. A Feminist Critique of the Man-made Environment* (Urbana: University of Illinois Press, 1995).
   On women in the architectural profession, see Francesca Hughes (ed.) *The Architect: Reconstructing her Profession* (Cambridge, MA and London: MIT Press, 1996); Katerina Ruedi, Sarah Wigglesworth, Duncan McCorquordale (eds), *Desiring Practices: Architecture, Gender, and the Interdisciplinary* (London: Black Dog Publishing, 1996); Ellen Perry Berkeley with Mathilda McQuaid (eds), *Architecture: a Place for Women* (Washington and London: Smithsonian Institution, 1989).
   For examples of studies which explore the significance of gender for our understanding of architecture in 'pre-modern' periods, see Alice T. Friedman, *House and Household in Elizabethan England: Wollaton Hall and the Willoughby Family* (Chicago and London: University of Chicago Press, 1989); Roberta Gilchrist, *Gender and Material Culture: The Archaeology of Religious Women* (London and New York: Routledge, 1994); Gülru Necipoğlu, *Architecture, Ceremonial, and Power: the Topkapı Palace in the Fifteenth and Sixteenth Centuries* (Cambridge, MA: MIT Press, 1992).

CHAPTER 1

A GRAVITY IN PUBLIC PLACES: INIGO JONES AND CLASSICAL ARCHITECTURE[1]

Christy Anderson

Architecture frames the measure of man. The contemporary photographer Karen Knorr offers the phrase 'The Search for the True Spirit of Antiquity' as a legend to her view of the interior of eighteenth-century Chiswick House[2] (Figure 1). This image, part of her series entitled *Connoisseurs*, frames an elegant and somberly dressed man within the vista of two highly ornate and classical door frames. The man, turned away from us and gazing out toward the garden, hides his identity and his emotions, while the architecture glows with gold against plain walls. Architecture bears the burden of expression, preserving personal anonymity even in an interior, domestic space. In this setting Knorr's use of the term 'antiquity' evokes both the ancient models used for this architecture as well as the noblesse of the man in the space. The presence of antiquity forms the past and anticipation of its true spirit frames the condition of the present.

Knorr's interest in this photograph is English classicism in the broadest sense, and she urges us to question the ways in which traditions and masculine identity are formed through the power of historical precedent and the inevitability of commonly held beliefs. Her photographs employ the language of classicism, its balance, proportion and symmetry. This is a visual language which carries with it the strength of patrimony and an irrefutable parentage.

In early seventeenth-century England the proponents of architectural classicism employed these attributes of inevitability and antiquity to promote its significance, using the vocabulary associated with masculine values in order to support classicism's superiority over a vernacular English architecture. In the early decades of the seventeenth century a small group of courtiers sang the praises of a classical architectural vocabulary in spite of the widespread preferences of architects, patrons and the general public for a style based on gothic forms and the continuity of native traditions.[3] (It was not until the eighteenth century that classicism, based on the work of the Italian architect Andrea Palladio, became a dominant voice in the eighteenth-century architectural circles of William Kent and Lord Burlington.) The language of masculinity was an important part of the architectural rhetoric of this stylistic shift for it associated architectural forms with gender and therefore with related debates about gender identity. This article looks at one moment in seventeenth-century English architectural history through an investigation of the language and connotations of visual style.

Within this story of the rise of classicism, the architect Inigo Jones (1573–1652) serves as the 'genius' who transformed English architecture and subsequently

Figure 1 *Karen Knorr, 'The Search for the True Spirit of Antiquity', 1986;
Cibachrome photograph, 39 × 39 inches. (Photo: copyright © 1986 Karen Knorr.
Reproduced by permission of the artist)*

English architectural history (Figure 2). His importance is equated with the great
political and military events of the period. A recent history of English classicism
begins with Jones as the first of the 'heroic' tradition of architects.[4] Classicism, the
Latin of architectural form, connected England with wider European developments,
especially with the interests of European courts. For some historians this marked a
coming of age in English political and artistic culture. 'For the English architects
from Inigo Jones down to the first quarter of the nineteenth-century reflect the
prosperity and the naval or martial pre-eminence of England. They are no more
inferior to those of the rest of Europe than was our reputation as an independent
kingdom. That is to say, they are not provincial.'[5]

Architecture before Jones – and continuing through the seventeenth century –
was a mixture of forms from a variety of sources, a combination of classical details,
heraldry and invented ornament. Two drawings demonstrate this contrast. In a gate
design by Jones for Hatton House in London (1622–1623), he used the classical
orders based on Continental models and the transformation of Roman precedent[6]
(Figure 3). The mode of representation, orthogonal projection as used by Palladio

ELEBERRIMVS VIR INIGO IONES PRÆFECTVS ARCHITECTVRÆ
MAGNÆ BRITTANIÆ REGIS ETC
Ant.van Dyck pinxit
R.V.Vorst sculp
Cum priuilegio

Figure 2 *R.V. Vorst after Anthony Van Dyck,* Inigo Jones, *engraving. (Yale Center for British Art, Paul Mellon Collection)*

and others, emphasizes the clarity and regularity of the design. Jones offers two alternatives for the Tuscan gateway, one on the left with rusticated bands; the other with smooth applied columns against the rusticated surface of the gate.

In contrast, a drawing by Robert Smythson from the end of the sixteenth century is also for a gate, but here the draughtsman is less interested in the

Figure 3 *Inigo Jones*, Elevation for a Tuscan carriage gateway for Hatton House, Ely Place, London, *1622–1623, pen and brown ink with grey-brown wash on paper (362 × 291 mm). Royal Institute of British Architects, London. (Photo: Conway Library, Courtauld Institute of Art)*

symmetry of the whole than in the inventiveness and exuberance of the ornament in the cresting (Figure 4). The bottom of the drawing is barely completed, in contrast to the even finish of the Jones design. Whereas Smythson manifests an Elizabethan aesthetic of wonder, Jones appeals to a more measured sensibility and the options offered to the patron. Although the drawing shows the changes made by Jones in the process of design, the addition of extra rustication along the cornice of the pediment, variations for the entablature mouldings along the right side of the page and so on, it is still intended to be a presentation drawing to the

Figure 4 *Robert Smythson,* Design for a Gatehouse, *sepia pen with brown wash, 8 × 7¾ inches. Royal Institute of British Architects, London. (Photo: Conway Library, Courtauld Institute of Art)*

patron. Jones signs the drawing in the upper right corner 'for my lo[rd] Stuard – for Hatton house 1622–1623'. The drawing was intended as a point of discussion for patron and architect, they could make choices about the degree of rustication and the placement of the inscription while examining the drawing. Jones's drawing was the medium for a client/patron relationship which highlighted Jones's specialized skill and knowledge in architectural design.

Restrained classical architecture, and the design process itself, were, for Jones, specifically connected with contemporary ideas of masculine self-presentation.[7] Jones made an explicit connection between architecture and masculinity in a note written soon after he returned from Italy and continental Europe in 1614. In the dead of winter, during the week of 20 January 1614, Jones must have been engaged in a period of some study and reflection on the nature of architectural ornament. On Thursday, 19 January, Jones wrote that

> As in dessigne first on Sttudies the partes of the boddy of man as Eyees noses mouthes Eares and so of the rest to bee practicke in the partes sepperat ear on comm to put them toggethear to maak a hoole figgure and cloath yt and consequently a hoole Storry wth all ye ornamentes

So in Architecture on must Studdy the Partes as loges Entranses Haales Chambers Staires doures windoues. and then adorrne them wth colloms. Cornishes. sfondati. Stattues. Paintings. Compartimentes. quadraturs . . .[8]

The body, and specifically the male body, is the model for architectural design and the organization of ornament. Following Vincenzo Scamozzi's interpretation of man as the model for the articulation of the exterior, Jones wrote 'the Aspecte of the fro[n]t more adorned the[n] the sydes. and least behind'.[9] Scamozzi was using the analogy as part of a series of general rules and reasons for the need for ornament in buildings, and why it should correspond to a logic based on the observation of nature, the hierarchies of society and the examples of God.

Jones would also have read about the human analogy for architectural design in his copy of Leon Battista Alberti's treatises on architecture and painting, books bound together on his library shelf.[10] Following on Vitruvius, Renaissance theorists including Alberti, Francesco di Giorgio and Filarete, all used the male body as the symbolic and literal model for a proportional architecture.[11]

On the following day Jones wrote on the theme of architectural decorum and the proper use of ornament. 'In all invencions of Caprecious ornaments, on must first designe the Ground, or ye thing plaine, as it is for youse, and on that varry yt, addorne yt, compose yt with Decorum according to the youse and the order yt is of.'[12] The building is to be built from the inside out, the bones organized first, with the appropriate dress added later according to the status of the building and based on the status of its occupant.

Jones then goes on to comment on the appropriate ornament for the interiors and exteriors of buildings. 'And to saie trew all thes composed ornaments the wch Proceed out of ye aboundance of dessigners and wear brought in by Michill Angell and his followers in my oppignion do not well in sollid architecture and ye fasciati of houses, but in garden loggis stucco or ornaments of chimnies peeces or in the inner parts of houses thos compositions are of necessity to be yoused.'

Composed ornament, such as that created by Michelangelo, and we can also add to this that type of ornament popular in northern Europe at the end of the sixteenth century, was to be limited to decorative elements on buildings. In the final section of this passage Jones equates this division in architectural decorum to the differences between masculine and feminine psychological make-ups:

For as outwardly every wyse man carrieth a graviti in Publicke Places, whear ther is nothing els looked for, yet inwardly has his immaginancy set free, and sumtimes licentiously flying out, as nature hirself doeth often tymes stravagantly, to dellight, amase us sometimes moufe us to laughter, sumtimes to contemplation and horror, so in architecture ye outward ornaments oft to be sollid, proporsionabl according to the rules, masculine and unaffected.[13]

A building should be the embodiment of *both* the masculine and feminine, exterior bearing the public face of *gravitas*, interior affected by the passions of 'nature hirself'. The interior is aligned with the emotions and the emotive, the feminine domain. The exterior gives nothing away, for this is, as Jones says, 'whear ther is nothing els looked for'. The distinction between the exterior and interior had been discussed by Alberti: 'In a town house the internal parts, such as the drawing rooms and dining rooms, should be no less festive than those of a country one; but the external parts, such as the portico and vestibule, should not be so frivolous as to appear to have obscured some sense of dignity.'[14] Jones, however, adds gender into this equation by specifically praising those qualities he associates with masculine architecture, equating a building's presentation with that of a man in the public domain. As men should present themselves with dignity and gravity, that is *gravitas*, so too should architecture. This note was written soon after Jones returned from his travels abroad in the company of Thomas Howard, the Earl of Arundel, whose sober personal appearance was thought at the time to represent a political conservatism that reinforced the status of ancient noble families in England.[15]

In the first years of the twentieth century Adolf Loos admired just this quality of restraint in the dress of English men. Mary McLeod has noted that it was this seemingly non-style of English men (in contrast to the dandyism of Germans) that offered a model for a new architectural style.[16] English clothing remained constant, we might say classic, because of its restraint and an English belief that clothing (like architecture) should represent an ideal vision in the public realm. This restrained taste was part of an aristocratic ideal, similar to the new standard for nobility embraced by Arundel and others three centuries earlier. Herman Muthesius wrote in *Das englische Haus* that 'the richer a man is, the more restrained his behavior, the more modest and inconspicuous he is'.[17]

The connection between architecture and ideals of masculine nobility were, however, already explicit by the early seventeenth century. The façade of a man – represented through costume and comportment – could define his nobility in the public arena. 'There is no one thing,' wrote Henry Peacham, 'that setteth a fairer stamp upon nobility than evenness of carriage and care of our reputation, without which our most graceful gifts are dead and dull, as the diamond without his foil. For hereupon as on the frontispiece of a magnificent palace are fixed the eyes of all passengers . . . by gait, laughter, and apparel, a man is known what he is.'[18] Or as Jones wrote in the margin of his copy of Scamozzi, 'a ma[n] [is] judged by his howse'.[19]

A strong façade was not just a passive reflection of nobility but rather was to be a role as a force over the interior. There was 'a double governance', according to Sir Thomas Elyot in *The Book of the Governor* (1531), 'that is to say, an interior or inward governance, and an exterior or outward governance. The first is of his affects and passions, which do inhabit within his soul, and be subjects to reason. The second is of his children, his servants, and other subjects to his authority.'[20] This was not, however, a golden age of opportunity for women's education. If knowledge is power, then for women that was confined within the home in the domestic pursuits. In Castiglione's *The Courtier*, a central text for Renaissance readers in what it meant to be a man, the emphasis for women was on social rather than scholarly skills, skills of the inside of the house rather than the outside: sewing, dancing, singing, entertainment.[21] Women learned what they learned in the home.[22] Gervase Markham in his *The English Housewife* (1615) described how men were to run the business of the estate, while the domestic activities of cooking, sewing and 'physicke' were in the women's domain.[23]

The believed instability of women, and their unsuitability for the affairs of business and the state, were attributable to their physical and inherent nature. Women were more changeable. They were affected by fluctuations of the moon and the imagination, or perhaps even from a deformity in the cranial suture (the sutura sagittalis), which did not allow humours to escape, thus leaving the brain subject to emotional attacks and the full force of the passions. Women were thought not to have the psychological control of men.[24] Their physic was colder and moister, and therefore more prone to illness than men, and made them weaker psychologically. These opinions were derived from a reading of Aristotelian thought and the metaphorical association of woman with mother earth, fruitfulness and fluctuations of the moon. This medical status of women had a bearing on their ethical status. The assumption of the frailty of body made women best suitable for the care of the young, and unsuitable for exposure to the outside world, natural justification for her exclusion from public life.[25] The ethical implications of this biology are qualities of passivity, receptiveness and mutability.[26] If identity and behaviour was extrapolated from biology then it could be seen as an integral part of the female nature.[27]

The volatility of the female character could be likened to the fluidity of the Elizabethan and Jacobean architecture, which exploited the infinite variety and fantastic effects that could be achieved when innovation was key. Like the architecture of many countries during the sixteenth century, English architecture had developed a rubric that encouraged masons and designers to freely adopt and adapt elements from a variety of sources for their projects, changing them, adding colour or new decoration, prizing invention above all else. The effect was to produce an aesthetic of wonder and amazement. Classical architecture, as it was understood by Jones, was a system of restraint and projection: the building expressed a public ideal that constrained the emotional expression in the interior spaces.

Women changed their fashions as they changed their residence throughout the year. The development of the London 'seasons' throughout the seventeenth century required women to change their appearance as they moved from country to town in an ever more regularized pattern of social migration between their various family residences (Figures 5 and 6). Their dress was ever more dictated by changing fashion conventions, and gave credence to the criticisms against excessive opulence that Queen Elizabeth had sought to regulate with sumptuary laws in the sixteenth century.[28] Wenceslaus Hollar's engravings of the seasons highlights the changing fashions of women, setting them like ornaments against the architectural landscape that signified the changing locations of society in town and country. Disassociated from their setting, yet simultaneously controlled by it, these elaborate etchings are fashion plates showing women in their 'natural state', with an external appearance as fluid as the changing seasons.[29]

English architecture in the classical tradition frequently employed imagery of dress and costume (and therefore class) when describing the difference between the orders. In 1563 John Shute, in the first book in English to present the orders as part of a larger system of architectural design, showed each order as expressive of a particular ancient God, thus following Vitruvius's explanation of the origin of the orders as derived from the qualities of the gods: 'The temples of Minerva, Mars and

Figure 5 *Wenceslaus Hollar,* The Four Seasons (full-length), Winter, *etching, 1644.* *(British Museum)*

Welcom sweet Ladis you doe bring Spring. That makes the Earth to looke so greene
Rich presents of a hopefull Spring As when see first began to teeme.

Figure 6 *Wenceslaus Hollar,* The Four Seasons (full-length), Spring, *etching, 1644.* *(British Museum)*

Hercules will be Doric since the virile strength of these Gods makes daintiness entirely inappropriate to their houses.'[30] For Shute the 'pillers, partelye for their beautye and comlines, partelye for their fortitude and strength, the writers of them, haue resembled and lykned to certain feyned Goddes and Goddesses.'[31] Each order is comparable to a body type represented by an archetypal deity.

By 1624, Henry Wotton, English ambassador to Venice and collector of drawings by Palladio, described their differences as:

> First, therefore the Tuscan is a plain, massie, rurall Pillar, resembling some sturdy well-limmed Labourer, homely clad, in which kinde of comparisons Vitruvius himselfe seemeth to take pleasure . . .
>
> The Ionique Order doth represent a kinde of Feminine slendernesse, yet saith Vitruvius, not like a light Housewife, but in a decent dressing, hath much of the Matrone. . . . Best knowne by his trimmings, for the bodie of this Columne is perpetually chaneled, like a thicke plighted Gowne. . . .
>
> The Corinthian, is a Columne, laciviously decked like a Curtezane, and therein much participating (as all Inventions does) of the place where they were first borne: Corinthe having been without controversie one of the wantonest Townes in the world.[32]

By equating the orders with contemporary English dress (that of the housewife, labourer and so on) Wotton translates a Continental architectural system into an instantly recognizable English system of class distinction. Like Hollar's plates of the season, described through the changes in dress, Wotton also includes the range of class that dress so often demarcates. Each of the orders is equivalent in his schema to a level of English society.[33] Wotton's treatise aimed to make the theory of Continental classicism applicable to English building practice, for as he states, 'all Nations doe start at Novelties, and are indeed maried to their owne Moulds', and if classicism was to make sense to an English audience it would have to be put in contemporary English terms.[34]

Jones invokes a dichotomy of masculinity/femininity in order to demarcate a difference in architectural style; classicism as appropriate for the exterior of buildings, mixed and invented ornament for interiors. He followed this pattern even at buildings intended for female patrons such as the Queen's House in Greenwich, built over a period of some 20 years from 1617 to the mid-1630s for Anne of Denmark, and then Henrietta Maria, queens of King James I and Charles I respectively. There the exterior included simplified Doric loggias and classical balustrades, while highly ornamented fireplaces modelled after French designs appear on the interior. Jones did not differentiate between houses for male or female patrons. All public building and spaces should ascribe to notions of masculine public decorum. For that purpose classicism was the appropriate architectural language.

Gender differences, presented as binary opposites, draw lines of demarcation between architectural spaces and stylistic differences. As Joel Sanders has recently written, '[The] opposition of public and private, upon which sexual binaries like male/female and heterosexual/homosexual crucially depend, is itself grounded on the prior spatial dualism, inside/outside. Through the erection of partitions that divide space, architecture colludes in creating and upholding prevailing social hierarchies and distinctions.'[35] For Jones, eager to establish his pre-eminence as court architect, such binary oppositions were extremely useful. Not only did Jones equate classicism with a pattern of beliefs valued by the court, he also drew lines of demarcation between his own work and that of other architects at court.

The traditions of English architecture, however, did not necessarily divide the masculine off from the feminine; symbols of each could be seen to inhabit the same form much as the classical was mixed with a variety of invented and copied ornament. This was easiest in paper architecture, as in *The Fairie Queene*, where Spenser's description of Alma's Castle is a creation of various shapes and properties:

> The frame thereof seemed partly circulare,
> And part triangulare, ô worke diuine;
> Those two the first and last proportions are,
> The one imperfect, mortall, foeminine;
> Th'other immortall, perfect, masculine[36]

Spenser's description of the House of Alma is ambiguous – it is as much a general notion of the varieties of architecture as it is a reference to the specific type of fantastic architecture as that of the Triangular Lodge, built by Sir Thomas Tresham (Rothwell, 1594–1597) as a meditation on the Catholic Trinity (Figure 7).

Shakespeare's King Lear could well proclaim that 'I dare do all that may become a man' (Act 1, vii), though this is a dare which the play then goes on to test at every opportunity. And Macbeth concedes in *his* very hesitancy that there does exist the possibility of an effeminate paralysis of inactivity on his part which will ultimately be contrasted by the masculine activity of Lady Macbeth. Macbeth makes a verbal pledge to act, but does not, and therefore leads to the question, does he also 'become a man'? Definitions of masculinity, and its varied manifestations, are at the heart of many cultural moments in early seventeenth century England. Susan Amussen has suggested how in the construction of masculinity in the years around 1600 there was a shift from a traditional model of manhood, based on violence, to a reformed notion of masculine power based on self-restraint and the recourse to law.[37] As Amussen notes, the reformed idea of manhood required economic, and one might add intellectual, resources to achieve this independent and self-sufficient status. Masculinity cannot be separated from class distinction.

Because classicism was based in antiquity, it required a wide educational training to understand its sources and significance. The architect, patron and public required a shared cultural knowledge to understand the references. The level of intellectual, literary and archaeological reference could run the gamut from a vague idea to particular and specialized knowledge. But along this continuum the introduction of architectural classicism by Jones assumed a level of educational experience that would be understood and cultivated by a cultural elite.

Jones's promotion of architectural classicism was predicated on the belief that it was the architectural expression of humanist educational ideals: rhetorical clarity, historical knowledge and the grammar of the Latin language itself.[38] Adolf Loos wrote that 'the architect is a builder who has learned Latin', and the educated language of education and architecture were the sign of both a masculine mode

Figure 7 *Triangular Lodge, Rushton (Northamptonshire), 1594–1597. (Photo: Christy Anderson)*

and new levels of professional behaviour.[39] These educational ideals formed the basis for the training of the male aristocracy for public service,[40] and Jones believed that architecture could similarly express these notions in built form.

Throughout his career, Inigo Jones sought to emulate the education of his patrons, providing through self-study what he had never had in formal training. The surviving books from his library indicate a concerted course of education in the standards of a humanist education: philosophy, ancient history, geography, mathematics, in addition to the technical architectural reading required for his profession.

Reading was at the centre of Jones's practice as an architect. Jones's careful and repeated reading of the treatises of Andrea Palladio, Vincenzo Scamozzi, Sebastiano Serlio and others provided the constant reference library of the vocabulary of classicism. Even these notes on ornament, quoted above, were interpretations by Jones of his reading. He had previously translated a passage in his copy of Giorgio Vasari on the life of the Florentine architect Baccio d'Agnolo, where Vasari had described how the architect's son, Giuliano d'Agnolo had replaced the outmoded 'tedesco', or gothic, windows of a palace with modern 'finestre inginocchiate'.[41] Jones translates the next passage of Vasari's text, writing that 'Architecture must be masculine, Solid, Simpull. And inriched wth ye grace of design and of a varied subject in the Composition that wth not for too little or too much of that in ye Order of architecture nor ye sight of the judicious.'[42]

In his notebook Jones transforms his translation of Vasari's text from 'solid and simpull' into 'sollid, proporsionabl according to the rules, masculine and unaffected'. The change in language, with the addition of masculinity and decorum into the equation, illuminates his thinking about the application of these ideals into English architectural practice. The trajectory of Jones's career at court depended in great part on his ability to fulfil the architectural needs of his patrons, in addition to simultaneously increasing demand for his 'new' architectural style based on Continental precedent and antique authority.[43] Solidity is opposed to fluidity, but in this context of talking about ornament it would have juxtaposed classicism to the flat, applied ornament used by Robert Smythson and others, as in the gateway design discussed above. In the details of the entablature, capital, base, etc. – that is, in all the elements of classicism – the ornament was understood as the expression of structural components in ancient architecture. Classical details were not meant to be applied but to represent an assumed innate order of architectural tectonics and proportionality.

'Solid and proportional' is also the language of science, and specifically Euclidian geometry. In early seventeenth century England the use of these terms in conjunction with architecture would have located the discussion in a specific context of theoretical discourse about architecture. In John Dee's 'Mathematical Preface' to the 1570 English translation of Euclid, architecture's seriousness as a field of study is based on its roots in science and mathematics.[44] Masons, of course, had always relied on mathematics as part of their art; and their libraries often contained copies of Euclid that were as much a sign of their education and status as they were a useful resource in their work.[45] And although Robert Smythson's grave monument described him as 'Architect and Survayor', even the most prominent of architectural designers before Jones rose through the ranks of the crafts of building (or surveying) by virtue of their professional development.[46] Many of the professions in England during the sixteenth century sought to improve the quality of their members' work and the status of their disciplines through education. The proliferation of books such as Leonard Digges's *Boke Named Tectonicon* (London, 1556) or Richard More's *The Carpenters Rule* (London, 1602) popularized the principles of geometry and their relevance to the building crafts. All of the related building and land crafts would benefit from their publication, as Digges stated in his preface, as they were written in order to show 'how to measure truly and very speedily all manor land, timber, stone, steeples, pillers, globes, board, glasse, pavement, &c. without any trouble, not pained by many rules, or obscure tearmes, nor yet with the multitude of Tables'.[47]

In discussing Jones's comments on gender, David Cast notes that the choice of language is key to understanding his interpretation of classicism and the serious-ness with which he approached his subject: 'The term "masculine", as used by Jones, is a part of this whole linguistic expansion, a word available in English already but transformed to evoke an ideal of artistic seriousness and authority to which any Italianizer would quite obviously agree, the notion of male superiority being so ingrained in this era that it becomes the common currency in language.'[48] One difficulty in the translation of Italian treatises into English was the lack of accurate terms to describe the parts of classical buildings. There was no exact equivalent, for example, for 'loggia' in English. An architectural style will not have a common currency if there is not the language of description to allow a common discourse between architect and patron, or architect and mason. Patrons at the court may have wished to build in the classical style and owned the architectural treatises; however, they still required the expertise of Jones, a professional architect, to negotiate the technical and visual language.

The signs of masculinity were many. If a man could be read through his speech, and certainly accent, then the shift in architectural language could well have been used in a similar vein. Architecture, like speech, could separate one group (or individual) from another. Ben Jonson wrote that 'Language most shows a man: speak that I may see thee. [for] . . . No glass renders a man's form, or likeness, so true as speech.'[49]

In advocating for the use of classicism in the public arena, 'where nothing els is looked for', Jones is not only praising classicism as a more masculine architectural style because of its ties to male educational experience, he is also promoting its masculine mode of textual reference. Classicism, especially in countries so distant from a ready reference of Roman antiquities, required that its practitioners and patrons use books as source material. For Jones, books – and highly developed reading skills – were at the core of his architectural practice. The survival of his library is the testimony to his careful study of words and images (Figure 8). Henry Peacham urged young gentlemen to use their books, write in the margins, appro-priate them as their own: '. . . for your owne use spare them not for noting or enterlining (if they be printed) for it is not likely that you meane to be a gainer by them, when you have done with them . . .'[50] To write in the margin was the mark of the scholar, and distinguished him from girls and gallants who carried their

22

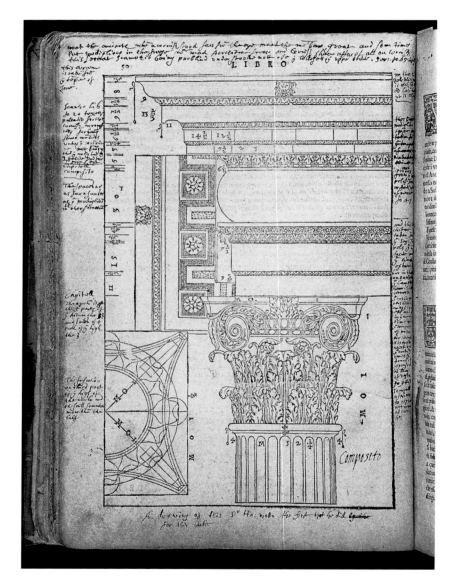

Figure 8 *Andrea Palladio,* I quattro libri dell'architettura *(Venice 1601), Bk. I, p. 50. Inigo Jones's copy. Worcester College, Oxford. (The Provost and Fellows of Worcester College, Oxford. Photo: Alan Buchanan)*

prayer books to church 'but for their outsides'. Annotating the text indicated a seriousness of study.

Classicism, and specifically Jones's practice of it, is marked by just such a mode of seriousness and scholarly method. Through the metaphors of gender, science and decorum he demarcates the boundaries of his scholarly understanding of the grammar and rhetoric of the orders. While this transformation of style may now seem an inevitable development, the strength of Jones's language suggests that this change required the support of an irrefutable theoretical authority. Allon White's observations on the hierarchy of discourse of 'high' and 'low' language are particularly apposite here.

> The language of most speech communities is stratified into 'high' and 'low' language. That is to say, there is a hierarchy of discourse which operates to distinguish certain language users from others on the basis of prestige and power. The 'high' language is normally associated with the most powerful socio-economic group existing at the felt centre of cultural power, and this language is mediated through institutions of education, religion, politics, and communications. The 'low' languages on the other hand are normally associated with the weakest socio-economic groups having limited control of dominant cultural agencies. Manual workers, women, adolescents, children, economic minorities, subcultures, and rural regions remote from the main centres all operate to a greater or lesser extent with 'low' languages in this sense.[51]

Classicism took on the role of 'high' architectural language through the work of its advocates in aligning its precepts with the seriousness of scholarly study and the ideals of masculine behaviour. What is not serious must be the trivial and the ephemeral. In her discussion of the materiality of the native English architecture, Lucy Gent notes that these issues of gender identity in architecture are often ignored 'for classicism tends to appropriate the language of purity, lucidity, beauty, and what is fundamental. It leaves to the Other impurity, obscurity, commodity and the trivial'.[52] Inigo Jones's architecture, as well as his practice of architectural theory, intersected with ideas of masculinity and succeeded in establishing a 'serious' language of design whose pedigree is irreproachable. The interest in architecture itself, and specifically classical architecture, became associated with a new gentlemanly ideal of the late Tudor period which praised humanistic education over military training. Henry Wotton may have written that 'I shall not neede to celebrate the subject which I deliver. For Architecture, can want no commendation, where there are Noble Men, or Noble mindes' in 1624, but his self-assurance belies a need to reassure those who may have yet doubted the ties between architecture and 'serious' masculine pursuits.[53] As Allon White suggests, 'the social reproduction of seriousness is a fundamental – perhaps the fundamental – hegemonic manoeuvre. Once the high language has attained the commanding position of being able to specify what is and is not to be taken seriously, its control over the language of its society is virtually assured.'[54]

Throughout the seventeenth century the taste for classicism came to define a gentleman as much as masculinity defined the significance of classicism as a style (Figure 9). Portraits such as this, showing William Style of Langley posed against his regular and geometrical Italianate garden, holding his surveying stick, and pointing to the globe at his feet project a vocabulary of masculine ideals. Every

Figure 9 *British School*, Portrait of William Style of Langley, *1636, oil on canvas, 80 × 53 inches. (Photo: Tate Gallery, London)*

other sign of status frames William Style's elegantly clad figure: the painted coat of arms in the window, the books open on the desk, the classical doorway arch. By the time of this painting in 1636, architecture in addition to dress and heraldry, had come to serve as a powerful form of public statement of nobility.

Serious architecture, like serious speech, asserts its importance by appearing to be above fashion and changing taste. In all periods, except in the most recent post-modernism of this century, proponents of classical architecture can assert that the reliance on symmetry and proportion, ornament from ancient models, and textual references transcended the vicissitudes of style that were fleeting moments in a long architectural history. (By highlighting the wilfulness of design, post-modernism treats these so-called innate truths with irony. Though it is difficult to say if there was any less seriousness than the belief in the essential integrity of the classical tradition.[55]) Yet, the introduction of classicism in seventeenth century England shows that this formation of a classical language was very much a marshalling of all the categories of gender, class and professional status that were already so powerful in the court circles where Jones sought patronage. Architecture gave a public and physical form to a changing ideal of masculinity as those ideas were just taking shape.

NOTES

1. This essay was written at the kind invitation of Louise Durning and Richard Wrigley for the Architecture and Gender Conference held at Oxford Brookes University (England) in October 1995. Since that time a shorter version has been published as 'Masculine and Unaffected: Inigo Jones and the Classical Ideal' in *Art Journal*, 56:2 (Summer 1997) 48–54. I am grateful to Georgia Clarke, Alice Friedman and Ellen Chirelstein for their many helpful suggestions.
2. Karen Knorr, *Marks of Distinction* (London: Thames and Hudson, 1991).
3. See my 'Learning to Read Architecture in the English Renaissance' in Lucy Gent, ed.), *Albion's Classicism: The Visual Arts in Britain, 1550–1660* (New Haven and London: Yale University Press, 1995), pp. 239–86.
4. Giles Worsley, *Classical Architecture in Britain. The Heroic Age* (New Haven and London: Yale University Press, 1995).
5. Sacheverell Sitwell, *British Artists and Craftsmen. A Survey of Taste, Design and Style* (London: B.T. Batsford, 1945), p. 20. I am grateful to Ellen Chirelstein for this reference.
6. John Harris and Gordon Higgott, *Inigo Jones: Complete Architectural Drawings* (New York: The Drawing Center, 1989), cat. no. 44, pp. 134–5.
7. This discussion of masculinity in the realm of architecture is indebted to the theoretical writings of scholars in a number of other fields. Among those works which I found particularly helpful were Maurice Berger, Brian Wallis and Simon Watson (eds), *Constructing Masculinity* (New York: Routledge, 1995); Jonathan Goldberg, *Sodometries. Renaissance Texts, Modern Sexualities* (Stanford: Stanford University Press, 1992); Peter Schwenger, 'The Masculine Mode', in Elaine Showalter (ed.), *Speaking of Gender* (New York: Routledge, 1989), p. 101ff; Eve Kosofsky Sedgwick, *Between Men. English Literature and Male Homosocial Desire* (New York: Columbia University Press, 1985).
8. Inigo Jones, *Roman Sketchbook*, fol. 76v. Now in the Devonshire Collection,

Chatsworth. This passage is cited and discussed by John Peacock, 'Figurative Drawings', pp. 285 in Harris and Higgott, *Inigo Jones*.

9. Against the text of Scamozzi: 'Così à punto l'Architetto, dee offervare la dispositione de gli ornamenti, e collocarli nelle parti più conueneuoli, e proprie dell'edificio: Intanto che l'aspetto principale di esso: ad imitatione del corpo humano, sia più ornato, che le parti da' lati, e meno il di dietro: il quale precetto fu molto osseruato da gli antichi, come vediamo nello opere loro' (Jones's emphasis). Vincenzo Scamozzi, *L'idea dell architettura universale* (Venice: Giorgio Valentino, 1615; Inigo Jones's copy at Worcester College, Oxford), II, p. 8.

10. Ibid.

11. See the discussion by Diana I. Agrest, 'Architecture from Without: Body, Logic and Sex', *Assemblage*, 7 (1988) 28–41.

12. Jones, Roman Sketchbook, fol. 76r.

13. Ibid.

14. Leon Battista Alberti, *On the Art of Building in Ten Books*, trans. J. Rykwert, N. Leach and R. Tavernor (Cambridge, MA: MIT Press, 1988), Bk 9, pt. 4, p. 300. I am grateful to Georgia Clarke for this suggestion.

15. Kevin Sharpe, 'The Earl of Arundel, His Circle and the Opposition to the Duke of Buckingham, 1618–1628' in Kevin Sharpe (ed.), *Faction and Parliament* (Oxford: Clarendon Press, 1978), pp. 209–44.

16. Mary McLeod, 'Undressing Architecture: Fashion, Gender, and Modernity' in Deborah Fausch, Paulette Singley, Rudolphe El-Khoury and Zvi Efrat (eds) *Architecture: in Fashion* (New York: Princeton Architectural Press, 1994), esp. pp. 57–60.

17. Herman Muthesius, *The English House*, trans. Janet Seligman (New York: Rizzoli, 1987), p. 149. Cited in McLeod, 'Undressing Architecture', p. 58 and n. 68 pp. 107–8.

18. Henry Peacham, *The Complete Gentleman*, ed. Virgil B. Heltzel (Ithaca: Cornell University Press for the Folger Shakespeare Library, [1634] 1962), p. 144.

19. Scamozzi, *L'idea*, I, p. 225. Jones annotates against this passage in Scamozzi: 'E pero non e punto spiacevole quel detto di Cassiodoro, che tale si crede esser il Padrone, quale noi vediamo esser costituita, & ordinata la sua casa: e certo non e cosa, che tra tutte le cure, o pubbliche, o private trapassi di giocondita, e piacere a quella del fabricare, e godere una bella, e comoda casa, essendoche e cosa da prudente, e da huomini grandi, e di grosse facolta.'

20. Sir Thomas Elyot, *The Book of the Governor* (London 1531, 1962), p. 183; cited in Katherine Hodgkin, 'Thomas Whythorne and the Problems of Mastery', *History Workshop*, 29 (Spring 1990) 21.

21. Alice Friedman, 'The Influence of Humanism on the Education of Girls and Boys in Tudor England', *History of Education Quarterly*, 25:1–2 (Spring/Summer 1985) 66.

22. Walter J. Ong, 'Latin Language Study as a Renaissance Puberty Rite', in his *Rhetoric, Romance and Technology. Studies in the Interaction of Expression and Culture* (Ithaca: Cornell University Press, 1971), pp. 117–18.

23. Friedman, 'Influence of Humanism', p. 66.

24. Ian Maclean, *The Renaissance Notion of Woman. A Study in the Fortunes of Scholasticism and Medical Science in European Intellectual Life* (Cambridge: Cambridge University Press, 1980), p. 41.

25. Maclean, *Renaissance Notion of Women*, p. 44.

26. Ibid.

27. See Sherry B. Ortner, 'Is Female to Male as Nature is to Culture?' in M.Z. Rosaldo and L. Lamphere (eds) *Woman, Culture, and Society* (Stanford: Stanford University Press, 1974), pp. 67–87.

28. Reed Benhamou, 'The Restraint of Excessive Apparel: England 1337–1604', *Dress*, 15 (1989) 27–37, cited in David Kutcha, 'The semiotics of masculinity in Renaissance England', in James Grantham Turner (ed.), *Sexuality and Gender in Early Modern Europe* (Cambridge: Cambridge University Press, 1993), p. 242.

29. On the Hollar engravings see Richard T. Godfrey, *Wenceslaus Hollar: A Bohemian Artist in England* (New Haven: Yale University Press, 1994), cat. no. 44, pp. 79–81.

30. Marcus Vitruvius Pollio, *The Ten Books on Architecture*, trans. Morris Hicky Morgan (New York: Dover Books, 1960), Book 1, ch. 2, para. 5, p. 15.

31. John Shute, *The First and Chief Groundes of Architecture* (London: Thomas Marshe, 1563), § Bii.

32. Wotton, *Elements of Architecture*, pp. 27–9.

33. See Keith Wrightson, 'Estates, degrees, and sorts: changing perceptions of society in Tudor and Stuart England' in P.J. Corfield (ed.), *Language, History and Class* (Oxford and Cambridge MA, 1991), pp. 30–52.

34. Wotton, *Elements of Architecture*, p. 14.

35. Joel Sanders, 'Introduction', in *Stud. Architectures of Masculinity* (New York: Princeton Architectural Press, 1996), p. 17.

36. Edmund Spenser, *The Fairie Queene*, II, ix, 22. On this passage see Alastair Fowler, *Spenser and the Numbers of Time* (New York, 1964), pp. 260 ff.

37. Susan Dwyer Amussen, '"The part of a Christian man": the cultural politics of manhood in early modern England' in Susan D. Amussen and Mark A. Kishlansky (eds), *Political Culture and Cultural Politics in Early Modern Europe. Essays Presented to David Underdown* (Manchester and New York: Manchester University Press, 1995), pp. 213–33.

38. On English educational practice, see among others, David Cressy, *Education in Tudor and Stuart England* (New York: St Martin's Press, 1976); Anthony Grafton and Lisa Jardine, *From Humanism to the Humanities. Education and the Liberal Arts in Fifteenth- and Sixteenth-Century Europe* (Cambridge, MA: Harvard University Press, 1986); J.H. Hexter, 'The Education of the Aristocracy in the Renaissance' in his *Reappraisals in History. New Views on History and Society in Early Modern Europe* (Chicago: University of Chicago Press, 1970), pp. 45–70; Lisa Jardine, 'Humanism and the Sixteenth Century Cambridge Arts Course', *History of Education*, 4:1 (1975) 16–31.

39. Loos is cited in Miriam Gusevich, 'The Architecture of Criticism: A Question of Autonomy', in Andrea Kahn (ed.), *Drawing/Building/Text* (New York: Princeton Architectural Press, 1991), p. 8.

40. Hexter, 'Education', esp. pp. 64–70.

41. Inigo Jones's annotation in his copy of Giorgio Vasari, *Le Vite del' Piu Excellenti Pittori, Scultori et Architettori* (Florence, 1568), p. 82. This copy is now in the collections of Worcester College, Oxford. See the discussion of this passage in Vanessa S. Chase, '"The Masculine Shew": The Country House as the Architecture of Masculinity in Late-Stuart England,' Master's Thesis, The Courtauld Institute of Art, University of London, 1991, pp. 12–15.

42. Ibid.

43. See the discussion of Jones's court career in J. Lees-Milne, *The Age of Inigo Jones* (London, 1953); John Harris, Stephen Orgel and Roy Strong, *The King's Arcadia: Inigo Jones and the Stuart Court* (London: Arts Council of Great Britain, 1973).

44. John Dee, 'The Mathematical Preface', in *The Elements of Geometrie of the Most Auncient Philosopher Euclide of Megara*, trans. Henry Billingsley (London, 1570).

45. The 1546 will of the mason John Multon specified the dispersal of 'all my portratures, plaates, books with all my other tooles and instruments'. W.J. Williams, 'Wills of Freemasons and Masons', *The Masonic Record* 16 (1936) 204; cited in Malcolm Airs, *The Tudor and Jacobean Country House. A Building History* (Stroud, Gloucs.: Alan Sutton Publishing, 1995), p. 54.

46. See John Wilton-Ely, 'The Rise of the Professional Architect in England' in Spiro Kostoff (ed.), *The Architect. Chapters in the History of the Profession* (New York and Oxford: Oxford University Press, 1977), pp. 180–208.

47. Leonard Digges, *A Boke Named Tectonicon* (London: John Daye, 1556), 'the pleasant profit or content'; cited in Eileen Harris, *British Architectural Books and Writers 1556–1785* (Cambridge and New York: Cambridge University Press, 1990), p. 182.

48. David Cast, 'Speaking of Architecture: The Evolution of a Vocabulary in Vasari, Jones, and Sir John Vanbrugh', *Journal of the Society of Architectural Historians*, 52 (June 1993) 187.

49. Ben Jonson, *Selections*, ed. Ian Donaldson (Oxford: Oxford University Press, 1985), p. 574.

50. Peacham, *The Complete Gentleman*, p. 54.

51. Allon White, '"The Dismal Sacred Word": Academic Language and the Social Reproduction of Seriousness', in his *Carnival, Hysteria, and Writing: Collected Essays and Autobiography* (Oxford: Oxford University Press, 1993), p. 122.

52. Lucy Gent, '"The Rash Gazer": Economies of Vision in Britain, 1550–1660', in Gent (ed.), *Albion's Classicism*, p. 378.

53. Wotton, *Elements of Architecture*, p. vii.

54. White, 'Dismal Sacred Word', p. 134.

55. See Peter Eisenman, 'The End of the Classical: The End of the Beginning, the End of the End', *Perspecta: The Yale Architectural Journal*, 21 (1984), 154–72.

CHAPTER 2

'O TOWER MOST WORTHY OF PRAISE!': THE PARADOX OF FREEDOM, CAPTIVITY AND GENDER IN LITERARY ARCHITECTURE OF SIXTEENTH-CENTURY FRANCE

Joanne Mosley

Architecture and literature enjoy a rarer relationship than other arts, since coexistence depends on compatibility of matter. But sixteenth-century France is a rich source of their interaction. Writers, courtiers and patrons lived in the ubiquitous presence of building projects, whether royal chateaux or family manors.[1]

Travel to Rome was a frequent literary adventure and the buildings were viewed as precious relics considering their ruinous state.[2] Du Bellay's *Antiquities of Rome*[3] is a monument of disappointment, and the use of the Forum as a cow field must have encouraged use of Horace's topos, 'Exegi monumentum', the durability of words more lasting than bronze.[4]

Interest in the professional architecture of Italy is reflected, from the 1540s, by the production of French translations of Vitruvius, Alberti and Serlio, as well as the home-grown works of De L'Orme, Bullet or Du Cerceau, which could be found in family collections throughout the land.[5] So too could the bestselling chivalric romances, in sales second only to the Bible and crammed with luscious descriptions of imaginary castles and palaces.[6] The impact of architecture is, of course, borne out by its memorable visual aspect which gave rise to the memory palace tradition, where buildings and their rooms were key tools in the art of memory.[7]

The two disciplines developed together in stature, with the creation, in mid-century, of Dorat's pléiade of poets, and De l'Orme's claiming the status of 'architect' rather than mason, a title long accorded to his Italian counterparts.[8] The accepted distinction was that the architect dealt in conceptual design and used his head, the mason dealt in tools and used his hands.[9] Collaboration took place between the most renowned poets and architects of the day for the royal entries, where the poets devised allegorical themes and the artists carried them out, leaving room for the verses of a Ronsard or a Dorat to adorn arches and fountains.[10]

The present paper examines the roles played by literary architecture in three major French writers of the sixteenth century – Rabelais, Montaigne and Marguerite de Navarre – and finally compares them with a contemporary Spanish classic by St Teresa of Avila.[11] Each of these authors uses an edifice to convey his or her central ideas, which in all cases are aspects of the theme of freedom and its opposite, captivity.[12] Buildings are particularly apposite to represent enclosure, and its various implications of escape, sanctuary or imprisonment.

Architecture is also a statement on gender. The literary critic, Patricia Meyer Spacks, argues in *The Female Imagination* that women's writing reveals that women do not feel free, but she links this phenomenon to a real, inferior social situation.[13] The social standing of the four authors under question is relatively comparable, and it is therefore possible, without ignoring context, to observe imagination as a psychological, rather than purely social, issue. Literary architecture is here applied as a yardstick against which to measure the perspectives of the two male and two female authors.

※ ※ ※

The Abbey of Thélème, often identified with the meaning 'the good life', is the climax of Rabelais's philosophical and comic novel of 1534: *Gargantua*.[14] This memorable episode occurs at the point where the giant Gargantua has won the Picrocholine war and is thinking up a worthy reward for Brother Jean who in one day alone had slain 13,622 men, armed with only the staff of his cross.[15] It is for this outstanding war hero that the Abbey of Thélème is conceived, and unlike the reward given to the people, which is mentioned only as 'a strong fort',[16] Thélème is examined in minutest detail: not least because the word 'abbey' does not convey what the author has conceived, and because each aspect of the building mirrors the ideas behind it.

The central idea is freedom, the Abbey being named after the Greek New Testament word, 'Thelēma', meaning 'free will'.[17] Informed by his stifling experience as a former monk, Rabelais challenges the necessity of enclosure. The importance he gives to free movement is seen from a comparison of Thélème with Brother Jean's own abbey, Seuillé: the latter is described as: 'well bolted and barred'.[18] Brother Jean is delighted to exchange Seuillé for Thélème, which will be different from all other abbeys for, as Gargantua says, 'First of all, . . . you mustn't build walls round it.'[19] Nor will there be any poverty, celibacy or obedience.[20]

Allusions to the cultured court of François I are legion, and it is the architecture which superimposes the court onto the monastic framework, for Gargantua's abbey is unmistakably reminiscent of Chambord, Blois or Amboise.

The reader is drawn into the aerial perspective of a hexagonal form, the number six symbolizing perfection,[21] and the huge round towers, each with six floors, each floor with 9,332 suites of rooms (a multiple of six), each suite with an inner chamber, closet, wardrobe and private chapel.[22] While an edifice of such proportions can only exist in the imagination or in fiction, the separate apartments were typical of the type of rooms at Chambord;[23] only later did chateaux contain the long stretches or *enfilades* of rooms which so struck Montaigne on his visit to Italy.[24]

Two features in particular are reminiscent of the Loire chateaux. The crowded skyline is a cross between pure symmetry and messy shapes, the latter a remnant of the French Middle Ages,[25] and conical roofs, protruding gutters and an array of gold figures, grotesques and small animals suggest Chambord. Also portrayed is a spiral staircase, like the one to be found at Blois or at Chambord where at least two men could climb it side by side. In Rabelais' narrative it is of fantasy proportions, allowing six mounted horsemen abreast to ascend it in full flight.[26]

The details of the building, being imaginary, are not subject to constraints of finances, materials or practicalities. A revealing example is the title of Chapter 53: 'How the Thélèmites' Abbey was built and endowed'.[27] In the first paragraph, the money for building the abbey is delivered; then, in the second paragraph, it appears that everyone has already moved in.

Rabelais's omission of detail is not a sign of ignorance, given his ability, evidenced throughout his work, for assimilating vast quantities of technical expertise on a wide range of subjects and deploying it for comic effect. He even had access to a ready source of architectural expertise during or just before the writing of *Gargantua*: working in Rome as the private secretary of the Cardinal Du Bellay, he became a close friend of Philibert De l'Orme; indeed, it is to the inspiration of De l'Orme that Anthony Blunt attributes the ingeniousness of Thélème's architecture.[28] The building detail which Rabelais does include is not very technical, perhaps in order to avoid pedantry, and it would have been familiar to any house owner: lead coping, gutters and pipes.[29] There is no mention of architraves, pediments or frontispieces which were an Italian fad, and Rabelais had no doubt heard De l'Orme's views on the loss of decorum occasioned by imitating ultramontane fashions in areas of France where certain materials were not to be found and the styles were inappropriate.[30]

The hugeness of the dimensions undoubtedly creates an impression of uninhibitedness. Notably, it is when the Abbey is described that the giant characters disappear from the story, as well as the larger-than-life Brother Jean, giving way to hundreds of inhabitants in miles of corridors. Perspective in particular conveys a sense of freedom, for the view of the abbey is always one which looks down and inwards: upon the walls and roofs and then into the details of the living quarters, containing every possible splendour of Rabelaisian plenty, from crystal mirror frames to embroidery and rhinoceros tusks.

The inhabitants of Thélème are aristocratic young ladies, noble handsome knights, and preachers of the Gospel. The emphasis is on equality of the sexes, and this situation is maintained in terms of occupation of space (three wings each) and activities (walking, hunting and riding in the purpose-built parks).

The insight into this utopian society, very different from that of Thomas More although a conscious echo of it, comes from the buildings rather than the actual people. The uniformity of free will converts into a passive drifting through life, evidenced by such inhuman statements as: 'If some man or woman said "Let us drink", they all drank.'[31] The community lacks the vibrancy of character; it is lifestyle rather than life and is gleaned by the reader in much the same way as visitors today take a guided tour of a stately home.

The building and its grounds speak for themselves, as it were. The inhabitants are known – or presumed – to read, because there is a library containing six shelves of books in six languages. They are known to swim in the pools, walk in the maze and play on the tennis courts because these things exist, but are not portrayed actually doing them. The indispensable army of servants is overlooked, probably because Rabelais chooses not to portray the humbler dwellings.

When Charles Lenormant in 1840 published his *Restitution of the Abbey of Thélème*,[32] he reconstructed Thélème with a ground plan and bird's eye view which, denuded of the luxuriant detail, appears to be an empty fortress or impregnable prison. The adjacent parks are similarly unwelcoming in the quest for accurate lines. Closer to the spirit of Rabelais are Gustave Doré's chaotic sketches, with protruding walls and many-sided towers, creating a sense of bustling rather than regimentedness.[33]

Rabelais's treatment contains both lines and detail, the idea of the architect and the trappings of the residents, perfect form clothed in luxury and comfort. With the equality of the sexes and the humanist reform so cherished by the great Valois monarch, Thélème appears to be a charmed world, a synthesis of many plenitudes and perfections.

Yet, not even this idealized abbey bears the promise of uninterrupted freedom, and its syntheses are but paradoxes in the light of real day. In his prologue, Rabelais likens his work to the Sileni of Alcibiades, which is particularly apt for Thélème:

> That is the reason why you must open this book, and carefully weigh up its contents. You will discover then that the drug contained within is far more valuable than the box promised; that is to say, that the subjects here treated are not so foolish as the title on the cover suggested.[34]

Close to an inscription instructing the fun-loving inhabitants of Thélème to live as they please is a bronze plaque on which are inscribed verses announcing the coming catastrophes when the good will be persecuted and the preachers of the Gospel will die. Thélème, like the real-life haven for humanist writers in courtly attire, is a threatened existence and is, after all, an enclosure, one which keeps enemies out: 'Enter not here, vile hypocrites and bigots', another inscription begins.[35] Thélème is home to a peace and freedom which will cease to exist once one looks outside.

* * *

Peace did come to an end. On 24 July 1570, at the height of the French civil Wars of Religion, Michel de Montaigne retired to a round tower in his family chateau. For the next eleven years he was able to relinquish the delicate, if not dangerous, position of Mayor of Bordeaux before royal command sent him back to his post. His retirement represented for Montaigne a hard-won freedom. This was the theme of the inscription which he had painted on his wall to commemorate his 38th birthday and a retirement dedicated to 'freedom, tranquillity, and leisure'.[36] Cicero had defined freedom as the power to live as one wished;[37] in this sense, the tower could be said to serve the same purpose as the Abbey of Thélème.

Montaigne's tower has become legendary, for scholars and tourists alike. It is also a literary event, for it symbolizes the author's solitary 'assaying', or testing out, of himself and the subsequent publication of the *Essays*.[38] In an early chapter, 'On solitude',[39] he yearned for space in which to be himself:

> So we must bring [the soul] back, haul her back, into our self. That is true solitude. It can be enjoyed in towns and in kings' courts, but more conveniently apart.[40]

It was with the hindsight of ten years of solitude that Montaigne wrote his chapter, 'On three kinds of social intercourse',[41] in which the tower is described. By this time, solitude is still prized but as a vantage point from which, unenslaved, one can understand the world better. This explains why the tower is climax to a chapter of an essentially social and unsolitary character: it considers in turn friendship and society, relationships with women, and reading books (this last part including the depiction of the tower and stressing the companionable nature of the authors on the shelves).

Montaigne describes his inner self as if in terms of the tower which had been his daily companion for so many years, and in keeping with his belief that architecture cannot be seen in separation from its inhabitants or function:[42] 'I would rather,' he writes, 'forge my soul than stock it up.'[43] The potential stock or furniture is books, those companions in solitude who can be either fellows in dialogue or causes of indoctrination.

It is notable that while a picture of the tower figures in almost every illustrated book on Montaigne and is revered as the seat of his philosophical reflections, its actual description by Montaigne is rarely quoted by critics. It is one of the rare passages of the *Essays* which are purely autobiographical, and its very reality appears to rob it of the potential of conveying other things.

The description of the tower is endowed with the realism of a proprietor surveying his own patrimony: 'My soul,' he writes, 'is satisfied and contented by this right of possession'.[44] And the tour to which he invites his reader is methodically orientated and filled with measurements and angles: from the first-floor chapel to the second-floor bedroom and dressing room, then to the third floor and the library and to its adjoining rooms where he spends all day every day. Rooms are referred to in connection with their commodities, the light they let in, the space they provide for the stacking of books. Speaking practically as an owner who would have appraised other residences with the consumer's eye, he contemplates the idea of himself having a gallery in which to pace about while thinking, but is deterred by the thought of the inconvenience such a building project would entail.[45]

The perspective – that of a man inside a tower, surveying its contents and the view – reveals a Montaigne who feels like the master, the use of possessives reinforcing his already quoted 'right of possession':

> At home I slip off to my library a little more often; it is easy for me to oversee my household from there. I am above my gateway and have a view of my garden, my chicken-run, my backyard and most parts of my house.[46]

This is the voice of the châtelain. Brantôme, the contemporary memorialist, expressed himself in similar lordly manner when contemplating a building project:

> Once, and against all good sense, I spent a long time planning to build a castle there in the form of a citadel to command over all the neighbouring places and roads. . .[47]

These outward views, noticeably in a different direction from the inward-looking ones of Rabelais's narrative, are made possible by the actuality instead of the symbolism of an edifice, whence to look outside is quite different from contemplating the outside world.

The power of property, combined with a physical commanding view, gives the Montaigne in his tower an essentially male voice, which differs from the frequently portrayed universal 'self' as human being. It is also – consciously or not – a purely male domain from which other people, in particular his wife and daughter, are excluded:

> There I have my seat. I assay making my dominion over it absolutely pure, withdrawing this one corner from all intercourse, filial, conjugal and civic.[48]

Montaigne associates confinement in a building with the religious life which both he and Rabelais consider a form of imprisonment. Yet neither author attributes the slavery of religious life to the actual physical incarceration within walls. For Rabelais, captivity is having to regulate one's life according to the sound of a bell;[49] for Montaigne it is being enclosed with other people. He writes:

> I have never considered any of the austerities of life which our monks delight in to be harsher than the rule that I have noted in some of their foundations: to be perpetually with somebody else and to be surrounded by a crowd of people no matter what they are doing. And I find that it is somewhat more tolerable to be always alone than never able to be so.[50]

The tower represents for Montaigne a purifying space providing for the elimination of external influences and allowing the authentic self to find freedom away from women, society and the undue influence of books. It is also love, worldliness and study which Marguerite de Navarre defines as her three *Prisons*.

* * *

The Prisons is arguably the summit of Marguerite de Navarre's literary output. Completed circa 1547, it recounts a journey from captivity to freedom, in which the narrator's stages of enlightenment are conveyed through fictional architecture: three different prisons from which the narrator escapes in turn.[51]

This protagonist is a male persona, which has the effect of reducing the work's autobiographical character and thereby of extending its reach. Yet there are obvious references to the author, such as descriptions of her family, and actual residences make a veiled appearance. Their influence on the creation of *The Prisons* may possibly be inferred in view of the surprising panegyric of her unlearned dullard first husband who had died twenty years previously, the Duke of Alençon: for Marguerite, this marriage had meant sacrificing magnificent chateaux, mirrored in the palace of Book II, for the fortified towers of the chateau of Alençon, today a state prison, resembling the monolith in Book I. She also sought refuge in her books, which may have inspired the fantasized library of Book III, and found freedom in enclosure, as did her mother-in-law in Alençon, also described in the third Book.[52]

The first of the three Books depicts a symbolic tower and its prisoner of love; on the surface, this is a conventional genre, which fact in itself is a strong reason for the narrator being male.[53] Prominence is given to the tower with which, anthropomorphically, the beloved is identified: there are such statements as: 'Your eye it was that held me, and your voice . . . /. . .bound me with rope';[54] 'on my knees I worshipped . . . that window',[55] and the panegyric:

> O tower most worthy of all praise, from you
> No other good can tempt me to depart[56]

In all three Books, edifices are hybrid, as when the narrator chooses the name of 'palace' to praise the tower:

> O lovely tower, delight-filled paradise,
> O radiant palace of the shining sun[57]

The term 'palace', too, is a mixture of positive and negative qualities for it also represents worldliness, as in this address to the tower:

> A fig for castles, palaces and towns,
> So ugly-seeming when compared to you![58]

The apparent ambiguity can, however, be resolved. The tower and palace, when praised, begin with an upper case letter in the French text and are called good or perfect – 'a tower so perfect in all parts',[59] the narrator says. But in the negative statement just quoted, they begin with a lower case letter and are said to be 'ugly'. The consistency of alternating cases suggests more than a printer's custom. More importantly, linking of the good with beauty and the bad with ugliness derives from Plato, who was introduced into France largely through the championing of Marguerite de Navarre.[60] This fact provides the philosophical dimension of the work, where the prison symbolizes the earthly body, from which the soul is trying to break free. The addition of the upper case letter to the edifices also renders the absolute perfection inherent in the Platonic Idea or perfect Form. But the tower is not the heavenly city.

A sense of its fragility is also conveyed by the mention of stones and bricks, for absoluteness cannot remain a seamless construction in the face of fragmentation. The tower is literally deconstructed, as the weather, exemplifying the topos of 'Exegi monumentum', sends it into ruins. The narrator exclaims to the former Beloved and to the reader:

> And I believed; those ancient walls, you vowed,
> Would stand and not a single brick be lost.[61]

> But that was not to be, for bolts and bars
> Began to break and fall[62]

With nowhere left to reside, he sheds the role of inhabitant for that of builder, the one who has made himself a prisoner of love: 'And all I find,' he writes, 'is my own handiwork'.[63]

In Book II, the royal palace, or prison of worldly ambition, is not constructed or inhabited by the narrator who now adopts the perspective of onlooker. The palace is noisy, bright and crowded, in contrast to the dark, quiet tower.[64] Bells and trumpet blasts can be heard, as well as the cry: 'This is the Court.'[65] Like the Abbey of Thélème, the lines and outlines of the palace are lost in an effusion of bustling detail.

In this Book, building becomes a theme in its own right. Architecture is cited as amongst the narrator's first discoveries. He says:

> Of architecture nothing had I known,
> Nor the delights of gold or painted forms
> Because my prison, ugly as it was,
> Had always seemed so perfect and so fair
> That I had never turned my eyes or mind
> To look on any building save my own.[66]

The prevalence of architecture over the reality of the story is illustrated in another flashback to Book I when he is reminded of his former Beloved, not by seeing a similar woman but a similar building, in the symbolism of a church, and this leads to the exclamation:

> . . . my prison was my church, . . .
> Altar and image, you alone were these,
> The end and aim of all my pilgrimage.[67]

The Book also uses architecture to make social comment, both through the narrator's desire for worldly glory – which includes wanting to build 'scores of houses'[68] – and through reflections based on his observation of interiors of buildings, such as the honours sought, and the pardons bought, by donors of church silver and reliquaries.[69] Running from the world for fear of losing his soul, yet arguably also in frustration at the unfulfilled desire to be creative – not one of the scores of houses gets built – the narrator retreats to his books.

The edifice of Book III is the *tour de force* of *The Prisons*. It is the one wholly fantasy construction and is introduced as such:

> Do not refuse to read about the third,
> That prison built and shaped by my own hands[70]

It is entirely man- or woman-made, with candle-light replacing the sun and moon. The narrative has all the creativity of that other fantasy construction, Thélème, but this time the actual building work is described:

I laid foundations for my prison first,
Then gradually the walls and pillars rose
As through long hours I toiled incessantly
And often studied far into the night;
For every pillar I used finest books.[71]

As with the rest of the work, the boundaries between fictional reality and fantasy are blurred, with literal study leading to the building of its symbol: the prison of the acquisition of knowledge for its own sake.

This prison consists of a laurel roof and pillars of books, each one representing a discipline of study. Colour abounds: poetry books are bound in green velvet studded with enamel flowers, mathematics in silver with engraved lines and circles, rhetoric in white satin, with black words emanating from a red open mouth. All the books reach up to the Bible, symbolically bound in lamb's wool, and it sits on top of theology, those books closest to the Spirit placed highest up in the pillar.[72]

The narrator's sudden revelation is the presence of God declaring to him: 'I am'.[73] This causes the destruction of this last prison, as the laurel leaves, symbol of worldly glory, are razed to the ground by the flame of the Holy Spirit. The piles of books, apparently supported by the roof, collapse from their position as walls and rearrange themselves, like so many building blocks, into a pavement on which the narrator walks away into freedom.[74]

At this point, the male identity of the narrator recedes and it addresses the reader as an equal soul:

O Nothing, in the All you are set free . . .
Gone are your fears of prison walls and bars[75]

With perfect liberty attained, the narrative ends and the architecture disappears. Buildings are not absolute but ambivalent entities, combining interior and exterior, enclosure and escape. They are also inseparable from their inhabitants, which is why a narrator who becomes 'Nothing' makes it impossible for even the most ideal of towers to exist.

* * *

There exists, however, an ideal edifice inside every person. This is the message of the *Interior Castle*, a work written in 1577 by Teresa of Avila, the Spanish mystic.[76] Instructed to find a novel way of explaining prayer but which was consistent with the teaching of the Catholic Church, she situated Christ at the heart of a crystal castle, which is a person's soul. The castle has seven levels, arranged like concentric circles around the absolute centre where Christ sits and waits patiently, invitingly, even sadly, hoping that the soul will want to make the journey to him.

The journey, which is that of prayer, begins at the very edge of the castle, in battle with the vermin and beasts, or worldly cares and worries, which try to prevent entrance to the castle. They even bear a resemblance to the soul, for in this state, both the person and the beasts are exterior rather than interior.[77] The person is therefore defined in terms of his or her positioning and as such is a generalized human being.

The interior conflict is reminiscent of Marguerite's *Prisons*[78] where a person engages in conflict in order to find escape from apparent, outer freedom and instal him- or herself inside a closed edifice. Teresa is also aware of this paradox when in another work she describes her monastery as a prison of freedom – 'O captivity / Of a great liberty'[79] – and she perceives her imagined castle as a means of escape from a real, concrete prison. Addressing the sisters, she writes:

> Considering the strict enclosure and the few things you have for your entertainment, my Sisters, and that your buildings are not always as large as would be fitting for your monasteries, I think it will be a consolation for you to delight in this interior castle since without permission from the prioress you can enter and take a walk through it at any time.[80]

The interior castle is depicted quite differently from static, cramped enclosure; it is a mobile, purposeful path, equivalent to the imagery of the ladder or ascent which was more common with mystical writers.[81] The end goal, God, is represented in terms of a king sitting at the heart of his palace,[82] or the sun at the centre of the castle, lighting up the gloomier rooms on the outer circumference.[83] The castle is thus the reverse of real buildings – and indeed of literary architecture based on possible buildings – where light is normally closest to rooms with windows and the interiors of towers are oppressively sombre. The perfection of the castle illumined in divine light makes it a prefiguration of the heavenly Jerusalem, whose inhabitants are first and foremost human souls.

* * *

The works examined show a curious relationship of text and architecture, where buildings are subsumed into writing and yet stand out from it, to the point, arguably, of being more memorable than the characters or personae. They are often described in detail but not with the technical architectural vocabulary which might be incongruous with literary, particularly reflective works. The conveyance of ideas is not limited to any one type of edifice: unsurprisingly, palaces are more courtly and towers solitary, although values of each depend on the authorial philosophy.

Notably, the personae do not always match the gender of the author: Rabelais's characters are mixed, Marguerite's narrator is male, Teresa's souls are genderless. Their role, as delineated by the buildings they inhabit, points to an equality of the sexes; it is significant that only in Montaigne's real-life situation are women excluded.

Beyond any statements or implications of equality, the gender of the authorial voice is more pronounced: Rabelais and Montaigne have a high or aerial view; Marguerite and Teresa are between windowless walls. Montaigne feels in command, Marguerite vulnerable. This is, of course, only a tentative indication of the gendered psyche, but with the exception of Teresa whose imagined castle grants freedom to physically enclosed women, there is little social reality to endorse the division of male and female perspective: Marguerite, after all, holds the highest social status.

The ordering of the texts reveals a progression not only of interiorness, but one of imaginary architecture raised from literary device to the status of a revelation. By virtue of its all-inclusive, transparent, and multi-dimensional form, the crystal castle can 'hold' the other edifices which run through it like a spiral staircase, as it were, and join it at the centre, which is the search for the truth and self-knowledge. After pushing past the vermin and beasts which roam around Teresa's castle, which are the worldly cares and vanities of *The Prisons*, there is the victory of the true interior revelation. The centre is also that of the utopian Thélème, where men and women are held in equality and are inherently good within. It is the victory of the interior man in his quest for self-knowledge, away from the noise of the world and even the foreign bodies of books which can rob the mind of authenticity. It is a castle where all contradictions are resolved and a place where interiorness and omni-sided views alike are safeguarded. It is perhaps the biggest paradox of all for text and architecture, for it is the victory of the spirit over space and matter.

NOTES

1. The royal palaces were known to all the king's subjects, whether they had seen them or not; Rabelais's description of his imaginary Abbey of Thélème as a thousand times more wonderful than Bonnivet (*Gargantua*, 1534 edition), Chantilly or Chambord (1542 edition) attests to the fame of these chateaux. Building was not, however, limited to families of particular standing; the title of Du Cerceau's manual of 1559 is revealing: *Livre d'Architecture . . . pour instruire ceux qui désirent bastir, soyent de petit, moyen, ou grand estat.* La Noue comments on the 'vehement passion' of his contemporaries for building; see *Discours politiques et militaires*, ed. F.-E. Sutcliffe (Paris and Geneva: Droz, 1967), p. 196.
2. Guide books to Rome and its architecture constituted a large corpus of travel literature. See Margaret M. McGowan, 'Impaired Vision: the Experience of Rome in Renaissance France', *Renaissance Studies*, 8:3 (1994) 244–55. See also: Eric MacPhail, *The Voyage to Rome in French Renaissance Literature*, vol. 68 (Saratoga, CA: Anma Libri (Stanford French and Italian Studies, 1990).
3. For the purposes of this paper, all titles and quotations will be given in English.
4. This commonplace was cited frequently by poets and in prefaces to works of history.
5. Important titles included: Alberti, *Architecture*, 1553; Colonna, *Hypnerotomachie ou Discours du Songe de Poliphile*, 1546; Serlio, *Le premier livre d'architecture*, 1545; Vitruvius, *Architecture*, 1547 (all the above translated by Jean Martin); Bullet, *Reigle générale d'architecture*, 1564 and 1568; Du Cerceau, *Les plus excellents bastimens de France*, vol. 1, 1576 and vol. 2, 1579; De l'Orme, *L'Architecture*, 1567.
6. See David Thomson, *Renaissance Architecture. Critics. Patrons. Luxury* (Manchester and New York: Manchester University Press, 1993), p. 84.
7. See Frances Yates, *The Art of Memory* (London: Routledge & Kegan Paul, 1966).
8. See Thomson, *Renaissance Architecture*, p. 131.
9. The difference between architect and mason had been explained by Alberti as, respectively, conceptual and material. De l'Orme, however, had insisted that the architect should also possess technical skill. See Doranne Fenoaltea, 'Doing it with Mirrors:

Architecture and Textual Construction in Jean Lemaire's *La Concorde des deux langages*' in B.C. Bowen and J.C. Nash (eds), *Lapidary Inscriptions: Renaissance Essays for Donald A. Stone Jr.* (Lexington, KY: French Forum, 1991), pp. 23 and 31, n. 14.

10. See Frances Yates, 'Poètes et artistes dans les entrées de Charles IX et de sa Reine à Paris en 1571' in J. Jacquot (ed.), *Les Fêtes de la Renaissance*, vol. I (Paris: Editions du CNRS, 1956), pp. 61–84.

11. Chronology has not been observed in order to examine Marguerite de Navarre after Montaigne and thus to group the two male and female authors together.

12. Literary architecture is a growing area of research. David Thomson, the architectural historian (*Renaissance Architecture*) has explored the controversy of fantasy architecture. Recent work, tracing aesthetic principles common to textual and architectural structure, includes: Doranne Fenoaltea, '*Si haulte architecture*'. *The Design of Scève's Délie* (Lexington, KY: French Forum, 1982); Cynthia Skenazi, 'Eutoie et Utopie dans *Le Temple de Cupidon* de Marot', *French Studies*, xlix (Jan. 1995) 17–28.

13. 'The fact that women may find their most significant freedom through fantasy or imagination need not imply any commitment to madness.' See Patricia Meyer Spacks, *The Female Imagination. A Literary and Psychological Investigation of Women's Writing* (London: Allen & Unwin, 1976), p. 314.

14. The Thélème episode (Chapters 52–58 of *Gargantua*) is arguably a free-standing episode and has been published separately: see Raoul Morçay (ed.), *L'Abbaye de Thélème* (Paris: Droz, 1934 and 1949). References to the original are taken from Rabelais, *Œuvres complètes* (*OC*), ed. Pierre Jourda (Paris: Garnier, 1962). English translations are from Rabelais, *The Histories of Gargantua and Pantagruel* (*HGP*) trans. J.M. Cohen (Harmondsworth: Penguin, 1955).

15. See Chapter 27: *OC*, pp. 111–12; *HGP*, pp. 100–1.

16. 'un fort chasteau' (Chapter 51): *OC*, p. 187; *HGP*, p. 148.

17. For further discussion of the debate on free will in relation to the Thélème episode, see M.A. Screech, *Rabelais* (London: Duckworth, 1979), pp. 187–94.

18. 'bien reserrée et fermée' (Chapter 27): *OC*, p. 106; *HGP*, p. 97.

19. 'Premierement . . . il n'y fauldra jà bastir murailles au circuit.' (Chapter 52): *OC*, p. 189; *HGP*, p. 150.

20. '[Item,] parce que ordinairement les religieux faisoient troys veuz, sçavoir est de chasteté, pauvreté et obedience, fut constitué que là honorablement on peult estre marié, que chascun feut riche et vesquist en liberté.' (Chapter 52): *OC*, p. 190; *HGP*, p. 151.

21. Ancient and modern mathematics also attributed mystical powers to the number six. See Screech, *Rabelais*, p. 189.

22. See Chapter 53: *OC*, p. 192; *HGP*, pp. 151–2.

23. Chambord was an early example of such *appartements*, which were to become the norm in French chateaux; see David Watkin, *A History of Western Architecture* (London: Laurence King, 1986), p. 211.

24. See Richard Sayce 'The Visual Arts in Montaigne's *Journal du Voyage*' in Raymond C. La Charité (ed.), *O Un Amy! Essays on Montaigne in Honor of Donald M. Frame* (Lexington, KY: French Forum, 1977), (pp. 219–41), p. 235.

25. See Anthony Blunt, *Art and Architecture in France 1500–1700* (Yale University Press and Pelican, 1993), pp. 16–18; Watkin, *History of Western Architecture*, pp. 210–11.

26. See Chapter 53: *OC*, p. 193; *HGP*, p. 152.

27. '*Comment feust bastie et dotée l'abbaye des Thelemites*': *OC*, p. 191; *HGP*, p. 151.

28. See Blunt, *Art and Architecture*, p. 84.

29. 'l'endousseure de plomb', 'goutieres', 'eschenaulx' (Chapter 53): *OC*, p. 192; *HGP*, p. 152.

30. De l'Orme sets these views out in Books I and VI of his *Architecture* (Paris, 1567); see Blunt, *Art and Architecture*, pp. 86–7.

31. 'Si quelq'un ou quelcune disoit: "Beuvons", tous buvoient' (Chapter 57): *OC*, p. 204; *HGP*, p. 159.

32. *Rabelais et l'Architecture de la Renaissance. Restitution de l'Abbaye de Thélème*, Paris, 1840. The plans referred to are reproduced in Thomson, *Renaissance Architecture*, Plates 38 and 39, p. 77.

33. Doré's abbey, which one can be forgiven for assuming to be Thélème, is included in Rabelais' *Œuvres*, Paris: Garnier, 1873 as the monastery of the Fredons in Chapter XXVI of *Le Cinquième Livre*, which is now generally assumed not to be by Rabelais. It does not include a written account of the new monastery. The illustration is reproduced in Rabelais, *OC*, p. 376.

34. 'C'est pourquoy fault ouvrir le livre et soigneusement peser ce que y est deduict. Lors congnoistrez que la drogue dedans contenue est bien d'aultre valeur que ne promettoit la boite, c'est-à-dire que les matieres icy traictées ne sont tant folastres comme le titre au-dessus pretendoit' (The Author's Prologue): *OC*, p. 7; *HGP*, p. 38.

35. 'Cy n'entrez pas, hypocrites, bigotz' (Chapter 54): *OC*, p. 194; *HGP*, p. 153.

36. See Donald M. Frame, *Montaigne. A Biography* (San Francisco: North Point Press, 1984), p. 115.

37. See M.A. Screech, *Montaigne and Melancholy. The Wisdom of the Essays* (London: Duckworth, 1983), p. 65.

38. This testing of the self is the meaning of Montaigne's title, the *Essais*.

39. Book I, Chapter 39.

40. 'Ainsin il la faut ramener et retirer en soy: c'est la vraie solitude, et qui se peut jouïr au milieu des villes et des cours des Roys; mais elle se jouyt plus commodément à part'; see Montaigne, *Œuvres complètes* [*OC*] ed. M. Rat (Paris: Gallimard (Pléiade), 1962), p. 234. All English translations of Montaigne in the text are taken from Montaigne, *The Complete Essays* (*TCE*) trans. M.A. Screech (Harmondsworth: Penguin, 1993), the present quotation on p. 269.

41. Book III, Chapter 3.

42. See Sayce, 'The Visual Arts', p. 237.

43. Book III, Chapter 3: *TCE*, p. 923. The original conveys clearly the idea of stock as furniture: 'j'aime mieux forger mon ame que la meubler', *OC*, p. 797.

44. 'mon ame se rassasie et contente de ce droict de possession.' (Book III, Chapter 3): *OC*, p. 806; *TCE*, p. 932.

45. See Book III, Chapter 3: *OC*, p. 806; *TCE*, p. 933.

46. 'Chez moy, je me destourne un peu plus souvent à ma librairie, d'où tout d'une main je commande à mon mesnage. Je suis sur l'entrée et vois soubs moy mon jardin, ma basse court, ma court, et dans la pluspart des membres de ma maison.' (Book III, Chapter 3): *OC*, p. 806; *TCE*, p. 933.

47. 'Je fus une fois et longtemps en dessein d'y faire bastir un chasteau en forme de citadelle, par despit, pour commander aux environs et chemins'; see Brantôme, *Œuvres complètes*, ed. L. Lalanne, vol. 10, 1881, p. 151 (quoted in Anne-Marie Cocula-Vaillières, *Brantôme. Amour et gloire au temps des Valois* (Paris: Albin Michel, 1986), p. 420.

48. 'C'est là mon siege. J'essaie à m'en rendre la domination pure, et à soustraire ce seul coin à la communauté et conjugale, et filiale, et civile.' (Book III, Chapter 3): *OC*, p. 807; *TCE*, p. 933.

49. See Rabelais, *Gargantua* (Chapter 52): *OC*, p. 189; *HGP*, p. 150.

50. 'Je n'ay rien jugé de si rude en l'austerité de vie que nos religieux affectent, que ce que je voy en quelqu'une de leurs compagnies, avoir pour regle une perpetuelle societé de lieu et assistance nombreuse entre eux, en quelque action que ce soit. Et trouve aucunement plus supportable d'estre tousjours seul, que ne le pouvoir jamais estre.' (Book III, Chapter 3): *OC*, p. 807; *TCE*, pp. 933–4.

51. References to the original are taken from Marguerite de Navarre, *Les Prisons* (*LP*) ed. Simone Glasson (Geneva: Droz, 1978). All English translations are from *The Prisons of Marguerite de Navarre* (*TPMN*) trans. Hilda Dale (Reading: Whiteknights Press, 1989).

52. One of Marguerite's biographers also interprets this transition in terms of imprisonment: 'Marguerite vivait auprès d'une mère et d'un frère très aimé, dans une demeure riante, à deux pas des fastes de la cour. La voici enfermée dans un sombre château médiéval, entre une belle-mère très pieuse et un mari illettré, d'esprit militaire.' See J.-L. Déjean, *Marguerite de Navarre* (Paris: Fayard, 1987). For descriptions of members of Marguerite's family in *The Prisons*, see Book III, ll. 2167–244 (Marguerite de Lorraine); ll. 2245–456 (Charles d'Alençon); ll. 2457–706 (Louise de Savoie); ll. 2707–864 (François I).

53. Works in this tradition include Froissart's *Prison amoureuse*; Diego de San Pedro, *Carcel de Amor* and the chivalric romances. See also Glasson's discussion in *LP*, pp. 15–18.

54. 'Si vostre œil fut mon lyen, et ma corde
    Vostre parler'.
    Book I, ll. 51–2: *LP*, p. 77; *TPMN*, p. 2.

55. 'A deulx genoulz, . . .
    Je l'adoroys'
    Book I, ll. 110–11: *LP*, p. 79; *TPMN*, p. 4.

56. 'O digne Tour d'avoir toute louange,
    Pour autre bien jamais je ne vous change!'
    Book I, ll. 137–38: *LP*, p. 80; *TPMN*, p. 4.

57. 'O belle Tour, ô Paradis plaisant,
    O clair Palais du soleil reluysant'
    Book I, ll. 121–2: *OC*, p. 79; *TPMN*, p. 4.

58. 'Fi des chasteaux, des villes, des palais!
    Au pris de vous, ilz me semblent tous laidz.'
    Book I, ll. 129–30: *LP*, p. 79; *TPMN*, p. 4.

59. 'si parfaict edifice'
    Book I, l. 128: *LP*, p. 79; *TPMN*, p. 4.

60. She commissioned original translations of Plato, who was a lively subject of discussion in her literary circles. See L. Clark Keating, *Studies on the Literary Salon in France, 1550–1615* (Cambridge, MA: Harvard University Press, 1941), pp. 15–16.

61. 'En m'affermant que ma prison antique
    Demourroit ferme, sans en rompre une brique'
    Book I, ll. 191–2: *LP*, p. 82; *TPMN*, p. 6.

62. 'Mais quoy! je viz et grilles et verroulz
    Rompre et lascher'
    Book I, ll. 253–4: *LP*, p. 84; *TPMN*, p. 7.

63. 'Mais je n'y voy que l'œuvre de mes doigtz'
    Book I, l. 272: *OC*, p. 85; *TPMN*, p. 8.

64. The critic, P. Sommers, emphasizes the paradox of movement which in worldly terms means freedom while in *The Prisons* it symbolizes the dissipation of the soul. See *Celestial Ladders: Readings in Marguerite de Navarre's Poetry of Spiritual Ascent* (Geneva: Droz, 1989), p. 93.

65. 'Lors j'entendiz ung qui dist: "C'est la court."'
    Book II, l. 254: *LP*, p. 105; *TPMN*, p. 26.

66. 'Jamais n'avoys congneu l'architecture
    Ne prins plaisir en dorure ou paincture,
    Car ma prison, bien qu'elle fust mal faicte,
    Trouvée avoys si belle et si parfaicte,
    Que je n'avoys œil ny entendement
    Jamais tourné sur autre bastiment.'
    Book II, ll. 149–54: *LP*, p. 102; *TPMN*, p. 23.

67. '. . . Ma prison m'estoit temple . . .
    Vous seulle estiez mon autel, mon ymaige,

Le but et fin de mon pelerinage.'
    Book II, ll. 225 and 227–8: *LP*, p. 104; *TPMN*, p. 25.
68. See Book II, ll. 155–9: *LP*, p. 102; *TPMN*, p. 23.
69. See Book II, ll. 231–48: *LP*, pp. 104–5; *TPMN*, pp. 25–6.
70. 'Ne refusez de veoir ceste derniere,
    Laquelle [fiz] et bastys de moymesmes'
    Book III, ll. 16–17: *LP*, p. 135; *TPMN*, p. 49.
71. 'Ceste prison par le bas commançay,
    Et peu à peu pilliers et murs haulsay.
    Par grand labeur et par long travailler,
    Par mainctes nuictz estudiant veiller,
    Tous mes pilliers de beaulx livres je fiz'
    Book III, ll. 31–5: *LP*, p. 136; *TPMN*, p. 50.
72. See Book III, ll. 37–300: *LP*, pp. 136–45; *TPMN*, pp. 50–7.
73. See Book III, l. 520: *LP*, p. 153; *TPMN*, p. 63.
74. See Book III, ll. 1537–42: *LP*, pp. 186–7; *TPMN*, p. 90.
75. 'O Rien, en Tout tu es en liberté, . . .
    Tu ne craindz plus d'estre mys en prison.'
    Book III, ll. 3129 and 3131: *LP*, p. 239; *TPMN*, p. 133.
76. The work is also known popularly by its subtitle of the 'dwelling places'. Teresa entitled
    her manuscript: *El Castillo Interior o las Moradas*. See Santa Teresa, *Las Moradas*, ed.
    T.N. Tomás (Madrid: Ediciones de 'La Lectura', 1922), p. xiv, n. (1). The first French
    translation was published in 1601, as part of the *Œuvres*, trans Jean de Brétigny and
    Dom du Chèvre (Paris: Guillaume de la Noue), 3 vols, and ran to several editions as a
    separate work with the title *Le traité du château ou demeures de l'âme*. See Jean
    Dagens, *Bibliographie chronologique de la littérature de spiritualité et de ses sources
    (1501–1610)* (Paris: Desclée de Brouwer, 1952), entry '1601'. All references to the work
    are taken from Teresa of Avila, *The Interior Castle* (*TIC*) trans. K. Kavanaugh and
    O. Rodriguez (New York, Ramsey and Toronto: Paulist Press (Series: The Classics of
    Western Spirituality), 1979).
77. 'They [exterior souls] are now so used to dealing always with the insects and vermin
    that are in the wall surrounding the castle that they have become almost like them.' See
    TIC, The First Dwelling Places, Chapter One, section 6, p. 38.
78. There is no implication that Teresa would have read Marguerite de Navarre, which
    would have been highly improbable.
79. 'Oh qué cativerio/De gran libertad'; see Thérèse d'Avila, *Œuvres complètes* (Paris:
    Desclée de Brouwer, 1989), 'Poesías', XXX, p. 1132.
80. See *TIC*, Epilogue, section 1, p. 195.
81. More famous examples include St John Climacus' *Ladder to Paradise* and the *Ascent of
    Mount Carmel* by St John of the Cross, co-founder of the Carmelite order with Teresa.
82. See *TIC*, The Seventh Dwelling Places, Chapter Two, section 11, p. 182.
83. See *TIC*, The First Dwelling Places, Chapter Two, section 8, p. 42.

CHAPTER 3

WOMAN ON TOP: LADY MARGARET BEAUFORT'S BUILDINGS AT CHRIST'S COLLEGE, CAMBRIDGE

Louise Durning

The pre-Reformation colleges of Oxford and Cambridge would seem to offer a promising subject for the architectural historian concerned to analyse the spatial construction of gender identity. These were exclusively masculine spaces; societies of celibate men, many of them ordained priests, living, eating, studying and worshipping in community, cared for by male servants and protected from female intrusion by force of statute as well as by their perimeter walls. However, the customary historiographical models employed in the analysis of these institutions have had little to say on the role of this gender-exclusivity as one of their defining features. Instead, the architectural history of the Oxbridge colleges has been dominated by a typological model, concerned with tracing the evolutionary morphology of the college 'type' and of its constituent parts – gatehouses, chapels, lodgings, halls – and moreover of classifying 'Cambridge' and 'Oxford' variants of the generic type. Though this model has its roots in nineteenth-century positivist historiography, specifically in the work of Willis and Clark, its normativizing strategies are still rehearsed in contemporary writing.[1]

My aim in this paper is to challenge this approach through a re-examination of one of these colleges and to open up instead a gendered reading of its buildings. However, in choosing this particular college I am deliberately seizing upon an anomalous case, one where the active intervention of a female patron places the presumed norms of collegiate design under stress. Christ's College, Cambridge was founded in 1505 by Lady Margaret Beaufort, Countess of Richmond and Derby (1443–1509) and mother of Henry VII.[2] The college buildings she commissioned reveal some atypical features in the treatment of spatial planning and sculptural decoration, features which have hitherto been submerged beneath the customary typological generalizations of collegiate history. In place of these, I will consider the novel design of the buildings as a response to the unusual representational demands of a powerful female patron, focusing specifically on the design of the master's lodge and on the heraldic sculpture of the gatehouse.

Christ's College was, in fact, a refoundation of an existing college, called Godshouse, established on the same site in the 1440s and absorbed into the new foundation. The establishment of the new college was the climax of a period of intense interest in Cambridge on the part of the countess, shaped and encouraged by her close relationship with Bishop John Fisher, her personal confessor and,

Figure 1 *Birds-eye view of Christ's College, Cambridge, reduced from David Loggan's print of c. 1688*

from 1504, Chancellor of the University. She endowed the university preacher-ships, and took an active interest in the affairs of other colleges, encouraging Bishop Alcock's foundation at Jesus. On the death of Elizabeth of York in 1503, she assumed *de facto* the role of patroness of Queens' college, manoeuvring Fisher's election as President.[3] Her specific interest in Christ's College may have been encouraged by its connection with Henry VI whom it claimed as 'founder'.[4] Through the countess's interventions, however, this small college was radically transformed. It was greatly increased in size and wealth and quickly provided with new buildings appropriate to its enhanced status.[5] Between 1505 and 1510 the college had acquired a complete quadrangle, closed on all four sides, containing all the necessary components of college life, including a grand gatehouse, a new master's lodging and hall and a sumptuous rebuilding and refitting of the college chapel (Figure 1).[6]

The comprehensiveness of this building scheme is in itself significant. Most of the medieval colleges acquired their sites and buildings piecemeal, sometimes over protracted periods, and only the wealthiest foundations such as New College, Oxford, founded by a Bishop of Winchester, or Queens' College in Cambridge, backed by royal patronage, had enjoyed the luxury of a complete scheme of buildings raised to a single plan.[7] However, the building programme at Christ's not only expanded the college accommodation but radically transformed its spatial organization, establishing with exceptional lucidity the hierarchical relationships between its component parts, a hierarchy which had, at its apex, the countess herself.

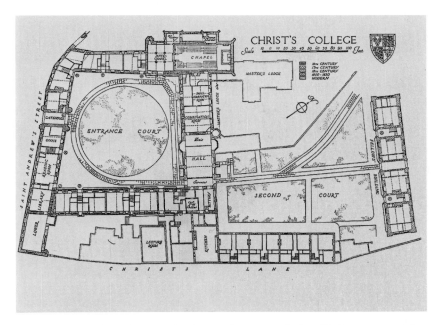

Figure 2 *Christ's College Cambridge. Modern ground plan (© Crown copyright. NMR)*

Standing under the gate and facing into the interior, the important foci of the college face the visitor across the expanse of the court. The chapel and hall are brought into a unified 'prestige' complex by a linking two-storey block of chambers usually known as the master's lodge (Figures 2 and 3). Yet this nomenclature masks its real function and interest for, as chapter six of the foundress's statutes makes clear, the upper floor of this new building was specifically designed to house a suite of rooms for the countess herself, the master being accommodated on the ground floor only:

> The Master himself, for the time being, we allow to occupy those lower rooms which are below the first floor rooms built for our use.[8]

This component of the college complex is unique among pre-Reformation Oxford and Cambridge college plans, providing the only known instance of rooms specifically reserved for a female occupant. Its presence disrupts the common assumption that the medieval colleges were exclusively masculine spaces.[9] Although they were not subject to monastic enclosure, the statutes of the colleges commonly contained injunctions against the presence of women within their precincts, a measure to safeguard both the reputation and the 'peace' of their communities.[10] Recent scholarship has begun to cast some doubt on the extent to which the ideals of statutory provision were maintained in practice; nevertheless, the emphatic

Figure 3 *Christ's College, Cambridge. View into the court with master's lodging.*
(Photo: Louise Durning)

inclusion of a female presence within the precincts of Christ's, embodied in its central building and proclaimed on its exterior by the oriel window which bears her coat of arms, is still an exceptional instance.[11]

It is surprising therefore that the Beaufort lodging has received little comment from previous historians. The existence of the countess's rooms is routinely noted in the many published accounts of the college and its buildings, but their significance has never been the subject of serious analysis. For Willis and Clark, for example, the master's lodge at Christ's was only one of many which served to demonstrate the typical 'Cambridge' plan, by placing the master's lodging next to the dais end of the hall, an analysis followed by the authors of the Royal Commission for Historic Monuments volumes on the buildings of Cambridge.[12] More recently, Jones and Underwood, in their biography of Lady Margaret, have discussed the importance of the lodge, emphasizing the extent to which this part of the college court 'was dominated by arrangements for her personal convenience', though they do not comment in any detail on its architectural significance.[13]

The Beaufort lodging (perhaps a less misleading term than 'master's lodge') is arranged in two superimposed suites. Both comprised three rooms, the timber partitioning of the master's rooms mirroring that of the floor above.[14] In the master's rooms, the chamber nearest the hall, usually known as the master's parlour, opened directly off the dais and probably also served as a meeting room for the master and senior fellows. This had its own separate door to the court, while the two inner rooms, the master's private chambers, could also be entered through a door beneath the carved oriel of the upper lodging.[15] Entry to the master's suite was made directly from the court but access to the countess's upper suite was more protected, provided by two turret staircases projecting from the rear of the lodge into the privy garden. One stair communicated with the dais end of the hall, the other, since demolished, provided access to the chapel. The internal arrangements of the rooms on each floor have been much altered, and a major restoration campaign of 1911 involved the complete reconstruction of the internal timber partitions, but when originally built the countess's suite contained a sequence of three interconnecting chambers: a large room next to the hall; an inner room (marked on the exterior by its oriel window); and a smaller room next to the chapel, which may have been subdivided into a bedchamber and oratory.[16]

The significance of this disposition of chambers is that it provided the countess, albeit in the limited compass of a college court, with the minimum necessary complement for an aristocratic lodging or apartment: antechamber, chamber and closet – a sequence of rooms necessary not only for convenience but also for the ritual expression of state. In the great houses of the medieval nobility, status relationships were enacted in spatial terms, through degrees of proximity and distance and the ceremonial crossing of thresholds. The authority of the occupant of the principal lodgings was embodied in the ability to grant or withhold access to one or more rooms in the sequence. The countess's chambers, visually central to the plan of the court externally, were also placed at the deepest level of access, a private self-contained zone, beyond the hall dais, protected from easy access by its turret stair, but enabling controlled entry to the antechamber or even great chamber for invited guests of appropriate rank. Doubtless, when the countess had lodged at Queens' College on earlier visits to Cambridge, more makeshift arrangements may have been necessary to accommodate her and her retinue, but in the new purpose-built lodging at Christ's she could more efficiently command the kind of dignified spatial setting to which she would have been accustomed in her own houses and palaces.[17]

The relationship between the Beaufort lodging and contemporary aristocratic domestic planning is further underlined by its arrangement into superimposed apartments. This introduced a new element into collegiate planning, the 'stacked' lodging. Simon Thurley, in his study of Tudor royal palaces, has analysed the fashion for this particular arrangement of elite accommodation in early Tudor court circles.[18] It was employed at Henry VII's new palace of Richmond (1497–1501), where the lodgings for the queen and the king were stacked one above the other, and in the royal guest lodgings built at Wolsey's palaces. Similar arrangements are found at a number of courtier houses of the period, notably the stacked ducal lodgings built at Thornbury Castle, Gloucestershire, for the Duke of Buckingham (1508–1521), and at Kenninghall, built for the Duke of Norfolk (1520s).[19] In both of these houses the ducal lodgings, differentiated by more elaborate fenestration, occupy the upper floor with the duchess lodged below. Significantly, Thurley located the earliest known English example of the 'stacked lodging' in one of Lady Margaret's own properties, Maxstoke Castle in Warwickshire.[20] This timber-framed building, erected in the late 1480s or early 1490s during her stewardship of the castle, has on each floor a large bay-windowed room with a smaller room beyond.[21]

In the stacked lodging at Christ's, the customary gender hierarchy which informed this disposition of rooms was reversed, or rather, in the absence of the conjugal couple which informed such planning, was redefined. Lodging the head of house on the ground floor also disrupted the customary spatial hierarchy of collegiate living. At every other college of the time, as indeed in the older Godshouse, the master could expect the privilege of a room or two on an upper floor.[22] Here, however, though relegated to the ground floor, he had the luxury of a suite of rooms in a commanding position. Indeed it could be argued that his status was elevated by inclusion in this new complex, ennobled by his subordination, but also his proximity, to the new household's female head.[23] Broad parallels have often been drawn between the quadrangular plan forms of medieval colleges and great houses, but here it would seem the college itself was transformed into a household by the presence of the foundress's chambers at its heart. The lodgings of the fellows and scholars, grouped around and below Lady Margaret's chambers, duplicated not simply the formal, but also the ritual, arrangement of spaces within the great house.[24]

The capacity to exceed the customary limits of the feminine which is demonstrated in the Beaufort lodging was mirrored in the ambiguities of the countess's gendered presence within the Tudor polity. Her customary title, 'Our Lady the King's Mother', honoured her as matriarch, but in the years following her son's accession to the throne Lady Margaret's public role, and her feminine identity, was radically transformed, enabling her to command a freedom of action and a degree of personal power unusual even for women of her class. By an Act in Henry's first Parliament in 1485, she was declared *femme sole*.[25] Though still married to her third husband, Thomas Stanley, Earl of Derby, this action redefined her legal identity as that of a single person, 'not coverte of anie husband' and brought with it the right to hold property and pursue actions at law in her own right. Seeking recognition as *femme sole* was a tactic more commonly exploited by urban businesswomen, allowing them to trade independently (and to protect their husbands from responsibility for their debts).[26] However, as Jones and Underwood have argued, 'for a married aristocratic woman to declare herself *femme sole* was quite unprecedented'.[27]

This action in common law was followed some years later by a process in canon law which further redefined the public boundaries of her gender identity. In 1498 or 1499, the still-married countess took a vow of perpetual chastity.[28] Vowed women were normally, though not exclusively, widows. In taking the 'mantle and ring' which were the visible signs of their special estate, vowesses remained within, but formally set apart from, the normal commerce of daily life. As Erler noted in her study of this practice, the motives informing the decision to vow could be complex, involving not only pious but economic considerations, bringing with it the freedom to control their own resources, 'control which the vow safeguarded from male intrusion in the form of pressure to remarry'.[29] The countess, as *femme sole*, was already in command of such material autonomy before she took her vow and, being in her late fifties, may have been thought unlikely to marry again. Though a spirit of pious self-dedication need not be wholly dismissed, it is significant that the immediate material effect of her vow was a separation from her husband and the setting up her own independent household and council centred on her new palace at Collyweston near Stamford.[30]

It is clear that, by the time of her Cambridge foundation, Lady Margaret, now in her sixties and at the height of her financial and political power, had for decades been acting as an independent authority. The power that came from her newly acquired royal status and financial independence, and which made the founding of her college possible, also conferred the symbolic power to reassign the limits of her public identity.[31]

Thus far, our concern has been to interpret the function of the Beaufort lodging. But the question of function needs to be addressed more widely. Why have such a suite at all? For what reason would a founder, far less a foundress, need to command purpose-built accommodation within their college? Though Lady Margaret's piety was legendary, it is unlikely that the rooms at Christ's were intended as a contemplative retreat.[32] A more likely explanation may be found in the larger role she played in the affairs of the university. Since the early 1500s the countess had exercised real authority in Cambridge not only as a powerful benefactress but as a lawgiver. As Malcolm Underwood has shown, it was to her court at Collyweston that, in 1501, an important dispute between the university and the town was referred for arbitration. The resulting agreement vested power in the countess to deal with any further disputes between town and gown.[33] Her rooms at Christ's College may therefore have been intended as a necessary base for her interests in Cambridge government and an appropriately grand arena for the reception of visitors and supplicants.

There could have been no more emphatic statement of Lady Margaret's authority in Cambridge than the new gatetower of the college, rising just opposite one of the city gates, and dominated by the lavish and colourful display of her arms (Figure 4). The embodiment of the foundress's presence in the spatial planning of the college was also amplified by the heraldic decoration of the buildings. Displays of her badges and arms visually punctuate the spaces of the college, marking its focal points – the heraldic themes of the gate were repeated on the oriel window of her principal chamber facing into the court. Though emphatic displays of heraldry, particularly on gateways and oriel windows, were a fashionable feature of aristo-cratic, episcopal and royal building works of late medieval England, the conspicuous scale of the display at Christ's, and its concentrated orchestration of dynastic information, particularly in the grand gateway, represent important innovations.

Here again, as with the Beaufort lodging, the unusual treatment of this part of the college has tended to be overlooked within the dominant typological modes of analysis. The tendency in the past has been to see the Christ's College gatehouse as exemplifying a stage in the stylistic evolution of the 'Cambridge' gate.[34] Like the layout of the lodging though, this too needs to be interpreted within the specific context of its founder's intentions. Such an interpretation demands that heraldry be taken seriously. The bright colours and imagery of heraldic insignia, though they offered much scope for decorative treatment, were not simply decorative embellishments. Coats of arms were heritable signs, proofs of descent, and of the right to titles and lands which that descent entailed and as such their

Figure 4 *Christ's College, Cambridge. Detail of gatetower. (Photo: Louise Durning)*

use was subject to legal control.[35] Thus a coat of arms was not only a representation of authority, the act of displaying it was in itself a concrete instance of that authority.

The dominant note of the display on the Christ's gate is the shield of the Beaufort family with Lady Margaret's personal crest of a ducally gorged eagle issuing from a coronet. The Beaufort shield, incorporating the arms of England within a blue and silver border, proclaimed their royal descent from John of Gaunt, son of Edward III and patriarch of the Lancastrian dynasty. The visual impact of the armorial shield is increased by the gigantic scale of the mythical beasts (yales) which support the shield, and by the carved 'backdrop' of foliage and flowers, including marguerites and forget-me-nots against which it is set. These flowers were the countess's personal emblems, punning allusions to her name and to her motto, *souvent me souvient*. These are emphatically the countess's own arms, not a simple repetition of her paternal arms, nor do they contain any reference to any of her marriages.[36]

The second major theme is provided by the large badges which appear on the upper tier of the gatehouse: the royally crowned red rose of the house of Lancaster and the coroneted portcullis of the Beauforts. They reappear, reversed, in the lower register filling the spaces behind the supporters, and the portcullis badge appears again below the arms in the 'tympanum' of the ogee label. The portcullis and rose were the royal livery badges, adopted by Henry VII on his accession, and instantly recognizable marks of the countess's regal status.[37] They are reiterated, on a smaller scale, in the paterae of the arch moulding together with other Lancastrian and Tudor badges and, in the label stops, the dragon and greyhound supporters of Henry VII.

This profusion of dynastic information, a complex interweaving of personal, familial and monarchical insignia, asserts the royal provenance of the college and its foundress. But it is also possible that the innovative manner in which this information was disposed, its visual rhetoric, also encouraged recognition of the college as a royal foundation. Sidney Anglo and Gordon Kipling, in their studies of Tudor cultural politics, analysed the consciously propagandistic manipulation of heraldic display within Henry VII's programme of dynastic affirmation and it would appear that Lady Margaret was equally concerned with self-representation in her own building works.[38]

The novelty of the sculptural programme at Christ's may be demonstrated through comparison with the near-contemporary gatetower of Jesus College, also in Cambridge, erected sometime between the late 1490s and 1507 (Figure 5).[39] Here is the same ogee label with string stepping up and round the finial but the heraldic shields are disposed as discrete elements on the façade. In general, architectural heraldry of the period tended to be contained within discrete architectural compartments, roundels, squares or quatrefoils. In the Christ's gateway, by contrast, the whole heraldic field is integrated within the lines of the architecture, the curving line of the ogee gable over the arch providing the base on which the supporters 'logically' stand. But the field itself is given an anti-architectural treatment, apparently adapted from the visual conventions of tapestry or manuscript illumination, with tufts of flora and suggestions of hummocks and hollows scattered

Figure 5 *Jesus College, Cambridge. Gatetower. (Photo: Louise Durning)*

over the background. The effect is strikingly similar to that of a cloth of estate, of
the kind familiar from later Tudor portraits such as the Hampton Court *Family
of Henry VIII* of c. 1545 or indeed Rowland Lockey's late sixteenth-century portrait
of the countess at St John's College.[40] The visual conceit of a gateway draped with
a (stone) cloth of honour seems a particularly appropriate invention. Gates were
crucial foci in the spectacle of late medieval ceremonies of entry and welcome
and would often be hung with hangings and tapestry on such occasions.[41] The cloth
of estate which, in court spectacle, framed the seated figure of the monarch or
prince also served to represent the continued presence of their authority in their
absence.[42]

The other distinctive and innovative feature of the display at Christ's is the use
of large-scale heraldic supporters flanking the central shield of arms. Though this
device was to become more common later in the century, the use of the full
achievement of arms (not only the shield but the crest and supporters) seems to
have been extremely rare in architectural sculpture before the first decade of the
sixteenth century.[43] Because of the disappearance of much work of this period it is
difficult to establish this with certainty, but, from the evidence of the few surviving
examples which predate the Christ's gateway, almost all were displays of the
reigning monarch's arms.[44]

The only near comparison in a collegiate context might be the Great Gate of
King's Hall in Cambridge, later absorbed into Trinity College (Figure 6). Here the
central achievement represents the arms of Edward III, founder of King's Hall,
supported by large heraldic lions and flanked, almost in the manner of a genea-
logical table, by the shields of his six sons.[45] The chronology of this building is,
however, uncertain and the heraldic embellishment may date either from the
1490s or after 1518.[46] If this is work of the 1490s it would serve to strengthen
the possibility that the Christ's gate was intended to be viewed within the context
of regal display.

Indeed, to find a comparably rich armorial scheme we have to turn to the royal
works, to Prince Arthur's Chantry at Worcester Cathedral (c. 1504), with its frieze
of Tudor badges (Figure 7), to the building of Henry VII's chapel at Westminster
Abbey (begun 1503), and the schemes to complete the buildings of St George's
chapel at Windsor and King's College chapel, Cambridge. The campaign to complete
Henry VI's unfinished chapel at King's was initiated at Henry VII's expense in 1508
but not completed until 1515.[47] As at Christ's, rose and portcullis badges are
liberally employed, decorating the turret caps and buttresses of the chapel, and
huge displays of Tudor royal arms and badges line the internal walls of the ante-
chapel. Most of this work, however, must have been completed after the building of
the gate at Christ's.[48]

A more immediate frame of reference, however, may have been provided in
another form of royal spectacle – the temporary architecture of royal pageants and
festivals, especially in the constructions made for the entry of Catherine of Aragon
into London in 1501 celebrating her marriage to Arthur, Prince of Wales and a key
triumphal moment in the establishment of the Tudor dynasty.[49] No pictorial
record exists of the six emblematic tableaux which marked the Spanish princess's
route into London, but an eye-witness account of the event, probably written by a

56

Figure 6 Trinity College, Cambridge (formerly King's Hall). The Great Gate.
(Photo: Louise Durning)

Figure 7 *Prince Arthur's Chantry, Worcester Cathedral. (Photo: Louise Durning)*

58

Figure 8 *Christ's College, Cambridge. Detail of oriel window to the Countess's chambers. (Photo: Louise Durning)*

herald, conveys a vivid sense of their appearance.[50] His description of the second tableau ('the castle of Policy, Noblesse and Virtue') is particularly suggestive in relation to the design of the Christ's College gate. It describes a pageant castle decorated with a profusion of royal badges and emblems. Above its gate, the king's arms were supported by a red dragon and white greyhound and flanked on either side by red rose badges 'half a yarde breadthe'.[51]

We have no account of the contemporary reaction to the countess's gate, but by considering its design against this background of royal works we may more easily judge the kind of framework of visual reference within which it was conceived and against which it would have been received.[52] Seen in this context, the use of the full achievement of arms for the display of the countess's personal armorial, a form associated with regal display and far outshining in its visual richness anything yet seen in Cambridge, must surely have been read as an emphatic statement of the authority of the foundress.

The assertion of the countess's lordship embodied in the spectacular gateway was continued and reaffirmed within the college itself. Her marguerites, portcullises and daisies were ubiquitous, worked into the windows, plate and vestments of her chapel and the woodwork of the hall screen.[53] They are also evident in the original book of statutes, whose illuminated initial letters contained a catalogue of her personal insignia.[54] Its most vivid assertion was, however, in the carved panels which marked the principal chamber of her apartment dominating the view of the interior (Figure 8). Its three panels show her achievement of arms in the centre with huge rose and portcullis badges in the lateral panels, all against a field of flowers and foliage.[55] Indeed it is tempting to suggest that this display may be the

ultimate source of the college legend, recorded by Thomas Fuller in the seventeenth century, in which the countess once appeared at the window to urge an
overzealous dean to lenience in his punishment of an errant student.[56] The 'folk-
tale' narrativizes the sense of presence and surveillance embodied in the heraldic
window, identifying the countess herself with her representation. Thomas Greene
has located the significance of heraldic communication within the wider culture of
ritual gesture and symbolic imagery by which authority was enacted and reproduced in pre-modern England. In the 'magical semiotics' of badge and shield, as in
the symbolic potency of crown, throne or staff of office, sign and referent collapsed
into one. The sign was indivisible from the person it embodied.[57] The heraldic
sculpture at Christ's not only inscribed the surfaces of the buildings with the
founder's marks of ownership but those marks themselves maintained the
presence of the foundress in her absence. It is significant that the same visual
conventions established at Christ's were repeated in the gatetower and oriel of the
countess's second, posthumous, college foundation at St John's, begun in 1511 and
overseen by Fisher (Figure 9).[58]

Alice Friedman, analysing the building works of a later generation of Tudor
widows, offered an analysis of the unconventional planning of Hardwick Hall which
could equally be applied to Lady Margaret's buildings at Christ's:

> Moving through these spaces or sitting in her chair of state, Bess of Hardwick became
> part of the spectacle; each space was designed to present an image through which she
> assumed the central role in an orchestrated representation of power . . . The country
> house took on a new and unique meaning at Hardwick because the gaze of authority it
> embodied was female.[59]

We have seen that, both in its spatial planning and in its visual enrichment,
Christ's College was organized around the representation of a female, if not conventionally feminine, presence. Empowered by a quasi-regal status that was both
maternal and 'masculine' (or at least 'neuter'), its foundress was able to renegotiate
and even reverse the gendering of spaces in the collegiate institution and to
dispose it as a stage for the representation of her authority.

But, in the final analysis, this focus on the exceptional presence of an exceptional female patron should encourage us, by its very extremity, to reverse the lens
and reconsider the 'norm' whose conventions were so spectacularly reordered
here. We still need to understand more about the functioning of the medieval
collegiate institution, of the meanings and limits of celibacy, and of the kinds of
masculinity constructed through such forms of community. How, for example, did
the organization of their spaces and rituals relate to the organization of the conjugal household or to the monastery? To understand the nature of these masculine
households will involve more than drawing formal similarities between their plan
forms or creating taxonomies of types. While social historians have only just begun
to find answers to some of these questions, architectural historians have hardly
begun to ask them.[60]

Figure 9 *St John's College, Cambridge. Detail of Gatetower. (Photo: Louise Durning)*

Notes

1. Robert Willis and John Willis Clark, *The Architectural History of the University of Cambridge and of the Colleges of Cambridge and Eton* (4 vols, Cambridge, 1886), reprinted in 3 vols, with an introduction by David Watkin (Cambridge: Cambridge University Press, 1988). Royal Commission for Historic Monuments (henceforward RCHM), *An Inventory of the Historical Monuments of the City of Cambridge*, 2 vols (London: HMSO, 1959). For more recent expressions of this model see, for example, J. Twigg, *A History of Queens' College, Cambridge, 1448–1986* (Woodbridge: Boydell Press, 1987), p. 130.

2. The most complete account of the countess's life and turbulent political career is in Michael K. Jones and M.G. Underwood, *The King's Mother: Lady Margaret Beaufort, Countess of Richmond and Derby* (Cambridge: Cambridge University Press, 1992). Henry VII was the son of Margaret Beaufort and her first husband Edmund Tudor, Earl of Richmond. Henry claimed the crown by right of military victory over Richard III at the Battle of Bosworth in 1485. Thus, though mother of a king, Margaret Beaufort had never herself been a queen.

3. See Malcolm G. Underwood, 'The Lady Margaret and her Cambridge Connections', *Sixteenth-Century Journal*, 13: 1 (1982) 65–81.

4. Godshouse was first founded in 1439 by William Bingham, Rector of St John Zachary in London. It was originally sited within the city but in the 1440s moved to a new site, just outside the city gates, in an exchange of lands with Henry VI who acquired the original site for the development of his own foundation, King's College. As a result of this, Henry VI was honoured as founder of the college. Both Henry VII and his mother took a close interest in manipulating the memory of the murdered Lancastrian king, attempting (unsuccessfully) to secure his canonization, and planning their joint burial chapel, Henry VII's chapel at Westminster Abbey, as a shrine for his relics. The foundation of Christ's was presented in the letters patent given by Henry VII in May 1505 as an act of filial piety, the Countess augmenting and finishing his foundation. See A.H. Lloyd, *The Early History of Christ's College, Cambridge* (Cambridge: Cambridge University Press, 1934), p. 341; Jones and Underwood, *King's Mother*, pp. 206–8.

5. Godshouse seems always to have been a small college, never having more than four fellows in residence. Under the new statutes given by the countess in October 1506 it was to become a house of sixty, comprising a master, 12 senior fellows and 47 pupil-fellows. This made it, in statutory terms, the largest college in the university after King's. See H. Rackham (ed.), *The Early Statutes of Christ's College, Cambridge* (Cambridge, 1927).

6. The most detailed building history of the college is given in Willis and Clark, *Cambridge* II, pp. 187–232 but see also RCHM, *Cambridge*, I, pp. 28–37. The building accounts are recorded in Lady Margaret's Household Accounts held in the archives of St John's College, Cambridge, especially D91.19, D91.21, D91.22. From their close study of these, Jones and Underwood calculated total expenditure on the building works from 1505 to 1509 at £1,625, with £432 spent in the first year alone: *King's Mother*, p. 224 and n. 75. The extent of the Godshouse buildings, and what was retained from them in the new college buildings, is not clear. For an attempt to reconstruct this see Lloyd, *Early History*, pp. 311–35. The original buildings were built in brick and clunch but in the course of the eighteenth century most of the façades were refaced in ashlar to a classicizing design. The hall was rebuilt by George Gilbert Scott in 1876–1879, following the original design, but the height of the roof, originally at the same level as the lodge, was raised by some six feet: RCHM, *Cambridge*, I, p. 32.

7. For New College, founded by William of Wykeham, see John Buxton and Penry Williams (eds), *New College Oxford, 1379–1979* (Oxford: The Warden and Fellows of New College, Oxford, 1979), esp. Chapters I and V. See also Twigg, *Queens' College*.

8. Rackham, *Early Statutes*, chapter VI ('Of the preferring of the worthy and of the

assignment of rooms'), p. 53. In the same chapter Fisher was appointed visitor to the college for life and was named as the only other person permitted to use the countess's suite, though there is no direct evidence that he actually did so. For discussion of Fisher's non-residence in Cambridge see C.N.L. Brooke, 'The University Chancellor' in B. Bradshaw and E. Duffy (eds), *Humanism, Reform and Reformation: The Career of Bishop John Fisher* (Cambridge: Cambridge University Press, 1989), pp. 57–60.

9. This changed from the mid sixteenth century with the post-Reformation abolition of clerical celibacy, and the potential for heads of houses to marry (though fellows still remained celibate). The spatial, political and psychological tensions this brought with it and the attempts made to find ways of accommodating women and children within the colleges will be analysed in my forthcoming paper, '"No Small Offence": Housing the Master's wife in the Post-Reformation Oxford College'.

10. For examples see John M. Fletcher and Christopher A. Upton, '"Monastic Enclave" or "Open Society"?: A Consideration of the Role of Women in the Life of an Oxford Community in the Early Tudor Period', *History of Education*, 16: 1 (1987) 1–9. Similar clauses are included in the statutes of Christ's, see Rackham, *Early Statutes* Chapter XXXI, 'Of the vicious manners forbidden to every fellow', p. 93. Separate colleges or hostels were, however, established by monasteries for housing monks of their own orders while studying at the universities. See J. Blair, 'Monastic Colleges in Oxford', *Archaeological Journal*, 135 (1978) 263–5.

11. See Fletcher and Upton, 'Monastic Enclave?'. Their analysis, based on a study of the Bursar's accounts of Merton College, demonstrates that the economic relationships between colleges and their locale of necessity brought the fellows into contact with female traders, college tenants and casual labourers.

12. Willis and Clark, *Cambridge*, III, p. 332; RCHM, *Cambridge*, I, p. lxxxvi.

13. Jones and Underwood, *The King's Mother*, p. 225.

14. Willis and Clark, *Cambridge*, II, p. 215.

15. This door, since filled in, is visible in Loggan's print.

16. A fourth chamber, a closet over the western end of the college chapel and looking down into it, may also have been intended for inclusion within the suite, though this was not completed until after the countess's death and was used by the master: RCHM, *Cambridge*, I, p. 27. Chapel closets were a common feature of aristocratic households of the period and one was included at Collyweston palace, linked to the countess's chambers by a timber gallery. Such a gallery seems to be indicated in the Loggan print of the college but the date of its erection is not known. See Michael K. Jones, 'Collyweston – An Early Tudor Palace', in Daniel Williams (ed.), *England in the Fifteenth Century*. Proceedings of the 1986 Harlaxton Symposium (Woodbridge: The Boydell Press, 1987), p. 135.

17. The countess visited Cambridge in 1505 and 1506, staying at Queens' College, where Fisher was President. It is not known which rooms she and her retinue would have occupied. See Twigg, *Queens' College*, pp. 134–6. She also visited in 1507 when she may have stayed at Christ's; Jones and Underwood, *The King's Mother*, pp. 223–4.

18. See Simon Thurley, *The Royal Palaces of Tudor England* (New Haven and London: Yale University Press, 1993), pp. 53–4.

19. Thurley, *Royal Palaces*, pp. 41–3. See also A.D.K. Hawkyard, 'Thornbury Castle', *Bristol and Gloucestershire Archaeological Society Transactions*, 95 (1977) 51–8. See also Maurice Howard, *The Early Tudor Country House: Architecture and Politics, 1490–1550* (London: George Philip, 1987).

20. Simon Thurley, 'The Domestic Building Works of Cardinal Wolsey' in S.J. Gunn and P.G. Lindsey (eds), *Cardinal Wolsey, Church, State and Art* (Cambridge: Cambridge University Press, 1991), p. 100.

21. Whether these rooms were intended for Margaret and Stanley or as a self-contained guest lodging is not clear. According to a survey taken of the castle in 1521 they were apparently left unfinished. N.W. Alcock, P.A. Faulkner and S.R. Jones, with a contribution by G.M.D. Booth, 'Maxstoke Castle', *Archaeological Journal*, 135 (1978) 216–18.

22. See Willis and Clark, *Cambridge*, III, Chapter 6 ('The Master's Lodge'), for a descriptive list of all known locations of master's lodgings at Oxford and Cambridge colleges.

23. In the Godshouse statutes the master was allowed 'the principal and best room' and this seems to have been on the street front. According to the Notary Public's record of the formal signing of the new Christ's College statutes in October 1506, the fellows met 'in a certain upper chamber belonging to the Master . . . near the gates'. Other indications in the new statutes of the increased status of the master are evident in an increased stipend and permission to keep one servant. See Rackham, *Early Statutes*, pp. 27, 57, 113, 137.

24. Whether or not the countess actually stayed in these rooms is immaterial to the interpretation of the spatial and visual logic of the plan, but there is some evidence that she may indeed have occupied them. The wording of the statutes implies that they were already finished by late summer or autumn of 1506 and would therefore have been ready for occupation by 1507, when she is next recorded in Cambridge. Moreover, an inventory of the contents of the chambers, taken after the countess's death, listed a number of her personal possessions still remaining within, including beds and over £300 worth of gold and silver tableware. See A.H. Lloyd, 'Two Monumental Brasses in the Chapel of Christ's College', *Proceedings of the Cambridge Antiquarian Society*, 33 (1933) 61–82. The inventory is transcribed on p. 75.

25. Jones and Underwood, *King's Mother*, p. 98.

26. For the law of *femme sole* see Caroline Barron, 'The "Golden Age" of Women in Medieval London', *Reading Medieval Studies*, 15 (1989) 39–40.

27. Jones and Underwood, *The King's Mother*, p. 99. They suggest a pragmatic motive for this manoeuvre as a means of preserving crown lands from falling into the hands of the Stanley family.

28. Jones and Underwood, *The King's Mother*, pp. 187–8. The original vow was made before Richard Fitzjames, Bishop of London, and was reaffirmed in 1504 after Stanley's death before John Fisher, Bishop of Rochester. The text of the second vow is reproduced in C.H. Cooper, *The Lady Margaret: A Memoir of Margaret, Countess of Richmond and Derby*, ed. J.E.B. Mayor (Cambridge, 1874), pp. 97–8.

29. Mary C. Erler, 'English Vowed Women at the End of the Middle Ages', *Mediaeval Studies*, 57 (1995) 157.

30. For the court at Collyweston, see Michael K. Jones, 'Collyweston'.

31. She also sought, and gained, papal dispensation to enter houses of enclosed monastic orders to converse with their inmates, as shown in a papal letter of 1504: 'he [Julius II] further grants that the countess, with six honest matrons, suitably attired, may as often as she pleases enter monasteries and houses of male religious even of the Carthusians and enclosed orders or of any others, have salutary discourse with them and take refreshment there . . . provided that they do not spend the night there', *Calendar of Entries in the Papal Registers relating to Great Britain and Ireland*, vol. xviii, pp. 1503–13, letter 120, 20 May 1504.

32. Erler lists a number of examples of vowed women living in or near nunneries but notes that in the 1530s a Lady Jane Guildford, who lodged at Gaunt's Hospital in Bristol, was forbidden to enter the cloister of the hospital ('Vowed Women', pp. 175, 182 and n. 86). Maurice Howard noted a tendency in the sixteenth century for lay patrons or stewards of monasteries to build, or have reserved for them, rooms in or near their precincts. These tended, however, to be separate from the cloister area; see Howard, *Early Tudor*, pp. 142–3. At Christ's, however, the Beaufort lodging is at the very heart of the community.

33. Underwood, 'The Lady Margaret and her Cambridge Connections', pp. 67–9.

34. See, for example, RCHM, *Cambridge*, I, p. lxxviii, where it is described as 'the apotheosis of the [Cambridge] gatetower'; Twigg, *Queens' College*, p. 130; Willis and Clark *Cambridge*, III, pp. 291–4.

35. Peter Hammond, 'The Importance of Heraldry in the Later Middle Ages', *Medieval History*, 2: 3 (1992) 90–8.

36. For the arms borne by her father, John Beaufort, Duke of Somerset, at St George's Windsor, which show swan and yale supporters, see W.H. St John Hope, *The Stall Plates of the Knights of the Order of the Garter* (London, 1901). Two late sixteenth-century posthumous portraits of the countess in the halls of Christ's and St John's Colleges show her arms impaled with those of Edmund Tudor.

37. This ostentatious stamping of the college with the badges of the king's livery takes on an added significance with the knowledge that the countess had licence to retain men for the king under fee (the only woman able to do so), and to issue the portcullis and rose badges which were the outward sign of that maintenance. See Jones and Underwood, *The King's Mother*, p. 81.

38. Sidney Anglo, *Spectacle, Pageantry and Early Tudor Policy*, Oxford-Warburg Studies (Oxford: Clarendon Press, 1st edn 1969, new edn 1997); Gordon Kipling, *The Triumph of Honour: The Burgundian Origins of the Elizabethan Renaissance* (Leiden: Sir Thomas Browne Institute/University of Leiden Press, 1977). For the countess's other building projects, see Jones and Underwood, *King's Mother*, pp. 104, 154–6.

39. RCHM, *Cambridge*, I, p. 84.

40. In a, now lost, stained glass window at the Greyfriars church, Greenwich, of c. 1506 the Countess was pictured against a cloth of estate powdered with portcullis and rose badges: Jones and Underwood, *The King's Mother*, p. 70 and n. 9.

41. See Anglo, *Spectacle*, esp. Chapter 1, for a description of Tudor royal entries.

42. For a near-contemporary statement of entitlement to a cloth of estate see 'A Boke of Precedence' (MS Harl. 1440, leaf II) transcribed in F.J. Furnivall (ed.), *Queene Elizabethe's Achademy, A Boke of Precedence, etc*. Early English Text Society, Extra Series, VIII (London: Trübner & Co., 1869), pp. 13–16.

43. Later examples include the gatehouse oriel at Hengrave Hall, Suffolk (dated 1538) or the gates of East Barsham Manor, Norfolk (c. 1520–30). Supporters seem not to have been used in armorial identification in England before the middle decades of the fifteenth century and appear first in stained glass and in manuscript illumination. Of the fifteenth century garter stall plates at St George's Windsor, only three make use of supporters, the earliest, interestingly enough, that of Lady Margaret's father. See Thomas Woodcock and John Martin Robinson, *The Oxford Guide to Heraldry* (Oxford: Oxford University Press, 1988), p. 96; Richard Marks and Ann Payne, *British Heraldry from its Origins to c. 1800* (London: British Museum Publications, 1978), p. 111.

44. Examples include the vault of the Divinity School at Oxford, completed in 1483, where the arms of Edward IV are given the place of honour in the central boss, distinguished from all others by the inclusion of supporters within the roundel. Similarly, the vault of the 'Fitzjames' archway at Merton College, Oxford (c. 1500) has, again in the central boss, the arms of Henry VII with dragon and greyhound supporters. See also the arms of Henry VI at the Bishop's Palace, Salisbury (1460s) and of Edward IV at Hertford Castle, in both cases framed in a small square tablet placed over the gate. The fireplace in the Bishop's palace at Exeter inserted by Bishop Courtenay (c. 1486) is more lavish, showing the arms of Henry VII and the Courtenay family. The only near non-royal comparison with the Christ's gate may be the heraldic gate from Hornby Castle (Yorks), now in the Burrell Museum in Glasgow. This is of uncertain date but probably early sixteenth century.

45. The supporters here are a retrospective attribution, supporters not being employed in heraldic display in the time of Edward III. See Woodcock and Robinson, *Heraldry*, p. 95.

46. Work on the King's Hall gate began in the 1490s but was left incomplete till a second building campaign resumed in 1518. It was further altered in c. 1600 when the statue of Henry VIII was installed on the street front. RCHM, *Cambridge*, II, pp. 215–16.

47. RCHM, *Cambridge*, I, pp. 102–3.

48. Ibid. The interior carving is dated c. 1512–1513. Though there is evidence of the involvement of the same workmen in some of these projects, notably William Swayne documented at King's Hall, King's College and Christ's, their similarities need not be understood as arising from this alone. It is unlikely that the design of such an important

display as the gatehouse at Christ's would have been left to the discretion of the sculptor and it is probable, given contemporary practice, that patterns would have been provided for the masons to work from. For Swayne, see John Harvey, *English Medieval Architects. A Biographical Dictionary*, rev. edn (Gloucester: Alan Sutton, 1984), pp. 291–2. For pattern books see Thurley, *Royal Palaces*, pp. 101–2. A smaller scale example of this use of patterns is found in the countess's own household accounts for 1503, which record a payment to a London painter for providing a drawing of a yale for the glazier working on the windows of her great chamber at Collyweston. See Jones, 'Collyweston', p. 135. The circumstances of this payment indicate the importance of heraldic accuracy. The drawing was to guide the correction of an error made by a previous glazier who had mistakenly represented the Beaufort yale as an antelope.

49. See Anglo, *Spectacle*, pp. 56–96. Though the pageants were erected by the city of London they were overseen by the king's commissioners.

50. Ibid., p. 58.

51. Ibid., p. 65.

52. Though some sense of its visual impact in the Cambridge streetscape may be suggested by the exaggerated scale with which the gatetower is drawn in Lyne's Map of Cambridge, published in 1574.

53. The richest items of chapel plate and vestements were bequeathed to the college from the countess's own household chapel after her death. The will was published in *Collegium Divi Johannis Evangelistae 1511–1911* (Cambridge: St John's College, 1911), pp. 103–26. See also R.F. Scott, 'On a List of Plate, Books and Vestments bequeathed by the Lady Margaret to Christ's College, Cambridge', *Communications of the Cambridge Antiquarian Society*, 9 (1899), 355–61.

54. The one surviving copy of the countess's original statutes still held by the college is also liberally illuminated with her badges and arms which were worked into the initial letter of each chapter. A further copy, now lost, was chained in the chapel as a reference text to be consulted by all members of the college though it is not clear if this was similarly decorated; see Rackham, *Early Statutes*, p. iv. The text of the statutes is written in the Countess's own voice (though their composition is usually attributed to John Fisher) and its opening words, 'Nos Margareta', are written in her own hand.

55. The corbelling of the window is further enriched with a secondary scheme of devices and badges, including fleur de lys, ostrich feathers in coronet, roses, portcullises and the initials HR (henricus rex).

56. 'Once the Lady Margaret came to Christ's College to behold it when partly built, and looking out of a window, saw the Dean call a faulty scholar to correction; to whom she said "*lente, lente*", gently, gently, as accounting it better to mitigate his punishment than to procure his pardon' (T. Fuller, *The History of the University of Cambridge*, ed. J. Nicholls, (Cambridge, 1840), p. 135).

57. Thomas M. Greene, 'Shakespeare's *Richard II*: the Sign in Bullingbroke's Window', in Lucy Gent (ed.), *Albion's Classicism. The Visual Arts in Britain, 1550–1660*, Yale Studies in British Art, 2 (New Haven and London: Yale University Press, 1995), pp. 313–23. See also Hammond, 'Importance of Heraldry'. For the uses of heraldic decoration in court architecture see Thurley, *Royal Palaces*, pp. 98–102.

58. See Jones and Underwood, *King's Mother*, pp. 235 and 246–9. Interestingly, Fisher's second set of statutes for the College of 1524 made the same provision for reserving rooms for himself in the master's lodging 'as the Foundress, in her gracious kindness, allowed me to do with respect to Christ's College'. J.E.B. Mayor (ed.), *The Early Statutes of St John's College Cambridge* (Cambridge, 1859), p. 273.

59. Alice T. Friedman, 'Architecture, Authority and The Female Gaze: Planning and Representation in the Early Modern Country House', *Assemblage*, 18 (1992) 54.

60. A model for such an analysis might be found in Rebecca Gilchrist's studies of medieval nunneries, especially *Gender and Material Culture. The Archaeology of Medieval Religious Women* (London and New York, Routledge, 1994) and in H. Hills's essay in this collection. For work by social historians on the collegiate experience see, for example,

66

Upton and Fletcher, 'Monastic Enclave'; James McConica, 'Elizabethan Oxford: the Collegiate Society' in McConica (ed.), *The History of The University of Oxford*, vol. III, *The Collegiate University* (Oxford: Oxford University Press, 1986); Victor Morgan, 'Cambridge University and "The Country", 1540–1640' in Lawrence Stone (ed.), *The University in Society*, vol. I, *Oxford and Cambridge from the 14th to the Early 19th Century* (Princeton NJ and London: Princeton University Press, 1974).

Chapter 4

Architecture as Metaphor for the Body: The Case of Female Convents in Early Modern Italy

Helen Hills

Female convents and their churches provide ideal sites for investigating the relationship between gender and architecture in early modern Europe. This is architecture designed and built for female patrons, to enhance female religious devotion and to foster the separation of women from both men and the competing demands of the world, and it was used almost exclusively by women – itself a remarkable fact in a field where information about audiences and users is notoriously hard to come by. Indeed, ever since convents became the focus of attention in the late nineteenth century, they have been considered crucial to the position of women in Europe. In 1910 Emily James Puttnam, herself the future president of a women's college, writing in *The Lady* waxed enthusiastic about convents. 'No institution in Europe has ever won for the lady the freedom of development that she enjoyed in the convent in early days', she writes. 'The modern college for women only feebly reproduces it.'

This paper explores the relationship between the architecture of female aristocratic convents in early modern Italy and the bodies they were built to house, seeking to link architectural discourse not simply to that of social hierarchy and exclusivity, but to the anxieties and unspoken fears circulating in the shadows of those discourses. I try to trace a path which avoids the present dichotomy between the 'heroic' and the 'passive' view of religious women and architecture, by drawing on the theoretical resources of Pierre Bourdieu and Lefebvre in particular. Bourdieu's concept of 'habitus' and Lefebvre's of spatiality help to inflect Foucault's still useful conceptualization of relationships between space and power.

Therefore, after briefly introducing the scholarship on early modern Italian convents, I move on to analyse their architectural organization in terms of the politics of sight, the threshold and social liminality. I then look more deeply at the relationship between flesh and stone, uncovering the connections between the clothing of bodies and the layered cloaks applied to the walls that housed them, their unclothing and the fear of their nakedness.[1] Finally, I discuss architecture as metaphor, specifically the architecture of aristocratic female convents as metaphor for the body of the aristocratic female virgin nun.

Conventual architecture is unusually redolent of the operation of power in space. We are familiar with the notion that techniques of power are invented to meet the demands of production, even in the broadest sense.[2] We should extend such a notion to include the production of religious devotion and to consider that production as significantly spatial. Conventual architecture relies not only on separation, exclusion and hierarchies of access. It depends to an unusual degree on what Foucault termed 'the optics of power' – the control of sight lines, the deliberate granting or stinting of visual access and carefully contrived asymmetrical viewing patterns. This chapter considers conventual architecture in relation to the optics of power.[3]

ARCHITECTURAL HISTORY AND CONVENTUAL STUDIES

Women were for many years more or less absent from architectural history and gender was, at best, an untheorized presence. More so than in any other area of art history, gender differences were assumed to be irrelevant to the concerns of architectural history much beyond the position of the cooker or the height of the kitchen sink.[4] In other areas of art history, the rediscovery of a significant number of neglected female artists and the representation of the female body were the principal subjects of feminist interventions from the 1970s, which led rapidly to the development and application of theories of representation, sexuality and gendered identities.[5] It was characteristic of the contributions of feminist art historians of that first generation to celebrate female creativity and to focus on female practitioners.[6] Although this work was useful and fundamentally changed our picture of artistic creativity, it tended towards an 'additive' approach to art history, in which female artists were merely added to a long list of their male counterparts. More recent feminist work has sought to go further, demonstrating that the consideration of gender in relation to artistic production is not simply a matter of making its social or cultural analysis more comprehensive. Instead it poses new questions, as well as opening to new interpretation material previously neatly packaged without any reference to gender.[7] The pattern was rather different in architectural history. Although the first wave of feminist scholarship concentrated on female architects and on historical and institutional obstacles to their training and emergence, much feminist scholarship bypassed architectural history, because architecture tends to be non-figurative and because very few architects have been female.[8] For those same reasons, scholars were forced to adopt or invent different modes of analysing architecture in relation to gender.[9] It is in regard to those later currents that conventual space poses such interesting questions: if it is careless to assume that a space almost devoid of men can be described as 'female', and if it is rash to suppose that conventual space is necessarily organized for the benefits of its female occupants, how do gender politics affect the organization and use of conventual space beyond the separation of the sexes?

Although the architecture of convents and their churches has received curiously little sustained attention, female convents have become quite fashionable in the last decade or so within certain scholarly communities, embracing religious studies, art history, social history, and producing new shoots moving in apparently all directions. While in 1988 Kathryn Norberg lamented the dearth of studies of women religious in early modern Europe, no similar lament could be voiced today.[10] In recent years, this area of scholarship has been transformed. Reflecting on the changes in scholarship with regard to religious women in late medieval Italy, in the decade before 1996, Roberto Rusconi argues that the study of women and religion 'has flourished as never before and changed in significant ways'.[11] Indeed a senior academic once scathingly characterized this development to me as 'a growth industry'. But it is not mere academic fashion; there are good intellectual reasons for this growing and focused interest. Here the continuing interest in feminism and gender issues intersects with renewed concern with religious devotion and practice and with emerging analyses of space. Concern with power and its operations and relationships has also come to focus on female convents as important interstices for the refraction and exchange of power within society. Concern with the relationships between female religious beliefs, religious practices, and sexuality and gender issues has intensified. Female mysticism and more generally female religious institutions throughout the medieval and pre-modern periods have been the subject of some of our most thought-provoking scholarship on gender, the body and society. Lively scholarship has opened to question the relationships between the body of Christ, the Eucharist and the body of the believers.[12] Reinvigorated discussions of the multifaceted varieties of Catholicism, the implications of Trent, the vexed issue of the 'Counter-Reformation' have illuminated similarities between Catholicism and Protestantism and have shown how changes in Catholicism and in the organization of the Catholic Church cannot be explained by reference to the Protestant menace.[13] There is increasing scholarly attention to the significance of conventual life and to the functions of convents for women and for female devotion, for family and for notions of female sexuality and virginity, and for the politics of the cities in which they stood.[14] A rich and complex picture is emerging.

The question of early modern female patronage in relation to the production of specific forms of architectural space has been much more productive ground than any search for long lost female architects of the same period. But until recently studies of female patrons in Renaissance and early modern Italy were almost exclusively reserved for secular patrons, and even when they did turn to ecclesiastical patronage, these studies tended to stop with details of aristocratic women's endowments to female religious houses. This has changed in the last decade, which has witnessed lively research on female patronage within convents.[15] Although scholars have examined conventual life from many different points of view, the architecture and decoration of convent houses and churches remains curiously under-examined. Most of the recent work on female convents and architecture has concentrated on nuns – usually singling out a few exemplary individuals – as patrons.[16] What is needed now is perhaps a different sort of feminist strategy that retains a concern with social history and with gendered patronage, but which locates these within contested fields of discursive formations. How do certain people and groups enter into spaces of representation, which spaces do they enter, and why?

While acknowledging that any discussion of this group of aristocratic female patrons cannot do full justice to the subtleties, the rich psychological variations, the infinitely complex texture of the constituent parts of their individual identities, it is important to consider these patrons as a group, rather than as separate studies of exceptional women. Such an approach will contribute to recent trends in patronage studies which are turning away from the celebration of individuals to broader questions of the relationships between the formation of class, gender, and other forms of group identity and cultural patronage.[17]

As Marilyn Dunn has pointed out, 'patronage by women was a common phenomenon, not an exceptional occurrence'.[18] And yet, as Cynthia Lawrence has indicated, studies of early modern patronage generally 'fail to establish or even to show much curiosity about patterns or trends in the way art is commissioned, collected, or valued by different individuals or groups at different times or under different circumstances'.[19] Studies of female art patronage have often limited the complexity of the identity of their subjects by emphasizing gender in isolation, as if their subjects were somehow necessarily female before all the other aspects of their manifold identities. Such an approach tends to flatten its subjects, so that the complexity of motives attributed to male art patrons may be replaced by a collapse of the subject into her gender.

Generally speaking, female patrons have received less subtle treatments in this respect than their male counterparts. Contemporary scholarship offers more nuanced interpretations of patronage by men, suggesting interconnections between their piety, their desires for social distinction, their political ambition and familial status. This is only partly due to the celebratory mode which has been adopted in relation to interventions by women. More seriously, it stems from a failure to appreciate the degree to which art patronage was a mode by which women could articulate quasi-independent positions for themselves. Even Marilyn Dunn, who takes pains to remark the degree to which chapels patronized by women in Seicento Rome 'commemorated their illustrious families' and who emphasizes the significance of these women's wealth and social standing as important factors behind both their *impetus* to act as patrons of art and their success in doing so, tends to view their patronage as spiritual or 'philanthropic' in its effects, and does not consider the art works patronized as helping to consolidate the power and prestige enjoyed by the women who commissioned them.[20] In other words, there is a reluctance to acknowledge the degree to which art patronage is not simply the product of social and political privilege, but actively helps to maintain that privilege.

Thus we have many female patrons whose patronage of religious art and architecture is explained almost exclusively in terms of their 'piety'.[21] While female piety and religious conviction are a crucial aspect of women's ecclesiastical patronage and cannot be reduced to political or other motivation, the assumption that 'piety' is causally separate and primary in relation to ecclesiastical patronage needs to be critically examined. Piety, isolated in itself, neither explains nor determines. As Craig Monson has observed, artistic activities, such as the patronage of churches and chapels and their decoration could form important impetuses in nuns' spiritual lives.[22] An analysis of piety reveals it to be more complex and less socially neutral than a simple model of piety-as-cause implies. Piety is anticipated, delayed, and traversed by social currents, and therefore needs to be analysed in relation to them.

Scholarship concerned with conventual life has tended to move in two divergent directions, with the left hand unaware of what the right hand is doing. Either scholars consider the spiritual and devotional aspect of convent women's lives, or they investigate the nuns' physical surroundings, the architecture of the monasteries and their place in their urban environment. Few have managed to bring these two strands together.[23] Broadly speaking, scholars have concentrated either on conventual life, the varied roles of convents, and on their inmates, more or less ignoring the architecture which framed these activities and defined conventual space as separate and set apart; or they have turned to the architecture and tended to read it in relation to religious devotion within the convent, again stopping short at the convent wall, or ascribed it to a single individual, an 'exceptional' female patron whose patronage is portrayed as innocent of the muddy complexities of familial and urban politics.[24] In this respect current scholarship is weakened by the fact that the relationship of nuns to the art and architecture which surrounded their lives and helped shape their beliefs has been relatively little studied.[25] Thus, we still lack detailed studies of convent architecture, planning, organization and decoration which attempts to relate these issues to the broader matters mentioned above.[26]

In short, scholars have tended either to idealize or to stigmatize convents. The former tends to promote readings of their architecture as signs of obedience, conformity and religious observance (their quiet halls, simple whitewashed corridors and private cells; their churches which emphasize eucharistic devotion) and to assume an identicality between an institution and a power system. The latter presents them in scandalous terms, in which their architecture becomes incidental and tends to be ignored – as centres of pent-up sexuality, passionate romance and intrigue, enclosures whose walls were only ever really intended to be straddled during spicy late night assignations and furtive wooings.

The exceptions to this rule have been mostly medievalists who have led the way in attempting to relate church decoration programmes either to female religious devotion or to their urban and social context.[27] The general consensus amongst historians and art historians is that in convents women were freer, more independent, and better educated than in any other sphere open to them; and it is generally taken as concomitant with that assumption that therefore the buildings which housed them would reflect these qualities of institutional autonomy, spiritual devotion, and religious dedication.[28] The reality was more complex and contradictory than this interpretation allows.[29] What is more helpful than framing the investigation in terms of positive and negative, with its implication of sudden change and fixed results, is to think more in terms of process, to examine how nuns themselves shaped their lives, how they interpreted what historians have tended to see as the conflict between family and convent, the opposition between the secular and the divine.[30] Hitherto the architecture of convents and their churches has been treated as separate from these issues and has received little attention.[31] It is vital to see convents as participating in the social fabric of which they form part, to consider the social and political and familial connections that seep through apparently impervious walls and vault over bolted gates and doors. In short, conventual architecture must be considered in relation to economic, political, religious, sexual and familial interests and concerns and one must not be reduced to another. In female convents urbanism and belief systems cross paths; here investigation into the early modern city, identities and issues of social class intersect.[32]

In a recent essay, Daniel Borstein, discussing the historiography of women and religion in late medieval Italy, argues that the recognition of women's significant role as 'consumers of the sacred' runs contrary to received wisdom 'which holds that women were pawns manipulated by men in the sociopolitical game of marriage alliances, and that those who were too ugly or too expensive to marry off were dumped in whatever convent would take them'.[33] Certainly, an emphasis on the absence of vocation for many nuns emerges sharply from the work of Pio Paschini, Luigi Fiorani and Carla Russo.[34] It is important, however, not to over-state either case. Indeed, an adequate explanation of female patronage in convents cannot arise from an analysis of the immediate reasons why they were there in the first place. As Marilyn Dunn has emphasized, 'women of the patrician class had little choice about their futures, regardless of whether that choice involved preference for marriage or the convent'.[35] What is needed instead is an awareness that their patronage was undertaken in relation to material, spiritual and socio-political circumstances and also helped to shape the very circumstances in which they found themselves. As Borstein writes, 'discerning the power of these pawns requires acute insight and careful attention to nuance – and paradox'.[36]

It is also true, however, that some feminist-inspired scholarship, drawing on the currents of 1970s academic feminism which valorized the contribution of indi-vidual women to art history, usually as artists, has tended to focus on the celebration of an extraordinary life, an exceptional artist-nun or female patron, at the cost of losing sight of the broader context in which such women operated. The result tends to be a picture of a few exceptional women acting courageously as patrons and artists in the firmament of baroque society, with, suspended below them in murky depths the undistinguished mass of women, mere cyphers. We need to think of women more sociologically – to relate those who were successful in determining specific architectural and artistic outcomes, and the precise chosen form of those artistic creations for which they were in part responsible, to broader dynamics within society and to the other women whose very presence often made possible the prominence of the few. The successes of the few must be interpreted in relation to their social rank and economic standing, to urban and familial politics and to social constraints. This paper contributes to this aim.

Recent work which rightly seeks to illuminate women's roles, strategies, responses to opportunities, challenges and obstacles perhaps also tends to obfuscate the limitations on their room for manoeuvre. Much current research still focuses on individual exemplary women.[37] Being quick to celebrate individual achievement may risk obscuring the limitations regularly enforced and imposed on women by systems of property ownership, ecclesiastical structures, and familial and theological discourses. The policing of convents through episcopal visitations early received scholarly attention; more recently the advantages convents presented to powerful dynasties in terms of surveillance of females have been illuminated in terms of urban politics by Elissa Novi Chavarria in particular.[38] But on the whole, research concerned with the social, political and economic circum-stances of convents tends to ignore the physical appearance of convents, their place in the urban fabric, their architectures and their decoration, just as studies of the architecture stop short at the convent walls.

I turn now to consider conventual architecture as metaphor, to find a path between the bifurcation of existing scholarship.

Architecture as Metaphor

The bifurcation existing in much scholarship between attention to nuns' social identities and religious practices and studies of the architecture which housed them cannot be amended by simply appending considerations of conventual architecture to existing interpretations of social organization within convents. Space does not merely provide the locus for social relations; it is primary to the construction of gendered and social identity. A more radical re-think of the model is required. Thinking about architecture as metaphor perhaps provides just such a model. If we think of architecture as a metaphor for the bodies it houses – that is, the architecture of an early modern aristocratic convent as a metaphor for the aristocratic female virginal body – we avoid some of the dichotomies discussed above. In other words, the advantage of conceiving of architecture as metaphor (or at least metonymy) for the aristocratic female body is that it necessarily and absolutely avoids the split from which the existing literature suffers between studies of the architecture and studies of the bodies it houses. In this model, the architecture stands in metonymically for the female body in the city, allowing an analysis of architecture as the site of a permanent battle, of deliberate and inevitable ambiguity, while avoiding the temptation to displace the investigation from the 'text' to the context.

Of course, it is vital to resist any simple collapsing of the built environment into metaphor alone. It risks too smoothly sliding behind a linguistic structure all the rough edges of material architecture and its production, from iconology to the division of labour in the building trades. Such an approach cannot provide an account of the architecture. But it can, at best, offer a way to cut through its apparent self-assured, self-contained detachment to expose its anxieties and uncertainties.

Space does not reflect gender; nor can it predict gender relations. Together gender and space may change meaning over time, according to changing cultural metaphors. Henrietta Moore has argued that architectural design and spatial organization help construct a representation of gender relations which presents privilege and authority as natural and pre-given: 'spatial representations help to produce and reproduce the distinctions on which the cultural constructions of gender are based. In other words, spatial representations help to support gender ideologies'.[39] Moore argues that 'the true nature of gender relations' is not represented spatially, but that it is 'the dominant male ideology' which is reproduced in space. The problem with this model is its rigidity in conceiving relationships between space and power. Bourdieu, Foucault and Benjamin in particular help to conceive rather more fragmented, contradictory and complex notions of these relationships. Bourdieu shows how even dominant power groups are fractured and contradictory, arguing that cultural capital may be at cross purposes with economic capital, so that the relationship between power and spatial representation will not be straightforward.[40]

But why should women as active social agents accept gender relations which oppress them? Are they forced to comply? Or are they complicit in their compliance? In *Outline of a Theory of Practice* Bourdieu suggests that 'agency', activities of individual social actors, support hierarchical systems of organization based on age and sex. So an individual is not necessarily aware of the consequences of their actions in any broad sense, or in relation to others. Actions which reproduce structural relations against their own best interests are produced by 'learned ignorance' or *habitus*, which lends agents a sense of order. So women acting on their *habitus* may well reproduce structural relations which determine their subordination to men, even while they may sometimes exploit their freedoms to initiate social change. Foucault describes how power grips us at the point where our desires and our very sense of the possibilities for self-definition are constituted.[41]

Although Bourdieu says relatively little about gender, *habitus* constructs gendered roles and identities especially through material culture. Space, the fundamental aspect of material culture, is, therefore, of central importance in constituting gender. It determines how men and women are brought together or kept apart; it participates in defining a sexual division of labour; its organization produces, reproduces and represents notions about sexuality and the body. Space determines and affects behaviour, just as the organization of space is produced by and in relation to behaviour.

In early modern Italy gender relations were organized in relation to the family. Property was transmitted predominantly along male lines, according to the principle of primogeniture. Idealized male and female roles are articulated in theological and religious discourses which elevated monogamy, female chastity, and fidelity. These conditions created a *habitus* for women in which their hunger for spiritual salvation assisted them in reproducing the structural gender relations of inequality through their own agency.

Female convents and their churches are places in which certain sorts of women are represented. Here I follow Griselda Pollock in her argument that '[r]epresentation is to be understood as a social relation enacted and performed via specific appeals to vision, specific managements of imaginary spaces and bodies for a gaze'.[42] It is time now to consider the organization of space of the convent in those terms.

THE INVISIBLE BODY

Monastic architecture was central to the social construction of difference between religious men and women, and even between men and women and between religious women from noble and non-noble families. Religious identities, sexual purity and social exclusivity were maintained through space, boundaries and architectural adornment. Architecture constructed the *habitus* which connected common interest groups. Convents were connected to the aristocracy through their material culture, to particular families through sites and donations, but above all they were connected to the *habitus* of aristocratic women.

In early modern Italy, architecture tended to work to render the body of aristocratic women, whether nuns or not, invisible. Patricia Waddy has shown how women of the highest status had their own separate apartments in Roman baroque palaces and how, although women could occupy the great apartments of a Cardinal and carry out diplomatic functions of entertaining and visiting, where there were men to do these tasks, then women's quarters were usually situated in the most segregated areas of the palace, looking towards the rear or inwards to an enclosed court or garden.[43] Unlike their husbands or brothers, women rarely had direct access from their apartment to the city (men's apartments often had small, private stairways and exits);[44] and women were hemmed in by a raft of female servants whose rooms abutted their apartments and had limited access to the rest of the palace.[45] As Saundra Weddle has aptly expressed it, the parental home, the marital home and the convent were the three types of enclosure available to respectable women.[46]

Peter Brown has discussed the relationships between celibacy and the opening of a public space in the person of the male regular in late antiquity.[47] Celibacy, symbolized by the tonsure, consequent upon the vows, created a public space within the body: celibate priests became accessible to others through the creation of public space in lieu of personal sexuality. The reverse was true of nuns. When early modern women gave religious sanction to their virginity, their celibacy was closer to concepts of chastity shared with upper-class, particularly aristocratic, secular women.[48] In Roberta Gilchrist's words, 'their bodies became private spaces'.[49]

Not only did nuns' bodies become private spaces, they became hidden, invisible. Consequently, the work of sustaining their presence within the city and within urban politics had to be carried by the architecture that hid them. In the case of virgin nuns, the architecture does not simply provide a public representation of an idealized social body, but it stands in metonymically for that body which is made publicly invisible through that very architecture. This is why conventual architecture is different from, say, the architecture of a palace, a school or a hospital. Unlike celibate priests who become asexual, nuns commit their virginity to the Church as Brides of Christ. Whereas monks' bodies become more public, nuns bodies became more private. Their inaccessibility was itself key and crucial, because their sensuality, unlike that of their male counterparts, was not simply banished, but was redirected towards Christ.

Part of the crucial significance of convents was that conventual communities were able to articulate a publicly recognizable presence in the city. Convents therefore represent the public face of a sanctioned female group. In addition, as Adrian Randolph has emphasized, the space of public worship was one of the few public spaces open to women. 'Indeed,' he writes, 'female public appearance was, more often than not, religiously sanctioned'.[50] While Randolph was thinking of women attending church services, listening to sermons, and their regular, pendular, journeys from home to church and back, his emphasis on the way in which the religious sanctioned female public appearance can be extended to conventual institutions more generally. How did architects sanction the presence of groups of rich and well-connected religious women in the heart of the city? What relationships were constructed between convent and city and between exterior and interior of the convents? In other words, how does architecture shape the social coding of sacred space?

SEPARATION, DISCIPLINE AND THE COUNCIL OF TRENT

Ironically, the Council of Trent's impact on conventual life was probably greater because it did not allow adequate time for discussion. Hurriedly, in the last session of the Council in December 1563, deliberations turned to female religious orders and to enclosure 'in a haste more similar to a flight than to a true and proper conclusion', without proper discussion or consensus.[51] The Council was uninventive, relied upon the resuscitation of earlier rulings, and left a trail of ambiguity and uncertainty in its pronouncements affecting female orders. Pope Pius IV wanted to finish the Council before his illness finished him; and his successor, Pius V, decided to abandon the publication of the Acts of the Council, as he feared controversy between the Molinists and the Thomists.[52] Issues discussed and determined ranged from financial provisions, to administrative organization, the election of abbesses to religious issues, such as the frequency of communion to be adopted by nuns.[53]

The most important decree, however, was the renewal of the Bull Periculoso (1298) of Boniface VIII, which required bishops to reinstate the strict enclosure of nuns (absolute prohibition against their leaving the convent, except in case of emergency), wherever it had been violate ('ubi violata fuerit'), and to preserve it wherever it was inviolate ('ubi inviolata est, conservari maxime procurent').[54] This opened gaping uncertainties about the correct measures to be taken with the open monasteries where enclosure had never existed.[55] Furthermore, Trent relied on the well-worn ways of reforming female orders: there was almost unanimous consent that reform should be determined by the general Superiors of the religious orders, who controlled most religious houses.[56] If the nuns resisted, the military could be called in. Nuns needed episcopal permission to set foot outside all convents at any time.[57]

It was easy enough to pass the decrees, but their implementation proved to be a vexed issue.[58] The struggles which raged before and after the Council throughout most of Italy focused on whether female convents were to be strictly vocational, part of the clerical order, as reforming bishops advocated, and answerable to the episcopacy; or whether they were to continue to provide the social function of harbouring superfluous daughters.[59] It is that tension that is apparent in conventual architecture of the period.

The process of ironing out abuses, and the strengthening of communal life, was never completely successful. Much more successful were attempts to enforce strict enclosure, measures to isolate convents from the outside world, with locks, bars, wheels and high walls. Sometimes this resulted in the extension of gardens and courtyards where, in compensation for rigorous enclosure, an image of the garden of Eden or of heavenly Jerusalem was created.[60] Architects steeped attention on the elements which became symbolic of enclosure. Desire to emphasize nuns' claustration was sharpened by the constant erosion of its distinction in practice, and by the contradictions and ambiguities inherent in the nuns' position.

After the Council of Trent, conventual enclosure – physical separation – became the principal means towards discipline. Enclosure produces what Foucault calls, 'the protected place of disciplinary monotony' within which space and time can be organized to suit the needs of the institution, without reference to the world beyond that enclosed.[61] Indeed, enclosure becomes the focus and subject of ecclesiastical tests of conventual obedience. The respectability and prestige of convents are measured not by the degree of religious devotion pursued by nuns therein, but by the effectiveness of their enclosure, the symbol of their separation from the world and the guarantee of the virginity of the disciplined bodies inside.[62]

VIRGINITY FORTIFIED

Gabriele Zarri formulated the term 'recinti sacri' or 'sacred enclosures' to describe how convents represent sacred spaces that assume a decidedly female character. But for her this female character remains steadfastly sociological in nature. It is my contention here that we should think of convents in more physical and architectural terms as representing the virginal aristocratic body within urban space.

This is not a new fusion. *Claustrum* depends on closure. C. Bologna has argued that it was great eleventh- and twelfth-century thinkers who made enclosure fundamental to monasticism, who identified the 'inside' of the body of the monk with the 'where of peace', with Augustine's *locus animae*.[63] The interiority elaborated by St Augustine is not simply the identification of a place outside of space. That 'place' is transformed through metaphoric praxis, since it can be spoken of only metaphorically. Exterior space therefore becomes a metaphor for interior space.[64] The convent becomes a metaphor for peaceful devotion and the exterior of the regular's body its sign. For women the sign of that devotion was their chastity, as the introduction to the statutes of the Franciscan convent of S. Maria Maddalena in Turin in 1671 indicate:

> So much did the Son of the Virgin like this virtue [chastity], that when he came to the world, he chose to be born to the purest Virgin that the human race boasted, and for this having to singularly shine in gestures, in words, and in behaviour of enclosed nuns, whose exterior shows very often the interior, because it exactly preserves it, the following statutes are made.[65]

'Enclosure is the principal thing as far as the vow of chastity is concerned' declares Alessandro de' Medici, Archbishop of Florence, in his *Trattato sopra il governo de' monasteri*, written in 1601.[66] Indeed, convent architecture above all obviously represents control over sexuality.[67] Just as the Decrees of the Council of Trent demanded sharp separation of the spheres, so the architecture of female monasteries responded with a rhetoric of fortification both in relation to its immediate urban context and the surrounding streets, and within the conventual churches which doubled as parish churches. That rhetoric was focused on those areas of the convent where contact between inmates and outsiders was most possible – doors and windows – the symbolic orifices – even covered walkways raised high above city streets to create separate passages of circulation. Paradoxically, then, apertures and points of access thereby became the most conspicuous parts of the convent (Figure 1).

Mary Douglas reminds us that 'we should expect the orifices of the body to symbolise its specially vulnerable points'. The same holds true of architecture. 'The mistake is to treat bodily margins in isolation from all other margins. There is no reason to assume any primacy for the individual's attitude to his [sic] own bodily and emotional experience, any more than for his cultural and social experience'.[68] Pronounced rustication on portals, narrow entranceways reached through cast iron gateways and up steep flights of stairs, heavy wooden doors flanked by wheels (*ruote*) which obviated the need for contact between human beings while allowing goods to pass to and from the convent, set up a clear sense of policed and controlled boundaries and apertures. Inside, bars, grilles, screens, curtains and choirs not only separated nuns from laity, but served to draw attention to that separation. Nuns' choirs and windows inside their churches were often framed by elaborate gilt iron grilles that billowed out into the space above the entrance to the church, resembling the elaborate cages of exotic birds (Figure 2). Architectural attention focused on the elements symbolic of enclosure.

Separate circulation routes allowed nuns to move around their convents, to circulate in cloisters, corridors, sheltered walkways, to move between convent and church, and even, in the case of some convents, to cross busy public thoroughfares in the centre of cities. The convent of S. Gregorio Armeno, for example, has a covered bridge forming part of the campanile tower, which allowed nuns to pass at *piano nobile* level from one part of the convent to another across the busy via S. Gregorio Armeno, without coming into contact with laity (Figure 3). Such walkways made individual nuns' bodies invisible to passers-by in the street below, but – paradoxically – reified and made the presence of the institutionalized nuns' bodies permanently present and visible in the city.

This is not an architecture of modest enclosure, but of fabulously advertised confinement. What mattered was not simply that daughters were respectably cloistered, but that their separation from the world – the guarantee of their virginity – was made visible to all.

Virginity had long been conceived in spatial terms. The metaphors of *porta clausa, claustra, hortus conclusus, fons signatus* used to describe virginity and its protection are themselves architectural, evoking a space defended, enclosed and sealed.[69] In 1427 Bernardino da Siena gave a sermon in which he imagined Madonna Clausura, as the virgin's doorkeeper, one of the virgin Mary's twelve handmaidens.[70] Bernardino seizes upon the metaphor of the window as signalling an orifice, open and available in his discussion of the Annunciation:

Figure 1 *Rustification suggesting fortification on the portal of the convent of S. Gregorio Armeno, Naples. (Photo: Helen Hills)*

Figure 2 *Syracuse, S. Maria delle Monache. Nun's choir. (Photo: Helen Hills)*

Figure 3 *The nuns' bridge across via S. Gregorio Armeno, Naples. (Photo: Helen Hills)*

> Let's talk of where the Angel found [the Virgin]. Where do you think she was? At the window or engaging in some other sort of vanity? O no! She was enclosed in a room, reading, to give an example to you, girls, so that you will never be tempted to stand either at the doorway or the window, but that you will remain inside the house, reciting Ave Marias and Our Fathers.[71]

The rhetoric of fortification of chastity had a long and respectable lineage in architectural theory. Writing in the mid fifteenth century, Leon Battista Alberti urges incarceration:

> [M]easures should be taken not just to dissuade the occupants from violating their chastity, but (more important) to make it impossible. For this reason all entrances must be barred, to prevent them from being entered, and those which are open must be watched, so that no-one can loiter there without arousing suspicion.[72]

Defence of the convent should be even tougher than that of a military encampment:

> A military camp with its rampart and ditches need not be defended as strongly as this, fortified, as it should be, with a high, unbroken wall, not even pierced by a single aperture through which temptations of the eye or incitement of the tongue might enter to weaken resolve, let alone actual people with designs on their chastity.[73]

Indeed, convents themselves were seen as bulwarks, physically protecting the city from divine disgrace. A city's safety could be strengthened by the intercessive prayers of religious, which in turn depended on the strength of its religious institutions. Nuns' bodies function like relics in that, like them, they enhance the spiritual significance of the place where they are housed. An ecclesiastical treatise on the role of women, written by Agostino Valier, Bishop of Verona, describes cloistered virgins as playing an important role in reconstituting the discipline of their city, by furnishing through their well-ordered respected convents a bulwark ('baluardo') against evil. Not everyone, of course, was happy with the situation. In 1719 Francesco Peccerillo decried the pervasiveness of convents throughout the city fabric in Naples: 'In short it is not necessary that a religious order should have, like Princes with their fortresses, a post for each quarter of the city'.[74]

With the determination to ensure that convents resembled prisons more nearly than places of prayer, emphasis shifted from virginity conceived as a moral and mental condition (back) to a conception of virginity as overwhelmingly physical.[75] With its carefully articulated concern for the physical enclosure of monastic space, the Tridentine Decrees shift the anxiety of inviolability previously focused on nuns' virginity onto the separateness of their space.[76]

ARCHITECTURE OF SEPARATION

Separation was crucial to female convents. Beyond the significant theological notion of symbolic separation from the world, central to the concept of a convent, separation assumed further social and ideological significance in relation to gender and social rank. Convents and their churches functioned to celebrate and represent God in the city, to house nuns in decorous comfort and style commensurate with their social rank, and to separate nuns from laity, clergy from nuns, virgins from their potential defilers. It is an architecture of definition through separation.

Conventual institutional and urban presence was defined principally through the architecture of convent buildings. Although convents were a massive physical presence within the city, lining streets from one end to the other, occupying entire blocks of the city centres, dominating prime squares, and towering over the city in height, nevertheless in terms of architectural treatment and handling, they deliberately appear to turn their backs on the city, presenting an appearance of indifference towards it, with their small-eyed exterior walls, and largely unadorned façades pierced by few grated windows. The often magnificent interior spaces of the churches themselves erupt unexpectedly from within those austere external shells. Here, where contact between nuns and public was physically closest, the greatest architectural orchestration was focused. Beyond the church, a system of screening, filtering and separation prevented deeper penetration within the conventual complex except to a few carefully regulated visitors. Certain areas were foreclosed to all but the nuns themselves (except in extraordinary circumstances, such as an official visitation), and sometimes only to an elite within them (such as the choir nuns who alone had access to the choir).

Grilled windows, *campanili*, *belvederi*, allowed nuns to look out into the city streets, over walls, into neighbouring houses, courtyards, cloisters; inside their churches *gelosie* and choirs, again grilled, gave them visual access to the congregation down below. They could see, without being seen, and without having physical access to what they saw. In many ways the convent emerges as what Foucault has called 'an apparatus of total and circulating mistrust'.[77] How may we interpret these unseen seeing eyes that the architecture of the convents represents? How is this female religious gaze effectively inscribed in social space? How does convent architecture function at once as the effect and the support of such a gaze? And how does being able to see, but not be seen, relate to the nuns' situation of enclosure? Power here is not wholly in the hands of one person or group (e.g. ecclesiastical authorities, the priest, senior nuns) to exercise over others; rather, it is a machine in which everyone is caught, those who exercise power just as much as those over whom it is exercised. Of course everyone does not occupy the same position; certain positions preponderate or are signalled as doing so by the architecture and permit an effect of control to be produced. But such ambiguities and uncertainties are embedded within conventual architectural organization, and are themselves an important aspect of its technology of power.[78]

That so much depended on the apparent and advertised respectability, chastity and virginity of the nuns' bodies provoked rampant anxieties resulting in regulations, visitations, inspections. The collective virginal body had to be protected – and visibly emphatically separated – from the bodies of potential violators, both sexual and social. Thus both laity and priests, servants and aristocrats were carefully regulated in terms of access to convents. The possibility of intimate bodily contact became the focus of surveillance, obstruction and fantasy.

Architectural organization was supplemented by detailed regulations attempting to control access, keep visitors separate from nuns, nuns separate from each other. A flotilla of rules and regulations sought to keep most people out of convents, allow in only a carefully chosen few, and to control where that select few might physically tread and what they might see. Spatial distinction between seculars and regulars is characterized by rules against the intrusion of unauthorized people ('passive cloister') and regulations against nuns leaving the cloister ('active cloister').[79] In April 1658 Archbishop Rubio of Palermo issued an edict stipulating that abbesses should ensure that lay folk could not see the nuns while they were dining, whether from 'the grates of the church, the parlours, the sacristy, or any other part'.[80] Alexander VII's Bull, published 20 October 1664, is characteristic of the concern with maintaining boundaries and separation. This Bull focused on the way and time in which it was licit for regular superiors of nuns and confessors to enter convents and stay there. It stipulated that confessors, whether ordinary or extraordinary, should enter enclosed convents as little as possible, and should be accompanied by a brother of old age and good *mores*. Anxiety about sexual relations between nuns and priests or confessors was constant, not only because of the close physical contact that religious functions made possible, indeed inevitable; but also because of the intimacy of the confessional relationship. Here the presence of a (supposedly) unsexual old man, functioning as a sort of prophylactic, is intended to guard against potential sexual contact. Likewise, attempts were made to guard against the widespread practice whereby nuns made gifts to their confessors.[81] Pius V's *Decori et honestati* decreed punishment by excommunication for those who broke enclosure and those who admitted outsiders into enclosed convents. Only fire, flood, plague or invasion justified egress.

The principal subject and object of conventual architecture is the body of the nun. The architecture frames and organizes relationships between the nun's body and God's Body (the Eucharist), between it and the familial body and the body politic of the city, both inside and outside its walls. The convent buildings themselves are a metaphor for the virginal upper-class female body. Even if outsiders were kept out, anxieties about unseemly physical contact lingered. Space inside the convent was subject to sharp hierarchical divisions.[82] Grilles and grates separated nuns' bodies from those of the congregation or priest, but not from each other. If communal conventual spaces were too confined, it was feared that nuns' bodies might rub together. This was the reason why the small grilled tribune at the east end of S. Gregorio Armeno in Naples was deemed unsuitable:

> [T]his, although oblong, because of its narrowness anyway bothered the ladies in reciting the Holy Offices, due to the confusion of their voices, and the heat, which the space accumulated in the summer, which sent the nuns' heads spinning, there being no more space between one lady opposite the next than six palms.[83]

Nuns' bodies were not to be at risk of touching each other or their heads would start to spin. Here is evident the fear of carnal pleasure sabotaging from within the whole precarious edifice of respectability, the fear of loss of control of mind and body that persistently and constantly threatened an institution dedicated to subduing them.

Silence, a precondition of a sealed body, was the ideal. Rules and regulations attempted to control when, where and to whom, nuns might speak.[84] Sixtus V stipulated in 1590 that permission of the Sacra Congregazione dei Regolari was required by regulars who wished to talk to nuns (of whatsoever order) in their parlatories, a rule which Urban VIII in 1623 and many Archbishops all over Italy were forced to reiterate.[85]

The myth of chastity and purity within their walls was too important outside them to allow truth to spill out. What happened inside should not be seen; nor should it be heard. The Constitutions of the Convertite degli Incurabili in Naples included a strict admonition in this regard:

> The visitor . . . having visited, admonished, and corrected the sisters as he will have done, in their presence must extirpate the visit from his mind (*abrusciare la visita*), so that their transgressions do not reach the ears of laymen, to whom it is not fitting that they should understand the troubles of religious women.[86]

Silence was intended to block rumour and scandal: worse than his 'carnal commerce' with a laysister of S. Marcellino was considered the possibility that Luca Coppola might lay pen to paper in its regard.[87] Even Archbishop Filomarino was wary as to what he committed to paper about his conventual visitations in Naples during the 1650s. When he criticized the strictly observant convent of S. Maria in Gerusalemme because the confessor's house stood between the convent and the church and sometimes nuns confessed before matins, during the night, Filomarino added darkly, 'I could add other things about which for respect of your Holiness and for not being able to trust the pen I shall be silent'.[88] Likewise when he interdicted the Neapolitan convent of Donnaregina, he dodged the law to avoid specifying the precise abuses so as not to make them known to lay people.[89] The rule of silence formed an invisible wall between the nuns and the world outside; it acted as a barrier, preventing truth seeping from one world into the other, part of the policy of the male ecclesiastical hierarchy of making the world dead to them and them dead to the world, sealing nuns inside, obstructing real understanding amongst outsiders of the lives and doubts and difficulties with which conventual inmates struggled. Silence, however, tends to breed not respect, but suspicion and fantasy, producing in turn a cycle of scandal and rumour, which necessitates ever more vigilant policing, deeper silences, darker shadows.

While conventual regulations focus on behaviour, conventual architecture was investigated during episcopal visitations. In 1648 Archbishop Filomarino ordered the nuns at S. Maria Regina Coeli to close up a room which had no apparent purpose. When he returned in 1652, he realized that the requested wall had only just been built. On this occasion, he was clement, but he frequently used excommunication and interdicts to achieve his ends.[90] Visitations attempted to banish all kinds of abuses. Small and dark corners inside convents were cautiously ferreted out by episcopal visitation. Their language and the preoccupation with routing out secrets and intimacy reveal as much about their executors as about the convents themselves. Consider the following passage by the Archbishop of Florence (1601):

> I have also in visits had an eye to check that through the convent there are no holes, through which from the church or from outside it is possible to see into hidden places, these are often made, and they are very dangerous, even if they are very small, because with threads it is possible to receive and send notes.[91]

Architecture is viewed as revealing probity or abuse. Convents were to be impermeable, because gaps or holes, however small, posed temptation, specifically sexual temptation. Convent walls, like the body of the nun smothered in a habit, were to be sheathed from temptation, made impenetrable. Architecture and the body are conflated.

Convents could not, of course, be completely sealed off from the outside world. Parts of the enclosed area were accessible, such as the parlour, or the *wheels*, or hallways. Again, architecture did a lot of the work of regulating separation here. Indeed, the interior organization of Alberti's prisons bears striking similarities to that of convents:

> There should be a hall, none too depressing, to serve as a vestibule for assembling those sent to be taught a discipline; beyond this the first entrances should be to the quarters of the armed guards, protected behind bars and a palisade; next there should be an open court, flanked by porticoes on either side, containing a large number of openings into several of the cells. Here the bankrupts and insolvent debtors should be kept, not all together, but in separate cells.[92]

The plan of the convent of S. Maria della Consolazione degli Afflitti dei Monache Riformate shows comparable assembly hall, entrances subject to easy protection, the exploitation of anterooms, and a cloister with openings to separate cells (Figure 4).

OPTICS OF POWER INSIDE CONVENT CHURCHES

The optics of power functioned externally – toward the city – and internally, within the conventual complex, but especially at the critical junctures and liminal spaces between the external and internal worlds. Although parlatories and sacristies were areas within convents which afforded considerable opportunities for contact between nuns and lay folk, the risk of unseemly contact, including eye contact, was felt with particular intensity with regard to conventual churches. Two groups of worshippers – lay and nuns – had to be kept separate from each other while participating in a shared Mass. Convent churches were therefore riven with sight lines and ecclesiastical authorities were alive to the potential for inappropriate visual encounters. For this reason, the opening and closing of churches was subject to particularly strict regulation.[93] But much of the regulating of contact during services was left to architecture. The architectural design of convent churches had to prevent lay folk from seeing the nuns while not preventing the nuns seeing the Mass.

The gaze has been theorized in terms of the asymmetrical power relations it produces – 'power through transparency' and subjection by 'illumination'.[94] But what did it mean to be looked at by a nun? Or to have your looking rendered

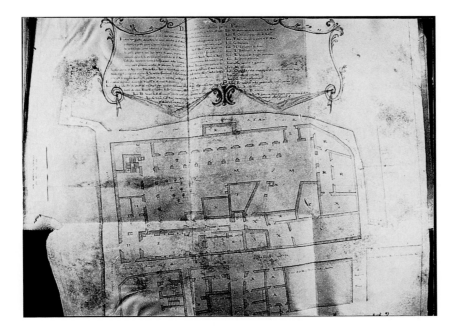

Figure 4 *Plan of the convent of S. Maria della Consolazione degli, Naples. (ASN, Mon. Sop., 4672, f.2bis)*

suspect and furtive? Was it at all comparable to being looked down on by the patron saints of the city, who usually line the skies of representations of cities of this period? As most saints came from religious orders, and given the notions surrounding virginity and the angelic choir, could it be that nuns were regarded as linked to saints, or as potential saints? Certainly they were regarded as intercessors on behalf of the city, as we have seen.

Adrian Randolph has argued that female sight was associated with seduction in fourteenth- and fifteenth-century Florence.[95] He quotes Francesco Barbaro, who called the gaze 'the most acute of all senses [. . .] and [. . .] from it, all motions of the person [body] arise'.[96] In Randolph's words, 'Sight, figured as the sensory linchpin, controls the entire body'.[97] Conduct books for women emphasize the importance of keeping their gaze lowered and modest, as do conventual regulations for nuns.[98]

INTERIOR VIEWING SYSTEMS – WITHIN THE CHURCHES

Nuns' churches did not arrange sinners equally under God's roof. They set nuns apart, as consecrated virgins, elevated and closer to God than the community gathered below them. Access to the Eucharist and to penance also separated the nuns from laity, driving deep wedges through the Christian community based on shared sin.

Roberta Gilchrist has observed that medieval convent churches were usually narrow aisle-less rectangles and suggested that this was because there was little demand for additional altars to be housed in side chapels, because nuns could not perform masses.[99] In early modern southern Italy, nuns' churches are also aisle-less rectangles, but they frequently do have side chapels. Of course, nuns could still not perform mass, but the Eucharist had become markedly more important, as a result of Catholic reform, and Trent, and it was of particular significance to women. The accommodation of lateral altars allowing the performance of many masses throughout the day and even simultaneously is crucial in this regard. The significance of lateral chapels goes further than this, however. Their presence indicates the degree to which, after enclosure, the monastery church was no longer considered to be the province primarily of the nuns themselves. In fact, nuns' bodily presence in the main body of conventual churches was greatly diminished; instead they became observers, suspended high up and participating in the services from within their own restricted spaces. They observed the masses conducted at the lateral chapels from the level of the clerestory from which they could also look down into the church through *gelosie* into the lateral chapels below.[100]

The significance attached to the female gaze makes all the more striking the elevation of enclosed women and the granting to them such dominant vistas in their churches, both along the nave and across the nave into lateral chapels – in both cases being able to survey the laity with ease (Figure 5). In turn, *gelosie* were emphasized and adorned materially, with highly wrought metal, gilded to draw the light. Many choirs were also treated in this way, as well as *coretti* looking into the church (Figure 6).[101] Thus conventual architectural decoration deliberately draws attention both to the invisibility of nuns' bodies and to their imperceptible looking.

The question of what nuns themselves should be allowed to see was hotly discussed and contested both before and after Trent.[102] San Carlo Borromeo's *Instructiones* (1577) sought to codify and formalize the relationship between the nuns in their choir and the performance of the mass.[103] Borromeo prescribes that an opening or grille, as long as the altar, should be set into the wall above the altar, so that the nuns in the inner church may see and hear Mass. Borromeo insists, however, that this opening should not provide views of anything else, such as glimpses of the street when the entrance door is open.[104] Control of sight was organized not only in terms of the building which contained the nuns, but also in terms of the nuns' bodies themselves. Thus two systems – body and building – functioned in parallel.

Rules governing convent nuns' sight lines in conventual churches were more restrictive than practice proved to be, at least in southern Italian convents. These rules relegated nuns to spaces in the back of the church or upper corridors behind grated and curtained openings which deprived them of a clear view of the church or even the mass celebrated in it.[105] In other words, the ecclesiastical authorities wanted to avoid the unimpeded gaze of nuns across the church and into the congregation, as corrupting to nuns, members of the congregation, or both.

Within their convents nuns could see, but not be seen. Conventual architecture granted the power of the gaze asymmetrically, affording nuns pleasures denied to

Figure 5 *View from nuns' choir of S. Maria Donna Regina, Naples, looking west towards the entrance. (Photo: Helen Hills)*

Figure 6 *Gilded nuns' choir balcony in Gesù delle Monache, Naples. Second half of seventeenth century. With kind permission of the Ministero per i Beni e le Attività Culturali*

laity. Grilles shielded nuns from scrutiny, rendered them anonymous, unidentifiable, and made snatched glimpses of a veil, a face, a hand, all the more tantalizing. A member of the congregation could only get a better view of the nuns if he stood very close to the grille and squinted through its gaps – that is only by conspicuously and deliberately peering into the nuns' spaces, an advertency which could not be private or hidden from others. The nuns' own looking was hidden; and it was liturgically endorsed. Although the nuns had liturgical reasons to look into the church, the congregation had no *good* reason to look at them. Mystery added aura to the institution of convents and to their inhabitants. Daniel Borstein sees women of that period as vigorously exercising 'the one form of authority they enjoyed: sacred charisma'. Hamburger and Randolph have provided useful accounts and analyses of the sexualization or charisma of sacred space, but neither was concerned with the organization of interior spaces of female convents in relation to those sexualized dynamics and to the force of the gaze, eroticizing or otherwise.[106]

Priests were ordered not to look into the faces of the women they confessed – Randolph suggests because of the fear of a woman's eyes. The danger of the female gaze helps to explain the lavish attention given to the grilles which screened the women, making their gazes invisible. But these devices did not prevent the women from looking. In fact, the screened *gelosie* and the raised choirs of baroque churches elevated the female gaze to unprecedented heights. Nor was the sacred space of the church de-eroticized by the grilles. The invisible presence of the nuns, who could be glimpsed indistinctly as they moved about and heard as they sang, was tantalizingly erotic; but the fact that they could not be clearly discerned and that their eyes could not be seen, meant that the eroticization became generalized, impersonal, as if emanating from the space as a whole rather than from an individual nun.

Thus conventual churches functioned like an inverse version of Foucault's famous panopticon.[107] Those who could see without being seen (like Bentham's supervisor) were the nuns, elevated and hidden behind screens. They were closer to God, closer to the officiating priest, and had privileged access to hidden spaces, denied lesser mortals. But those whom they could see, the congregation, who could not see them in their turn, who occupied the lower level of the church and were barred from the convent's interior, had freedoms denied to the nuns. Unlike Foucault's model which allies the gaze to forces of control and surveillance, where the gaze is identified with power, conventual visual economies depend on a notion of the gaze as debasing to their most valuable currency. What was at issue was protecting the virginal nun *from* the impure and potentially defiling gaze – both from her own looking, but especially from the looking of others. In both systems visibility is a trap and the fear of that trap can be exploited. In both systems invisibility is the guarantee of order, being seen without seeing, or seeing without being seen ensures that the subjects of the architecture are the objects of information, not subjects in communication.

RICHLY DECORATED CONVENT INTERIORS

Conventual church interiors generally contrast dramatically with their exteriors, just as nuns' external appearance concealed the rich treasures of their spiritual dedication and virginity. Whereas conventual exteriors were de-adorned, austere and shut-off from public contact, the interiors of the churches are frequently fabulously decorated, richly adorned, and open to the public (Figure 7). Here Gadamer's views on ornament are useful. Gadamer argues that architecture, no less than the other arts, has an ontological role of 'representing'. Ornament is

Figure 7 *Palmero, S. Caterina. Interior looking east. (Photo: Helen Hills)*

crucial in this regard. Ornament is not something to be regarded – as architectural historians have almost invariably perceived and treated it – as something additional, extra, applied. Ornament is to be taken as seriously as structure and is as revealing of social relations as spatial organization, style, or the tectonic. 'Ornament,' he argues, 'is part of presentation. But presentation is an ontological event; it is representation.'[108] The rich interiors of conventual churches can be read as representations of the trousseaux of the spouses of Christ.

Convent churches were the space where the convent met with the city, where men and women could come to worship and where they would be reminded of the presence of the nuns above them and around them, but separated from and invisible to them, in spaces that were contiguous, but not continuous, with theirs.

The richness of the decoration of aristocratic convent churches thus publicly demonstrated the familial, worldly and spiritual riches of the nuns. Paintings, gilt stucco, coloured marble revetment which adorned the church walls evoked not just the heavenly reward awaiting redeemed humanity, but, physically separated the congregation from the nuns, became, as it were, a rich and splendid cloak for the nuns. Here architecture, rather than the female bodies it shields, is adorned. The bodies of aristocratic young women were made austere and stripped of their rich finery. That rich costume was transferred to convent church walls. Conventual regulations inveighed against 'precious clothes' or clothes that were elaborately fashioned (*vesti preziose [e] fogge di vestire addobbato*), rings or earrings and 'other secular profanities'.[109] Architecture takes their place, a substitute, working by metonymy, replacing the ascetic body of the invisible virgin with the richly adorned body of the church.[110] Thus these virginal churches come to represent redemption, not only for the virgin who has dedicated her life to God, but for the members of its congregation who worship there and for the city where it stands. Thus conventual churches are monumental in Lefebvre's sense: 'Monumental space offered each member of a society an image of that membership, an image of his or her social visage.'[111] To Lefebvre the monument thus effects a 'consensus', and this, in the strongest sense of the term, renders it practical and concrete. 'The element of repression in it and the element of exaltation could scarcely be disentangled; or perhaps it would be more accurate to say that the repressive element was metamorphosed into exaltation.'[112]

CHRIST'S BODY AND THE NUN'S BODY

At the centre of the Mass, protected in a pyx, was the most sacred body of all. Although conventual regulations devote more attention to the bodies of nuns, liturgically the body of Christ remained central. Indeed, celebration of that body was what made enclosure particularly vulnerable, bringing as it did into the midst of the nuns contact with the priest and the presence of the congregation. The transubstantative nature of the Eucharist had, of course, been reaffirmed at Trent, renewing vigour in the cult of the Eucharistic host.[113] The belief that God was present in the Eucharist more literally than in any other sacrament enhanced the importance of attending mass.[114] Significantly, women's veneration of the Eucharist was more pronounced than that of men.[115] Christ was their Bridegroom; with the Mass their bodies became as one, a sweet foretaste of the ecstasies of Heavenly union. The practice of removing the Eucharist in order to punish nuns for non-compliance with the Decrees of Trent and the absolute terror and horror that that removal provoked vividly illustrate both nuns' intense devotion to the sacrament and the Church hierarchy's exploitation of that devotion.[116] When the convent of S. Gregorio Armeno in Naples was deprived of its Eucharistic host in March 1565 as punishment for not obeying archiepiscopal instructions, Fulvia Caracciola, a nun in the convent, described the church as 'like a widowed house' ('una casa vedovata') and the nuns as 'lost sheep, without a place where they could rest'.[117]

Just as the body of the nun was subject to tightest control, so was the body of Christ. All kinds of restrictions focused on the altar and position and visibility of the host. The 'ostiola' where the sacrament was ministered was expected to conform to the dimensions established by the Sacra Congregazione; and if it were found to be smaller, then it had to be enlarged.[118] The Archbishop of Florence, Alessandro de' Medici, goes to some length to stipulate the requirements of a suitable grate for communion in his treatise on conventual government (1601):

> Its opening should not exceed one palm, whether of thick stone cut so that the nun's face cannot reach the skin of the outside wall, but may remain so/in such a way inside, that the priest cannot see the eyes or forehead of the kneeling communicant nun.[119]

Again architectural requirements were reinforced by regulations governing the nuns' behaviour and dress:

Having prepared to receive this most august Sacrament [. . .], they will approach the little window two by two, with faces covered by the veil, in such a way however that the mouth is conveniently left uncovered, so that the priest can, with every ease, and without any danger of any inconvenience, administer the Sacrament.[120]

HABITUS: THE NUN'S BODY

How do the nuns manage to represent themselves as women, aristocrats and virgins in the design of their surroundings? The allure of rich materials, comfortable furniture, soft bedlinens, and beautifully decorated cells is apparent not only from the inventories of individual cells which record the rich furnishings, but also from conventual regulations which try to instil a respect for austerity and denial of the body. For example, in seven Diocesan Synods held by Archbishop Filomarino in 1642, 1644, 1646, 1649, 1652, 1658 and 1662, there were 38 decrees regulating the behaviour of nuns, which included stipulations that they should refrain from ornaments and not keep paintings, carpets and other such objects in their cells. Likewise the Constitutions of the convent of S. Giuseppe delle Eremitane call for nuns' cells to be furnished with no more than a bed, a chair, a wardrobe, an image of the Crucifix, the Madonna, and one other image depending on the nun's devotion, and a holy water stoup.[121] Despite such regulations, nuns' bodies could be wrapped in and surrounded by clothes and furnishings of beauty and comfort. After her death in 1675 the two cells of sister Maria Giacinta Tomacelli, a nun at S. Maria Regina Coeli, contained two mattresses, four pillows, four new rochets, two covers (one of new *rosciato* (a pink or purple cloth), one of linen, a crucifix of gilt copper, a reliquary, another reliquary of Pius V, the Office of the Virgin, a diurnal, two ebony writing desks, one large and one small, an ebony sideboard, 13 blocks of sweet peach syrup (*percopata*), 13 new chairs, a wash-hand basin with a green bowl with a green ewer, 16 small faience plates, two large dishes, one old cover of *rosciato*, a *canna* in length of Camray cloth. And she also owned 35 paintings of religious subjects which had been housed in the choir and in the sacristy and 23 small altar furnishings ('which are placed on the choir altar').[122] The possessions of D. Teresa Capano at the same convent included a silver watch and a crown; and Signora D. Elisabetta del Tufo who died probably in the 1640s left possessions including books, a coffee-mill, crystal objects and china, twelve paintings, and a clock.[123] Against the prescriptions of austerity and unworldliness, these objects insist upon comforting and stimulating the body and soul, satisfying appetites and affording human contact.

The richness of decoration of the walls of convents was equalled – at least occasionally – by the splendour of refreshments and entertainments at parties within those walls. 'Ricreationi' are a recurrent, sometimes exorbitant, expense in conventual accounts.[124] At S. Maria Egiziaca a Pizzofalcone, parties were held regularly for two days every month. In 1646 the Vice-queen obtained a papal licence to visit female monasteries together with 24 ladies and in S. Chiara they were offered a 'most sumptuous repast of sugary things'.[125] Special parties were held when nuns took the veil, often causing scandal and prompting episcopal warnings.[126] At Donnaregina when the daughter of the Duke of Martina took the veil, the church was filled with representatives of the nobility and the Viceroy himself gave his arm to the girl to lead her to the church of the convent.[127] Splendid parties celebrated the visits of dignitaries;[128] and dinners to celebrate liturgical feasts could assume the lavishness of secular banquets.[129] Fuidoro's commentary on Filomarino's attempts at reform indicate the scale of the practice:

> he prohibited there the creation during the solemn feasts of the dedications of monasteries of gatherings of ladies and gentlemen which create in the church more of a profane abuse of a nuptial feast than of devotion, with [the practice of] bringing in cordials, cups of sweet things and almond paste: it was more of an uproar than an ecclesiastical feast.[130]

In short, sugary sweets, music, feasts and display emerge as among the most pressing concerns of nuns in convents in baroque Naples. Saporific seductions of the body permeate conventual documents. References to drinking, eating and temptations to the palate are quite common. Elisabetta del Tufo's exotic coffee-mill has already been mentioned. And the convents were renowned for their rivalries in speciality sweet-making. Sweets not only stimulated sensory indulgence within the convent, they also effected commerce with the outside world. Sweet sticky cakes, manufactured by virgins, given as favours in return for favours, left sticky trails along their paths of passage in and out of convents, to the mouths of monks, nobles and priests. The sealed and secretive convents oozed enticing luxury sweets, which served both to exoticize their internal secrets, including the nuns themselves, and to bind their clients to them in this exotic and sticky exchange. While S. Chiara produced syrupy egriots or morello cherries, little pears in jars, *mostaccciuli* (a spiced cake laced with must), lasagne, and fritters known as *zeppole*, the nuns of S. Maria Maddalena turned their hands to marzipan 'bricks', and those at S. Maria Egiziaca to 'prison biscuits'; the speciality of Regina Coeli was candied fruit, such as citron and peach.[131] The exchange of sweets and glances in the erotic economy of convents alarmed the Archbishop of Palermo sufficiently to rule that during Good Friday celebrations 'all conventual grates should be locked so that [nuns] may not be seen by people from outside and nobody may give things of sugar, or anything else for similar effect'.[132]

Meanwhile, the sugar economy greatly strengthened the convents financially. Discussing the problem of the sugar economy at the Sapienza in Naples, the Sacra Congregazione dei Regolari observed:

> a large part of the aforementioned sweets go for the exactions of the entries of the convent, and they make notable presents to diverse persons for having the payment of the Court and City, of which the convent has 124,000 scudi in capital. Furthermore, a portion of the sweets is given for law-suits and to other people who serve the convent, such as lawyers, procurators, clerks, officials, collectors, ecclesiastics (*chierici*), servants of the convent, doctors, surgeons, sacristans, and other similar persons.[133]

The quantities were considerable, indicating that convents were highly penetrated. The same document reveals that up to 40 jars were given to the nurse of S. Paolo for the Theatine Fathers, 40 jars for the SS. Apostoli, and 20 for Santa Maria dell'Angeli.[134] During the Revolt of Masaniello, large gifts of sugar and sweets were made to lawyers, procurators and so on, to prevent attacks on convents.

Food occupied a central point in conventual life also in relation to female devotion.[135] The indulgence of the sweets must be seen in the context of the transubstantative Mass and of the regular fastings that marked many feast days in the conventual calendar. Fridays were a day of fasting for most convents. At S. Giuseppe delle Ermitane in Naples fasting also occurred during Advent and on the eve of Epiphany, Ascension, Corpus Domini, the Purification, the Birth of the Virgin, and the eve of S. Agostino.[136]

COVERING THE BODY

Clothing was the outward sign that revealed the body's state to be virginal, privileged, in a state of contrition or transience. Dressing and undressing, concealing and revealing themselves, removing their signs of virginity, transforming themselves and their environments through draping themselves in strange clothing, erecting *apparati*, draping statuary, bringing the lifeless to life – in various ways nuns layered fabrics over their bodies and the architecture surrounding them to suggest, to celebrate and to hide.

If the female gaze was dangerous, so too was the female body. Keeping it covered was an act of piety towards the heavenly bridegroom, a form of self-protection for the nun. This is how Sister Celestina Raineri's biographer and priest described her *pudeur*:

> From the great love that this virgin harboured towards purity originated also her very jealous guardianship of her body, not allowing, in so far as possible, that any part of it should be uncovered to human eyes.[137]

Nuns' bodies, sealed in chastity, had to be covered to protect them from corruption. Convent regulations insisted on this:

> And so that the internal chastity of the mind may shine in the exterior, in conversation, in the choir, in the parlatory, and in going about the convent, they should hold the hands in their sleeves, or at least under their scapulars.[138]

In their account of the life of Sister Maria Carafa, founder of S.M. della Sapienza, Francesco Maria Maggio and the Prioress of the Sapienza, Sister Angelica Caterina Carafa, dedicate considerable energy to the question of veiling the face. This was a matter about which Maria Carafa felt strongly. She wanted the virgins at S. Maria della Sapienza to cover their faces 'since it could avail them nothing to be seen by men'.[139] She quoted a hermit saint fleeing from the sight of his relations: *Si homines video, Angelos videre non possum* (If I can see men, I cannot see angels).[140]

Maggio cites a number of biblical sources in support of veiling: The Song of Songs, when the Lord says to his Heavenly Wife, 'I shall lead you in to solitude, and there shall I speak to your heart'; and Genesis 20, 'Ahimelech, King of Gerara, when he married Abraham and Sarah, he gave them many presents. To Abraham he gave sheep, cows, servants, and maids, but to Sarah he gave a veil to cover her face.' He also turns to Tertullian, cap.15, 'con fugit ad velamen capiti, quasi ad galeam, quasi ad clypeum'.[141] Significantly, Maggio claims that Maria Carafa wanted nuns to veil their faces because of their role as altars of God. St Ignatius, in his first letter to the nuns of Tarso, called nuns 'Altare Dei'; and St Jerome in letter 8, after having spoken of the altar of the temple, writing to a virgin, puts it like this: 'Et de altari transiam ad Altare'.[142] Likewise Maggio cites Giacomo Corono in *Clypeus Patientiae* to support the view that just as altars are covered, so should nuns be: 'sicut enima Altare debet esse omnino coopertum, sic Monialis & Mulier Deo sacra & dicata'.[143]

Maria Carafa justified her order that all the nuns at the Sapienza should cover their faces in terms of carnal love. Their Heavenly Husband was jealous of them, she claimed. Such a claim locates the nun's body – specifically her face – as the site of potential contest between spiritual and mundane bridegrooms. Maggio suggests that the *Hortus Conclusus* and *fons signatus* of Song of Songs are comparably covered. St Jerome in his 22nd letter to Eustace writes, 'Zelotypus est Iesus; non vult ab alijs videri faciem tuam'.[144] The veil therefore signalled that Christ was the nun's bridegroom, but it also became a sign in itself, an acknowledgement of the beauty and temptation of the nun's face beneath it. Thus – in truly Foucauldian fashion – the practice of veiling tended to suggest the sexual allure of the veiled enclosed nun. Just as the nun's body had to be veiled when she was at risk of contact with others, as during communion, so conventual architecture had to be veiled at points of especial porosity. For instance, a Florentine synodal law of 1517 required convents to cover grates with a veil when professed nuns were speaking with a man unrelated to them.[145]

Just as the habit itself signified the dedication of the body to the Heavenly Spouse, so within the convent specific clothing designated the distinctions between boarders, novitiates and choir nuns. Certain clothing had to be donned to enter the choir on feast days and this was what endowed nuns with the active and passive voice and granted them a share in conventual property.[146] In fact, the significance of the choir was always marked by appropriate clothing:

> On ferial days mass was said in the choir with a black cloak, without which you could not say a single line in that place.[147]

Thus clothing represented a privileged position within the hierarchy which was itself conceived spatially (in relation to the choir).

Dressing and undressing in non-conventual clothes seems to have exercised a strong attraction to the nuns, just as seeing nuns dressed up fascinated others. Fra Cirillo da Varese, for instance, allowed the nuns of S. Chiara in Naples inside the church on 15 May 1650 to perform a play, a comedy with nine characters, dressed in secular clothing, of which he and his brethren were spectators.[148] Such activities were liminal, drawing attention to the relationship between the body clothed and unclothed, the sacred and the profane (there is no such thing as profaneness in itself), the way in which the habit, the sign of virginity, could be removed and replaced by a sign of its absence. Thus the dressing and undressing can be seen as a way of turning virginity inside out, exploring its limits and its limitlessness. Did that secular sign threaten the virginal body, undermine it, or even strengthen it? If it strengthened the nuns, then it did so in a way unacceptable to the ecclesiastical authorities who took a very dim view of such proceedings, concerned as usual to eliminate ambiguity and ambivalence. Two synods (1646 and 1649) forbade nuns from putting on plays, even if they were religious, in their churches and from dressing up in women or men's clothing.[149]

Nowhere is the fascination with dress played out more clearly than during the rituals of monacation. Before taking the veil, the girl withdrew to her parents' house; when she next entered the convent, it would be the day of her official taking the veil and its celebration:

> the most select servants have to serve to adorn her as magnificently as can be imagined: her head is crowned with brilliant jewels, she is placed into a splendid coach and taken to the church whose hallways are gracefully decorated with hangings.[150]

Nuns dressed not only their own bodies, but the statuary and architecture of the convent. During festivals nuns dressed statues of saints in rich clothes and jewels. This led to nuns borrowing furnishings and to attempts by the Church (for instance, by Synodal Decree in 1660 and 1662) to limit convents' spending on *apparati* and using anything that did not belong to them.[151] Again we see here the fear of commerce and exchange as corrupting the conventual body (even as economic exchange was positively encouraged by ecclesiastical authorities eager to ensure that convents' finances broke even).

Like the nun's body, conventual architecture was dressed and specially adorned to mark feasts and transitions. Lavish *apparati* on church façades advertised to the city the rituals of the rites of passage for nuns, such as monacation. In 1732, for example, for the monacation party for Signora Ullone at Donn'Albina in Naples, the church was magnificently adorned. Four *canne* of *broccato camorcio* adorned the entablature of the atrium; five *canne* of pale blue brocade with a deep blue background hung in the atrium and in festoons within the church itself; while the most magnificent brocade – eight canne of white brocade with a green background, worked in silver – decorated the church façade to advertise in the city the special event taking place inside.[152]

Such adornments served to underline the liminality of the proceedings, as a young woman left the secular world and entered the enclosed world of the cloister for the rest of her life. The decorations temporarily transformed the church and its entrance into a celebratory space, linking the church with the street, with colourful and expensive cloth paid for by the monacand's family – and thereby also making visible the link between the family outside and the convent inside.[153]

CONCLUSION

Conventual buildings represented nuns' bodies metaphorically and metonymically. The austerity of their outer walls paralleled the austerity of the monastic habits, while the richly decorated interiors represent the precious balsam of virginity. The denial of the corporeal endlessly evoked it, while architecture and the body of the nun occupy mimetic fields. The internal organization of conventual churches was particularly redolent of the optics of power and the temptation and fear of sight, its architecture emphasizing separation from the laity and ambiguously both consolidating and fragmenting the religious body. The coverings of walls, habits and pyx that reveal and conceal the bodies of Christ and of the nuns function metonymically and metaphorically in a system of mutual representation.

The fortress-like appearance of convents strengthened and urbanized discourses of chastity; emphasis on enclosure and separation, both inside the conventual church and out, visibly forged segregation and exclusivity in relation to lay people and implied – while simultaneously obscuring – the nuns' intimacy with the Divine. The promise of their presence was constantly suggested by angelic singing from the choir, sounds muffled behind screens, an indistinct glimpse snatched between grilles, but always obscurely, never directly; conventual architecture served to shatter and fragment, to tantalize and obscure, to disembody and to mystify. The spectacular richness of convent church decoration advertised not only the familial and institutional wealth (and influence) to which nuns had access, but celebrated their bodily presence, too, as virgins, quasi-angelic, a divine urban resource, which could be tapped but never fully possessed.

ACKNOWLEDGEMENTS

I am grateful to the J. Paul Getty Trust for a Postdoctoral Fellowship 1998–1999 which allowed me to undertake the research and writing of this article. Helpful suggestions from Mary Pardo, Marcia Pointon, Mike Savage and Richard Wrigley have improved the text. Bibliographic assistance was unstintingly provided by François Quiviger. Graceful translations are by Mary Pardo; otherwise they are mine.

NOTES

ASN: Archivio di Stato, Naples
ASP: Archivio di Stato, Palermo

1. Richard Sennett's *Flesh and Stone: the Body and the City in Western Civilization* (London: Faber & Faber, 1994) was path-breaking in attempting to tell a history of the city through people's bodily experiences.
2. See especially in this regard, M. Foucault, *Surveiller et punir: Naissance de la prison* (Paris, 1975), trans. A. Sheridan *Discipline and Punish: The Birth and Death of the Prison* (London, 1977).
3. Lefebvre is key in thinking of space as socially and historically produced. See especially, H. Lefebvre, *La Production de l'espace*, trans. D. Nicholson-Smith, *The Production of Space* (Oxford, 1991), esp. pp. 1–60, 68–168.
4. Women's groups and feminists have long been active in architectural design; but

established architectural history, especially of early modern Europe for years blithely disregarded the implications of gender for architectural design, meanings and interpretation. Influential textbooks and surveys, such as S. Gideon, *Space, Time and Architecture* (Cambridge, MA, (1959) 1980), C. Norberg-Schulz *Baroque Architecture* (Milan, 1979), or Spiro Kostof's *A History of Architecture* (Oxford, 1985) ignore the implications of gender entirely, even at a time when their counterparts writing about other forms of visual art production were hard put to avoid at least a passing reference.

5. K. Petersen and J. Wilson, *Women Artists: Recognition and Reappraisal from the Early Middle Ages to the Twentieth Century* (New York, 1976), was one of the key publications in bringing the work of female artists to the attention of a wide public during the 1970s and R. Parker and G. Pollock's, *Old Mistresses: Women, Art and Ideology* (London, 1981) began to guide the debate beyond simply adding women to the canon of artists to considering the relationships between art history and the treatment of women in art.

6. The historical relationship between feminism and art history has been plotted many times elsewhere. See, for instance, N. Broude and M. Garrard, 'Introduction: Feminism and Art History' in N. Broude and M. Garrard, *Feminism and Art History: Questioning the Litany* (New York, 1982), pp. 1–18; N. Broude and M. Garrard, 'Introduction: The Expanding Discourse', in N. Broude and M. Garrard (eds), *The Expanding Discourse: Feminism and Art History* (New York, 1992), pp. 1–26.

7. Rozsika Parker and Griselda Pollock's *Old Mistresses: Women, Art and Ideology* (London and Sydney, 1981), marked an important milestone in this directional shift.

8. See, for instance, D. Hayden, *The Grand Domestic Revolution* (Cambridge, MA, 1982); C. Lorenz, *Women in Architecture: a Contemporary Perspective* (London, 1990); A. Garland, 'A Woman's Place', *Building Design* no. 664 (June 1983) and 'Getting an Even Deal for Women', *Building Design*, no. 675 (Feb. 1984). Amongst the exhibitions on the subject, 'The History of Women Architects', organized by the Union Internationale des Femmes Architectes Sektion Bundesrepublik e V., in Berlin in 1986 and 'That Exceptional One', an exhibition of work by female architects from 1888 to 1988, touring in the USA 1988–1990, were particularly important. An outstanding applied analysis of architecture designed by men in terms of gendered identities remains M. Roberts, *Living in a Man-Made World* (London and New York, 1991). The reasons why architectural history has proved more or less impermeable to many of the intellectual currents which have transformed the rest of art history, such as post-structuralism, would be interesting to discuss.

9. Feminist research concerned with the construction of gender roles through architecture has tended to focus on the modern domestic sphere, e.g. M. Roberts, *Living in a Man-made World* (1991), and R. Hirschon (ed.), *Women and Property – Women as Property* (London, 1984); much of this work viewed spatial arrangements as a simple reflection of social relations (e.g. S. Kent, *Domestic Architecture and the Use of Space* (Cambridge, 1990)). Structuralism encouraged the trend to use formal analysis to read architecture like a separate language. Though useful in providing a language in which to articulate spatiality, this approach failed to consider meanings within specific cultural contexts and overlooked the added complication that space does not simply map existing social relations, but helps to construct them – indeed, has a primary role here. Much of the newer scholarship concerned with precisely such problems comes from the USA and continues to focus almost exclusively on nineteenth- and twentieth-century, mostly domestic, architecture. See, for instance, B. Colomina (ed.), *Sexuality and Space* (Princeton, 1992); Agrest *et al.* (eds), *The Sex of Architecture* (New York, 1996); Coleman *et al.* (eds), *Architecture and Feminism*, 1996.

10. K. Norberg, 'The Counter Reformation' in J. O'Malley (ed.), *Catholicism in Early Modern History* (St. Louis, 1988), p. 134.

11. Rusconi, 'Women Religious in Late Medieval Italy', p. 305.

12. See especially, C.W. Bynum, *Holy Feast and Holy Fast*, p. 204, and Bynum, 'The Female Body and Religious Practice in the Later Middle Ages', *Zone 3: Fragments for a History*

of the Human Body, vol. 1 (New York, 1989), pp. 178–82. For female religiosity and the Eucharist in the baroque period more generally, see especially E.A. Matter, 'Interior Maps of an Eternal External' in U. Wiethaus (ed.), *Maps of Flesh and Light: the religious experience of Medieval Women Mystics* (Syracuse, 1993), pp. 60–73; E. Rapley, 'Women and the Religious Vocation in Seventeenth-Century France', *French Historical Studies*, 18: 3 (1994) 613–31.

13. Areas previously outside the main spotlight of religious historical research have been addressed. Monastic orders, new and reformed, male and female, as well as more informal religious organizations, like confraternities, are important subjects in these debates. For a useful overview of recent developments in early modern Italian religious historiography, see S. Ditchfield, 'In search of local knowledge', *Cristianesimo nella Storia*, 19 (1998) 255–96. Particularly significant in shaping the debate has been the work of Paolo Prodi and Adriano Prosperi (see, for instance, P. Prodi and W. Reinhard (eds), *Il Concilio di Trento e il moderno* (Bologna, 1996) and A. Prosperi, 'Riforma cattolica, crisi religiosa, disciplinamento: un percorso di ricerca', *Annali dell'Istituto storico italo-germanico in Trento* XIX (1993) 401–15.

14. In an inspiring article Frederick McGinness discusses the relationships between post-Tridentine Catholicism, chastity and the Eucharist, 'Roma Sancta and the Saint: Eucharist, Chastity, and the Logic of Catholic Reform', *Historical Reflections*, 15–1 (Spring 1988) 99–116. I have discussed the implications for conventual church architecture in baroque Naples in 'Cities and Virgins: female aristocratic convents in early modern Naples and Palermo', *Oxford Art Journal* 22: 1 (1999) 29–54.

15. See, for example, M. Bevilacqua, *Santa Caterina da Siena a Magnanapoli* (Rome, 1993); S. Boesch Gajano, *Luoghi sacri e spazi della santità* (Turin, 1990); M. Dunn, 'Nuns as Art Patrons: the Decoration of S. Marta al Collegio Romano', *Art Bulletin*, 70: 3 (1988) 451–77; M. Dunn, 'Piety and Patronage in Seicento Rome: Two Noblewomen and their Convents', *Art Bulletin*, 76: 4 (1994) 644–63; M. Dunn, 'Women as Convent Patrons in Seicento Rome' in C. Lawrence (ed.), *Women and Art in Early Modern Europe* (Pennsylvania, 1997), pp. 154–88; V. Sola, 'La decorazione marmorea della chiesa di S. Caterina del Cassaro in Palermo', *B.C.A. Sicilia – NS: AA*, III 7 IV (1993–94) fasc.i-II-III-IV, 11–23; C. Valone, 'Roman Matrons as Patrons: Various Views of the Cloister Wall' in C. Monson (ed.), *The Crannied Wall: Women, Religion, and the Arts in Early Modern Europe* (Michigan, 1992), pp. 49–71; C. Valone, 'Women on the Quirinal Hill', *Art Bulletin*, 76: 1 (1994) 129–46; M.-A. Winkelmes, 'Taking Part: Benedictine Nuns as Patrons of Art and Architecture', in G. Johnson and S. Matthews Grieco (eds), *Picturing Women in Renaissance and Baroque Italy* (Cambridge, 1997), pp. 91–110.

16. Jaynie Anderson claims that this is broadly true, too, of female patronage in the Renaissance: 'With the exception of some "superwomen", like Isabella d'Este and the abbess Giovanna da Piacenza, women patrons have suffered a particular form of death: they have been ignored, not only by historians of patronage, but more curiously, until recently, by feminists as well.' She also points out that there is no authoritative scholarship on patronage studies for the history of art patronage from Renaissance historiography to the present. J. Anderson, 'Rewriting the history of art patronage', *Renaissance Studies*, 10: 2 (1996) 129, 137.

17. This shift in emphasis owes much, directly and indirectly, to the work of the French sociologist, Pierre Bourdieu, especially to his *La Distinction. Critique sociale du jugement* (Paris, 1979).

18. Dunn, 'Spiritual Philanthropists', in C. Lawrence (ed.), *Women and Art in Early Modern Europe* (University Park, Penn., 1997), p. 155.

19. C. Lawrence (ed.), *Women and Art in Early Modern Europe: Patrons, Collectors, and Connoisseurs* (University Park, Penn., 1997), p. 2.

20. 'Chapel decoration was one of the primary areas of focus for the patronage of noblewomen nuns like those at S. Ambrogio della Massima and S. Lucia in Selci, for instance, for these chapels both commemorated their illustrious families and added to the spiritual decorum of these churches'; 'Empowered by wealth and social position,

supplemented by the key elements of a supportive network of other spiritual women, both past and present, and a persistent personal determination, these Seicento matrons were successful patrons, whose philanthropic activities significantly contributed to both the spiritual and artistic life of Rome'. Dunn, 'Spiritual Philanthropists', pp. 156 and 188.

21. See, for instance, Dunn's earlier work, such as 'Nuns as Art Patrons' (her subsequent work allows her female subjects greater complexity) and Valone, 'Women on the Quirinal Hill'. Jaynie Anderson makes a similar point about interpretations of the art patronage of Renaissance widows. J. Anderson, 'Rewriting the history of art patronage', *Renaissance Studies*, 10: 2 (1996) 129–38.

22. He regards it as significant that, for instance, Suor Maria Domitilla Galuzzi's visions should have begun soon after the redecoration and adornment with new icons of the chapel where she meditated. Monson, *The Crannied Wall* (1992), p. 6.

23. Jeffrey Hamburger diagnosed the problem in relation to medieval enclosure thus: 'A history of the art and architecture of female monasticism requires a social history of female spirituality in the Middle Ages. Neither, however, has been written, perhaps because each is integral to the other.' *Gesta*, XXXI/2 (1992) 126. In fact, the split between an analysis of practice and an analysis of architecture holds true even for much of the recent work on gender and domestic architecture. Recent studies concerned with the intersection of these themes too often treat the buildings by way of plans or photographs and leave practice – what actually went on inside those buildings – out of consideration all together. This is the principal weakness of Beatriz Colomina's otherwise valuable essay, 'The Split Wall: Domestic Voyeurism' in Colomina (ed.), *Sexuality and Space*, pp. 73–130.

24. Questions of female devotion, female sanctity, its production, its nourishment, its definition, its regulation and its propagation are also important foci for research. This work was stimulated by important studies which located sanctification within broad sociological analyses, such as the influential work of Weinstein and Bell and Sofia Boesch Gajano (D. Weinsten and R. Bell, *Saints and Society: the two worlds of Western Christendom, 1000–1700* (Chicago and London, 1982); S. Boesch Gajano and L. Sebastiani (eds), *Culto di Santi, istituzioni e classi sociali in età preindustriale* (Rome, 1984). Gabriella Zarri has illuminated the relationships between 'holy women' and their society, considering the legends of their lives in relation to the cultural contexts that gave them life and circulation, the relations of canonization proceedings, and the groups that promoted their cults (G. Zarri, *Donne e Fede: santità e vita religiosa in Italia* (Rome, 1994); Zarri and other scholars have been attentive to the connections between rapidly developing Italian urban cultures and particular forms of religious devotion (Zarri, 'Le Sante Vive', *Annali dell'Istituto storico italo-germanico in Trento*, VI (1980) 371–445 and Zarri, *Il Monachesimo femminile in Italia dall'alto medioevo al secolo XVII*, Convegno del Centro di Studi farfensi VI, Verona, 1995). The significance attached to charismatic figures who became the centre of attention for whole cities and were endowed with various supernatural and life-saving powers, including those of prophecy and insight (which were regarded as typically female), indicates the significance of charismatic women and reveals that popular ideals were embodied in the penitential practices and prolonged fasts of female mystics, as well as in the austerity of self-denying hermits.

25. Scholars have more energetically investigated artwork and music produced by nuns inside convents. See, for example, J. Hamburger, *Nuns as Artists: The Visual Culture of a Medieval Convent* (Berkeley and London, 1997) and C. Monson, 'La Pratica della musica nei monasteri femminili bolognesi' in O. Mischiati and P. Russo (eds), *La Cappella Musicale nell'Italia della Controriforma* (Cento, 1989), pp. 143–60.

26. This quality tends to mar Craig Monson's otherwise exemplary introductory chapter to *The Crannied Wall* (1992, pp. 2–7); and although Roberta Gilchrist, in an unusual study of female convent churches of the later Middle Ages, argues that space and material culture are 'fundamental in constituting gender' and that space 'reproduces attitudes towards sexuality and the body', her study fails to demonstrate this in detail;

R. Gilchrist, *Gender and Material Culture. The archeology of religious women* (London and New York, 1994), p. 17. Exceptions to this general rule include the work of Carolyn Valone, Marilyn Dunn, Caroline Bruzelius (especially Bruzelius, 'Queen Sancia of Mallorca and the Convent Church of Sta. Chiara in Naples', *Memoirs of the American Academy in Rome*, XL (1995), pp. 69–100). Unfortunately, such scholarship concerned with the early modern period has overwhelmingly focused on Rome and northern Italy (e.g. J. Mann, 'The Annunciation Chapel in the Quirinal Palace', *Art Bulletin*, 75: 3 (1993), 113–34. 1994; C. Valone, 'Women on the Quirinal Hill' Dunn, 'Nuns as Art Patrons' and 'Piety and Homage').

27. Roberta Gilchrist's *Gender and Material Culture: The Archaeology of Religious Women* (London, 1994) marked an important step in terms of thinking about architecture (often in ruinous form) in relation to gendered identity. Caroline Bruzelius' work subtly examines the relationships between architecture and patronage, religious beliefs and gender in medieval Naples (C. Bruzelius, 'Hearing is Believing: Clarissan Architecture, ca. 1213–1340', *Gesta*, XXXI/2 (1992) 83–91; and 'Queen Sancia of Mallorca and the Convent Church of Sta. Chiara in Naples', *Memoirs of the American Academy in Rome*, XL (1995) 69–100). See also the very useful collection of essays in C. Bruzelius and C. Berman (eds), *Gesta*, XXXI/2 (1992), which is focused on the architecture of medieval convents.

28. This approach was sparked by Joan Kelly's influential article, 'Did Women have a Renaissance?' in J. Kelly, *Women, History and Theory* (Chicago, 1984), pp. 19–50. Gerhard Williams, for example, argues that the Reformation left women increasingly confined within the familial sphere, but Italian Counter-Reformation religious institutions for women provided a viable and respectable alternative to marriage and sometimes additional scope for female agency. G. Williams in C. Monson (ed.), *The Crannied Wall* (Michigan, 1992). See also R.L. Greaves (ed.), *Triumph over Silence. Women in Protestant History* (Westport, CT, 1985); K. Norberg, 'The Counter Reformation and Women: Religious and Lay', in J. O'Malley (ed.), *Catholicism in Early Modern History* (St Louis, 1988), p. 133; J. Delumeau, *La Peur en Occident (XIVe–XVIIIe siècles)* (Paris, 1978), p. 408.

29. For a judiciously balanced viewpoint, see Craig Monson's introduction to C. Monson (ed.), *The Crannied Wall*, pp. 2–7.

30. William Christian's exemplary work on local religion and sacred space emphasizes process, including 'sacrilization as a process', drawing attention to how the wish of some religious to individuate sharply between, for example, a sacred place or a profane place, readily results in documentary evidence that is systematically biased and can consequently easily affect the interpretations of even those disinterested in those organizations that confer or protect sacredness. W. Christian, 'The Delimitation of Sacred Space and the Visions of Ezquioga, 1931–1987', in S. Boesch Gajano and L. Scaraffia (eds), *Luoghi sacri e Spazi della Santità* (Turin, 1990).

31. In 1977 Luigi Fiorani, in an important article on nuns and monasteries in Rome during the period of Quietism, lamented the neglect of this important subject in Seicento studies of Rome (L. Fiorani, 'Monache e Monasteri Romani nell'Età del Quietismo', *Ricerche per la storia religiosa a Roma*, 1 (1977) 63. Given the large and increasing numbers of convents and of nuns in Rome during this period, there is still, perhaps, a relative scholarly neglect. However since 1977, important work, including Fiorani's own, has thrown much light on the problems and circumstances of female religious orders in Rome.

32. These considerations have come to the fore in particular in the excellent scholarship on female religious devotion in early modern France. See especially P. Chaunu, *L'église, culture et société: Essais sur réforme et contre-réforme* (Paris, 1984), p. 401; E. Rapley, *The Dévotes: Women and the Church in seventeenth-century France* (Montreal, 1990), p. 5; H. Brimond, *Histoire littéraire du sentiment religieux en France, depuis la fin des guerres de religion jusqu'à nos jours*, vol. 2 (Paris, 1933), pp. 36ff; J. Dagens, *Bérulle et*

les origines de la Restauration catholique (1575–1611) (Paris, 1952), p. 105; and N. Davis, *Society and Culture in Early Modern France* (Stanford, 1975), p. 85.

33. D. Borstein, 'Women and Religion in Late Medieval Italy: History and Historiography' in D. Borstein and R. Rusconi (eds), *Women and Religion in Medieval and Renaissance Italy* (Chicago, 1996).

34. P. Paschini, *I monasteri femminili, Problemi di vita religiosa in Italia nel Cinquecento* (Padua, 1960), p. 58; L. Fiorani, 'Monache e Monasteri Romani', *Ricerche per la storia religiosa a Roma*, 1 (1977), 63–111, pp. 73–6; and C. Russo, *I Monasteri Femminili de classura a Napoli nel secolo XVII*, pp. 49–53.

35. Dunn usefully provides examples of seventeenth-century Roman aristocratic women who protested that they would have preferred a religious life but were forced to adopt a secular one. Dunn, 'Spiritual Philanthropists', p. 156.

36. Borstein, 'Women and Religion in Late Medieval Italy', pp. 8–9.

37. This is in part a consequence of the tendency within early feminist scholarship to 'celebrate' exceptional individual women, but the concentration on nuns' biographies draws on a particularly rich literary tradition, dating back through the sixteenth century to the medieval period. Jodi Bilinkoff argues that such accounts are a continuation of medieval hagiography. She suggests that the reluctance to use the word 'hagiography' (it rarely occurs in modern historiography in relation to lives of post-medieval women) betrays prejudices amongst historians rather than marked changes in the nature and functions of the lives themselves. J. Bilinkoff, 'Navigating the Waves (of Devotion): toward a gendered analysis of the Counter-Reformation', unpublished paper discussed at the North Carolina Research Group on Medieval and Early Modern Women, Chapel Hill, 16 November 1997. An impressive list of published lives of exemplary women is given in the 'Repertorio' in G. Zarri (ed.), *Donna, Disciplina, Creanza Cristiana dal XV al XVII Secolo* (Rome, 1996) pp. 407–705. Influential and recent biographical accounts include E. Zanette, *Suor Arcangela: Monaca del Seicento Veneziano*; Medioli, *L'Inferno Monacale di Arcangela Tarabotti*; S. Cabibbo and M. Modica *La Santa dei Tomasi: storia di Suor Maria Crocifissa (1645–1699)* (Turin, 1989); A. Jacobson Schutte (ed.), *Cecilia Ferazzi, Autobiografia di una santa mancata* (Bergamo, 1990); S. Andretta, *La Venerabile Superbia: ortodossia e trasgressione nella vita di Suor Francesca Farnese (1593–1651)* (Turin, 1994). The biographies of a remarkably large number of nuns were published soon after their deaths. These nuns were usually exemplary and often died in fame of sanctity. Typically, the biography itself, generally written by a confessor or a member of the nun's own family, is an attempt to promote the chances of beatification or sanctification of the woman involved. Examples published in early eighteenth-century Palermo include, A. Mongitore, *Compendio della Vita e virtu della Serva di Dio Suor Rosaria Caterina alias detta di Gesù, Palermitana, Religiosa Domenicana nel Ven. Monastero di s. Vincenzo Ferreri nella Terra di Carini* (Palermo, 1718); *Vita della Serva Soro Celestina Raineri Palermitana Sorella Professa nel Venerabile Monastero del Cancilliere di questa felicissima, e fidelissima Città di Palermo sotto la Regola del Patriarca S. Benedetto; scritto da un riv. sacerdote Divoto del detto Ordine e dedicato al Da D. Sebastiano Raineri, fratello della medesima* (Palermo, 1734); *Vita della Serva di Dio Suoro Teresa Benedetta Monaca Professa del Ven. Monastero di s. Gio. Battista detto lo Riglione nel secolo D. Caterina Gerbino, e l'Agras De' Baroni di Gulfnta, e Marchei dell'Agonia* (Palermo, 1744). Clearly, such authors are not disinterested bystanders, but often stood to have their own reputation, or that of their family, considerably enhanced as a result of their close involvement with a saint. Useful discussions of the problems involved in interpreting 'Lives' of nuns which were written by their confessors can be found in Alison Weber, *Teresa of Avila and the Rhetoric of Femininity* (Princeton, 1990); J. Coakley, 'Friars as Confidants of Holy Women in Medieval Dominican Hagiography' in R. Blumenfeld-Kosinski and T. Szell (eds), *Images of Sainthood in the Middle Ages*; E. Ann Matter, 'The Personal and the Paradigm: The Book of Maria Domitilla Galluzzi' in Monson (ed.), *The Crannied Wall*, pp. 87–103; and

Anne J. Schutte, 'Inquisition and Female Autobiography: The Case of Cecilia Ferrazzi', in Monson (ed.), *The Crannied Wall*, pp. 105–14.

38. C. Russo *I Monasteri Femminili di claudiera a Napoli nel secolo XVII* (Naples, 1970); Elissa Novi Chavarria, 'Nobilta di Seggio', *Dimensioni e Problemi della Ricerca Storica*, 2 (1993), pp. 84–111; M.A. Visceglia, *Il Bisogno di Eternitá: i comportamenti aristocrati a Napoli un etá moderna* (Naples, 1988).
39. H. Moore, *Space, Text and Gender*, (Cambridge, 1987), p. 188.
40. An arresting example is Damien Hirst's new London restaurant Pharmacy designed to *épater les bourgeois*. It demonstrates that cultural and economic capital do not overlap – he uses cultural capitalism to slap economic capital in the face. And the irony is, of course, that being slapped in the face attracts the rich punters.
41. Gramsci's notion of hegemony also illuminates these apparent paradoxes of people acting against their own interests. He argues that consensus is developed between dominant and subordinate groups through the process of hegemony, which may be very slow and gradual. Subordinate groups, which may include women, subscribe to dominant values, symbols and beliefs, which are part of an encoded value system which is maintained through institutional and individual action. But interest groups, such as aristocratic female religious, may also develop views which differ from prevailing orthodoxies.
42. G. Pollock, 'Feminism/Foucault – Surveillance/Sexuality', in N. Bryson, M.A. Holly and K. Moxey (eds), *Visual Culture: Images and Interpretations* (Hanover and London, 1994), p. 14.
43. P. Waddy, *Seventeenth-Century Roman Palaces: Use and Art of the Plan* (Cambridge, MA and London, 1990), pp. 25–31. In their wing of Palazzo Borghese, for instance, Virginia Borghese had rooms towards the garden of Palazzo Borghese, while those toward the street were taken by her husband, Giovanni Battista Borghese. Ibid., pp. 85–6.
44. Consider the spiral staircase which allowed Giovanni Battista Borghese to come and go from Palazzo Borghese's north-west wing unobserved.
45. The presence of an apartment of women attendants was the principal feature distinguishing female from male apartments. The women had individual rooms, a common kitchen and dining room, and a *rota* to allow them to receive food and supplies without having contact with men. Waddy, *Seventeenth-Century Roman Palaces*, pp. 29–30.
46. S. Weddle, 'Enclosing Le Murate: The Ideology of Enclosure and the Architecture of a Florentine Convent', unpublished PhD, Cornell University, 1997, p. 40.
47. P. Brown, 'Late Antiquity' in P. Veyne (ed.), *A History of Private Life: from Pagan Rome to Byzantium*, 1987, pp. 267–70. Brown points out that 'for active men to come to create a "public" space in their own bodies through the renunciation of marriage, such public space had to be palpable (even attractive) and the community's need for a public space defined in this drastic manner, in the persons of its leaders, had to be very urgent indeed'. Ibid., p. 270.
48. R. Gilchrist makes the same point in relation to medieval nuns and secular women of the upper classes. Gilchrist, *Gender and Material Culture*, pp. 167–9.
49. Gilchrist, *Gender and Material Culture*, p. 19.
50. A. Randolph, 'Regarding Women in Sacred Space', in G. Johnson and S. Matthews Grieco (eds), *Picturing Women in Renaissance and Baroque Italy*, (Cambridge, 1997), p. 17.
51. The Count of Luna addressed this remark to the congregation itself: 'si maravigliava molto che per venire alla fine del Concilio si procedesse in una fretta, che pareva più simile a fuga che a vera e legittima conclusione'. Quoted by R. Creytens, 'La Riforma dei monasteri femminili dopo i Decreti Tridentini', *Il Concilio di Trento e le Riforma Tridentina: Atti del Convegno Storico Internazionale* vol. I (Rome, 1965), pp. 51–2.
52. In fact, it was not until 1880 that the full sources were revealed. H. Jedin, *History of the Council of Trent*, vol. 2, trans. E. Graf (London, 1961), p. 503; J. Morris, *The Lady was a Bishop: the hidden history of women with clerical ordination and the jurisdiction of bishops* (London, 1973), p. 151.

53. *The Canons and Decrees of the Sacred and Occumenical Council of Trent*, trans. J. Waterworth (New York and London, 1848) (Sess. 25, Cap.V), p. 240.

54. 'Bonifatii VIII constitutionem, quae incipit *Periculoso*, renovans, sancta synodus universis episcopis sub obtestatione divini iudicii et interminatione maledictionis aeternae praecipit, ut in omnibus monasteriis sibi subiectis ordinaria, in aliis vero Sedis Apostolicae auctoritate clausuram sanctimonialium, ubi violata fuerit, diligenter restitui, et, ubi inviolata est, conservari maxime procurent, inobedientes atque contradictores per censuras ecclesiasticas aliasque poenas, quacumque sappellatione postposita, compescentes, invocatio etiam ad hoc, si opus fuerit, auxilio brachii saecularis . . . Nemini autem sanctimonialium liceat, post professionem exire a monasterio, etiam ad breve tempus, quocumque praetextu, nisi ex aliqua legitima causa, ab episcopo approbanda, indultis quibuscumque et privilegiis non obstantibus.' *Canons and Decrees of the Council of Trent* (Sess. 25, Cap.V), 240. On *Periculoso* see J.A. Brundage and E. Makowski, 'Enclosure of Nuns: the decretal *Periculoso* and its commentators', *Journal of Medieval History*, 20 (1994) 143–55 and E. Makowski, *Canon Law and Cloistered Women: Periculoso and Its Commentators, 1298–1545*, Studies in Medieval and Early Modern Canon Law, vol. 5 (Washington, DC: The Catholic University of America Press, 1997).

55. The Council ruled that professed nuns, or 'sanctimoniales' (itself an ambivalent term since it was not clear whether it included tertiaries), not be allowed out of the convent, except for a legitimate cause and with episcopal approval. The rulings were based on the mistaken assumption that nuns who took the three solemn vows necessarily abdicated their free will, even in those cases where the rule allowed nuns to leave the convent. In fact, this renunciation had not been demanded by the popes from Sixtus IV onwards, when the solemn vows were changed to simple vows and regular tertiaries had been recognized as true professed nuns. In the event Pope Pius V (1559–1565) interpreted the Fifth Canon of Trent much more rigidly than the way proposed by the Curia. Pius chose to return to Boniface VIII's legislation and to recognize one single category of true convents, in which nuns took the three solemn vows and observed strict enclosure. This resulted in the abolition of all the open monasteries which had been officially recognized by the Church from the time of Sixtus IV. Pius V was strongly supported in this more radical and aggressive interpretation by cardinals of the Congregation of the Council, especially by Cardinal Carlo Borromeo who claimed that reform of convents was impossible without a uniformity preventing jealousies between convents. R. Creytens, 'La Riforma dei monasteri femminili dopo i Decreti Tridentini', *Il Concilio di Trento e la Riforma Tridentina: Atti del Convegno Storico Internazionale Trento 1963*, vol. I (Rome, 1965), pp. 50–3, 60, 64, 65.

56. Creytens, 'La Riforma dei monasteri femminili', p. 49.

57. In various ways Pius V and Gregory XIII rigidified the rulings of Trent still further. For further details, see Creytens, 'La Riforma dei monasteri femminili', pp. 69–70.

58. Problems of enforcement rippled throughout the post-Tridentine Church where the end was willed, but not the means. This was nowhere more true than with regard to female convents, because of the sharp divergence between lay and clerical conceptions of their function. See A.D. Wright, 'The Religious Life in the Spain of Philip II and Philip III' in W.J. Sheils (ed), *Monks, Hermits and the Ascetic Tradition*, Studies in Church History, vol. 22 (Oxford, 1985), pp. 252–74.

59. A.D. Wright, 'Venetian View of Church and State: Catholic Erastianism?', *Studi secenteschi*, 19 (1978) 96–7.

60. G. Zarri, 'Recinti sacri. Sito e forma dei monasteri femminili a Bologna tra '500 e '600' in S. Boesch Gajano and L. Scaraffia (eds), *Luoghi Sacri e spazi della Santità* (Turin, 1990), pp. 381–6.

61. M. Foucault, *Surveiller et punir* (Paris, 1975), trans. A. Sheridan *Discipline and Punish* (London, 1977), p. 141.

62. This was how scholars discussed enclosure during the fifteenth and sixteenth centuries in Italy. Paolo da Certaldo, for example, discussed enclosure as necessary to preserve 'the reputation of chastity', the perception of a woman's virtue, which he considered a

'delicate thing': 'tenera cosa è nelle femine la fama della castità, è come fiore bellissimo'. Paolo da Certaldo and V. Branca (eds), *Mercanti Scrittori* (Milan, 1986), p. 10.

63. C. Bologna, 'L'"Invenzione" dell'Interiorità (spazio della parola, spazio del silenzio: monachesimo, cavalleria, poesia cortese)' in S. Boesch Gajano and L. Scaraffia (eds), *Luoghi sacri e spazi della santità* (Turin, 1990), pp. 243–66.

64. Augustine speaks of 'eyes of the soul', 'ears of the soul'. So 'body'/'soul', 'exterior'/'interior', 'surface'/'depth' become the expressive modes of a dialectic of knowledge and communication that claim to spread beyond the traditional confines of the inexpressible.

65. 'tanto piacere al Figlio d'Iddio questa Virtù, che venendo al mondo, volse nascere dalla Vergine più pura, che vantasse il genere humana, e per questo dovendo singolarmente risplendere ne gesti, nelle parole, e ne portamenti delle Religiose Claustrali, ne quali l'esteriore dimostra ben spezzo l'interiore, perche essatamente si custodisca, si fanno li seguenti statuti'. *Regola o Costitutioni delle M. Reverende Monache del Terzo Ordine di s. Francesco, dette Convertite del Monastero di S. Maria Maddalena nella città di Torino* (Turin, 1671), p. 33.

66. 'la clausura è cosa principale per conto del voto della castit'. Quoted by Weddle, 'Enclosing Le Murate', p. 247 n. 347.

67. Foucault argues that architecture changes late in the eighteenth century:

> A fear haunted the latter half of the eighteenth century: the fear of darkened spaces, of the pall of gloom which prevents the full visibility of things, men and truths. It sought to break up the patches of darkness that blocked the light, eliminate the shadowy areas of society, demolish the unlit chambers where arbitrary political acts, monarchical caprice, religious superstitions, tyrannical and priestly plots, epidemics and the illusions of ignorance were fomented. The chateaux, lazarets, bastilles and convents inspired even in the pre-Revolutionary period a suspicion and hatred exacerbated by a certain political overdetermination.

From being concerned with making manifest power, divinity and might through palace, church and stronghold, architecture began to tackle new problems, using the disposition of space for economico-political ends. In this regard, especially in schools, he argues that control over sexuality becomes inscribed in architecture. Foucault, *Power/Knowledge*, pp. 148, 150, 153. I find Foucault's discussion stimulating, but many of the ideas which he locates as eighteenth-century developments reach back much earlier, even if the architectural forms he individuates as being their fullest articulation are eighteenth century.

68. M. Douglas, *Purity and Danger: An Analysis of Concepts of Pollution and Taboo* (London, 1966), p. 121.

69. Saundra Weddle includes a useful discussion of the ideology of enclosure in her unpublished PhD, 'Enclosing Le Murate', pp. 29–39.

70. Bernardino da Siena, *Prediche volgari sul campo di Siena* (1427), vol. 2, ed. C. Delcorno (Milan, 1989), pp. 859–88.

71. 'Ma diciamo da [sic] la trovò l'Angiolo. Dove credi ch'ella fusse? A le finestre o a fare qualche altro esercizio di vanità? Eh no! Ella stava inserrata in camara, e leggeva, per dare esempio a te fanciulla, che mai tu non abbi diletto di stare nè a uscio nè a finestra, ma che tu stia dentro in casa, dicendo delle Ave Maria e de' Pater Nostri.' C. Delcorno (ed.), *Prediche volgari*, p. 862.

72. *The Architecture of Leon Batista Alberti in Ten Books*, trans. J. Leoni (London, 1755), p. 128.

73. Ibid.

74. 'E non è necessario in somma, che un ordine di Religiosi abbia, come fanno i Principi colle fortezze, un posto per ciascuna contrada della Città.' F. Peccerillo, *I Ragioni per la Fedelissima, ed Eccellentissima Città di Napoli circa l'Impedire la Fabbrica delle Nuove Chiese e l'acquisto, che gl'Ecclesiastici fanno de' beni de' Secolari* (Naples, 1719), p. 9.

75. The best discussions of the tension between conceptions of virginity as moral and physical (exemplified above all by St Augustine and St Jerome) are to be found in the special edition of *Quaderni Storici*, n.s.75, XXV, n.3 (1990) edited by G. Fiume and L. Scaraffia, devoted to virginity. See in particular their 'Premessa', pp. 701–14; A. Boureau, 'L'Imene e l'Ulivo. La Verginità femminile nel discorso della Chiesa nel XIII secolo', pp. 791–803; and G. Sissa, 'La Verginità materiale. Evanescenza di un oggetto', pp. 739–56. See also J. Bugge, *Virginitas: An Essay in the History of a Medieval Ideal* (The Hague, 1975) and C. Atkinson, 'Precious Balsam in a Fragile Glass: The Ideology of Virginity in the later Middle Ages', *Journal of Family History*, 8 (1983) 131–43.

76. Indeed convent architecture resembles that of prisons in other ways also, just as their organization and functions parallel contemporary prisons in arresting ways. It is striking that the first time prisons were used for punishment, and long-term punishment at that, in France was in relation to women guilty of fornication, adultery or prostitution (that is sins of concupiscence). This constituted what Philip Riley has described as 'the cornerstone of Louis XIV's attack on prostitution' in 1684. Not only did his ordinance link prostitution with sin, requiring physical penance and spiritual conversion, but it also established the connections between sin, punishment and imprisonment in relation to women found guilty of prostitution, fornication and adultery. In itself the refashioning of imprisonment to police women's chastity is significant. It is even more noteworthy that the women's prison of the Salpêtrière was run along lines reminiscent of a convent. Seventy-five lay 'soeurs', assisted by eight priests, ran the prison. Prayer, devotional reflection and spiritual exercises were allotted in fifteen-minute intervals between cleaning, weaving and carding wool. The sisters (chaste, unmarried and widowed women who received a pension and lifelong employment within the prison) administered discipline, led the prayers and recorded the prisoner's penitential progress. Borromeo's *Istructionum* was amongst the literature used to determine whether women were truly contrite. Riley argues that female imprisonment at the Salpjtrihre, where penance, conversion and spiritual instruction were linked, was overridingly religious in character. At Bon Pasteur, a private refuge in Paris for 120 women, lust (not sloth) was the capital sin. Those women chose to expiate their sins by accepting a life of mortification, silence, obedience and work. P. Riley, 'Michel Foucault, Lust, Women and Sin in Louis XIV's Paris', *Church History*, 59 (1990), pp. 41, 43. The picture is complicated by the fact that a considerable number of convents were converted to prisons, especially in France after the Revolution. J. Evans, *Monastic Architecture in France* (Cambridge, 1964), p. 4.

77. Foucault, *Power/Knowledge*, p. 158.

78. The phrase is Foucault's and comes from his discussion of the 'Panopticon' from which I have drawn many of my ideas. C. Gordon (ed.), *Power/Knowledge*, p. 148. Foucault argues that 'the classical age discovered the body as object and target of power'. He acknowledges that even before the eighteenth century the body had become the object of imperious investments, but identifies concern with the body to have been focused on 'elements of behaviour or the language of the body' rather than 'the economy, the efficiency of movements, their internal organization' which it later became. Foucault argues that what was earlier restricted to monasteries, armies and workshops came to be extended in the seventeenth and eighteenth centuries to be general formulas of domination. For Foucault this is 'an uninterrupted, constant coercion, supervising the processes of the activity rather than its result', which is exercised according to a codification that partitions time, space and movement as closely as possible. These 'disciplines' Foucault sees as making possible attentive control of the body's operations, allowing the constant subjection of its forces and imposing upon them a relation of 'docility–utility'. These controls were different from slavery, from service and vassalage. Foucault regards the eighteenth-century regulation of bodies as different from asceticism or monastic discipline, in that these sought to achieve renunciations rather than increases in utility and had as their principal aim 'an increase of the mastery of each individual over his own body'. Foucault, *Discipline and Punish*, pp. 136–7.

79. Gilchrist, *Gender and Material Culture*, p. 152.

80. *Editto*, Palermo, April 1658, n.p.

81. Any priest who received such presents risked having his licence to hear confessions revoked. Cardinal Filomarino was charged in 1652 by the Sacra Congregazione dei Regolari with checking the accounts of convents of Regina Coeli and the Sapienza in this regard. Russo, *I Monasteri Femminili*, p. 91.

82. I have discussed elsewhere the organization of the nuns' choir with regard to social hierarchy within the convent. Hills, 'Cities and Virgins', *Oxford Art Journal*, 22: 1 (1999) 29–54.

83. 'quale quantumque bislungo, a d'ogni modo p[er] l'angustia rendeva incomodo alle Signore nella recita de' Divini Ufficj p[er] la confusione della voce, e p[er] il Calore che acquistava in istato, che all SS[uo]re veniva a vacillare la testa, non essendo altro intervallo tra l'una Sig[nor]a dirimpetto all'altra, che palmi sei'. ASN, Mon. sop., S. Gregorio Armeno, 3430, f.116v.

84. For instance, an *Editto* issued by Archbishop Rubio in Palermo in February 1664 threatens nuns who speak to anyone apart from their mothers, fathers, brothers or sisters without written permission from the Vicar General with the deprivation of active and passive voice for four months. *Editto*, Palermo, 1664, p. 1.

85. For example the Archbishop of Palermo rehearsed the threats in April 1654 (*Editto*, Palermo, 1654). Enforcing the regulation was bound to be difficult, but had been made more so by Urban VIII's granting to Ordinaries the exceptional right to grant a licence giving permission four times a year to a regular monk wishing to talk to a nun to whom he was related in first or second degree.

86. 'lo visitatore . . . visitato, admonito, et correto che haverà le sorelle, in loro presentia debia abrusciare la visita, acciò le loro transgressioni non vadino alle orecchie de' laici, alli quali non conviene intendere li secreti de' religiose', *Costituzioni delli Convertite degli Incurabili*. Quoted by Russo, *I Monasteri Femminili*, pp. 103–4, n. 281.

87. Russo, *I Monasteri Femminili*, p. 104.

88. 'potrei dire altre cose che per riverenza della Santit' Vostra e per non potersi confidare alla penna taccio'. Quoted by Russo, *I Monasteri Femminili*, p. 84.

89. 'senza osservar le solennit' de jure et specificar cause per non pubblicarle alli secolari', quoted by Russo, *I Monasteri Femminili*, p. 104.

90. Russo, *I Monasteri Femminili*, p. 73.

91. 'Ho ancora nelle visite havuto l'occhio per il monastero non seino fori, per ii quali di chiesa o di fuori si possa vedere in luoghi occulti, di questi sene fanno spesso, e sono cosa molto periculosa se ben fussino piccolissimi, perché con fili si possano ricevere e mandare polizze'. Alessandro de Medici, 'Trattato sopra il governo de' monasteri', f. 88. Quoted by Weddle, 'Enclosing Le Murate', p. 253 n. 359.

92. Alberti, *On the Art of Building*, p. 140.

93. See, for instance, Russo, *I Monasteri Femminili*, p. 74 for Archbishop Filomarino's stipulations with regard to Neapolitan convent churches. In Palermo Archbishop Rubio ordered that conventual church doors must be locked before two o'clock at night and must not be opened on Good Friday before dawn; *Editto*, Palermo, 1658, n.p.

94. Of course the most famous discussion of these issues is Foucault's of the Panopticon.

95. Randolph, 'Regarding Women in Sacred Space', pp. 38–41.

96. F. Barbaro, 'De re uxoria liber' in (ed.) E. Garin *Prosatori latini del Quattrocento* (Milan and Naples, 1952), p. 125.

97. Randolph, 'Regarding Women in Sacred Space', p. 39.

98. For the post-Tridentine linking of government of the soul with good household management and other female virtues, see E. Casali, 'Economia e Creanza Cristiana', *Quaderni Storici*, 41 (1979) 555–83. For models of female aristocratic behaviour, see M.A. Visceglia, *Il Bisogno di Eternità*, pp. 141–74.

99. Gilchrist, *Gender and Material Culture*, p. 97.

100. In turn, this suggests that the absence of aisles was determined less by lack of demand for separate masses than by the importance of seeing the mass unimpeded by columns

and aisles from the *gelosie* up above, as well as by the emphasis on 'visual cleanliness', the avoidance of places which might accommodate scandalous assignations.

101. For instance, at S. Francesco a Pontecorvo gilt metal adorned both choirs and the coretti: 'sopra di detta porta è il sudetto coro da officiare con sua gelosia intagliata, e posta in oro [. . .] vicino [all'altare Maggiore] è altro coro dà officiare, ed intagliata, à guisa dell'altro Coro Già descritto [. . .] Dalla parte di sotto il cornicione di detta Chiesa vi sono sei coretti con loro gelosie indorate'. ASN, Mon. Sop. 4540, f.7v.

102. Caroline Walker Bynum's observation that early Italian vitae of female saints sometimes stress seeing the Eucharist over eating it is arresting in this respect. Bynum, *Holy Feast and Holy Fast*, p. 140.

103. Charles Borromeo's *Instructiones fabricae et supellectilis ecclesiasticae* (1577), Chapters XXXII and XXXIII, p. 87.

104. Borromeo, pp. 87 and 91. The window of the main altar had been discussed in the First Provincial Council of 1565, but Borromeo extended regulations further than that Council. E.C. Voelker, 'Borromeo's Influence on Sacred Art' in J. Headley and J.B. Tomaro (eds), *San Carlo Borromeo: Catholic Reform and Ecclesiastical Politics* (London, 1988), p. 187, n. 30.

105. Franca Camiz makes this point clearly in her article, 'Virgo-Non Sterilis', but she appears to be unaware of the wide discrepancy between proscription and practice. Camiz, 'Virgo-Non Sterilis: Nuns as Artists in Seventeenth-Century Rome' in G. Johnson and S. Matthews Grieco (eds), *Picturing Women in Renaissance and Baroque Italy*, p. 142.

106. J. Hamburger *Nuns as Artists* (Berkeley, 1997).

107. The principle of the panopticon is an annular building with a watch tower at its centre, and cells around its periphery. Backlighting allows the supervisor to watch the prisoners in the cells, but they cannot see whether they are being observed or not. Thus the architecture participates in the system of surveillance. See M. Foucault, *Surveiller et punir* (Paris, 1975), trans. A. Sheridan, *Discipline and Punish* (London, 1977), p. 200.

108. G. Gadamer, *Truth and Method*, trans. J. Weinsheimer and D.G. Marshall (London, 1989), p. 159.

109. The quotation comes from regulations issued by the Neapolitan Sacra Congregazione dei Regolari about clothing permitted to *educande*. Russo, *I Monasteri Femminili*, p. 67.

110. Katie Scott embarks on a stimulating discussion of the relationship between architectural decoration and body adornment in *The Rococo Interior: Decoration and Social Spaces in Early Eighteenth-century Paris* (New Haven, 1995).

111. H. Lefebvre, *The Production of Space*, trans. D. Nicholson-Smith (Oxford and Cambridge, MA, 1991), p. 220.

112. Lefebvre, *The Production of Space*, p. 220.

113. *Canons and Decrees of the Council of Trent*, Session XIII, caps. 1–8.

114. J.A. Jungmann, *The Mass of the Roman Rite: its Origins and Development* (London, 1959), pp. 93–104; J. Bossy, 'The Mass as a Social Institution, 1200–1700', *Past and Present*, 100 (1983) 29–61.

115. C.W. Bynum, *Holy Feast and Holy Fast*, p. 204 and idem, 'The Female Body and Religious Practice in the Later Middle Ages', *Zone 3: Fragments for a History of the Human Body*, vol 1 (New York, 1989), pp. 178–82. References to cravings for frequent communion are common in *vitae* of individual nuns of the baroque period. See, for instance, the following examples from Palermo: *Vita della Serva di Dio Sor[or] Celestina Raineri palermitana* (Palermo, 1734); *Vita della Serva di Dio Suoro Teresa Benedetta Monaca Professa del Ven. Monastero di S. Gio. Battista detto lo Riglione* (Palermo, 1744); A. Mongitore, *Compendio della Vita e Virtù della Serva di Dio Suor Rosaria Caterina* (Palermo, 1718). Also on female devotion and the Eucharist in Palermo, see A. Mongitore, *Palermo Divoto di Maria Vergine*, vol. II (Palermo, 1720). For female religiosity and the Eucharist in the baroque period more generally, see especially E.A. Matter, 'Interior Maps of an Eternal External' in U. Wiethaus (ed.),

Maps of Flesh and Light: the religious experience of Medieval Women Mystics (Syracuse, 1993), pp. 60–73; E. Rapley, 'Women and the Religious Vocation in Seventeenth-Century France', *French Historical Studies*, 18: 3 (1994) 613–31.

116. ASN, mon. sop., S. Gregorio Armeno, 3435, 130v–135r.

117. 'rimanendo p[er]ciò la Chiesa, come una casa vedovata, e le povere monache come smarrite pecorelle, non havendo luogo dove riposare potessero, giache l'uso loro era sempre di frequentare il S[antissi]mo Sacramento'. ASN, mon. sop., S. Gregorio Armeno, 3435, f.134v.

118. Russo, *I Monasteri Femminili*, p. 103.

119. 'Non ecceda un palmo di apertura, sia di grossa pietra, tagliata in modo che la faccia delle monache non possa venire su la pelle del muro di fuori, ma resti talmente dentro, che con il braccio messo dentro comunichi il sacerdote; sia l'altezza tale che il comunicante stando la suoro inginocchioni non vegga nè gli occhi nh la fronte.' Alessandro de' Medici, 'Trattato sopra il governo de' monasteri', quoted by Weddle, 'Enclosing Le Murate', p. 252, n. 357.

120. 'Preparate dunque à ricevere quest'Augustissima Sacramento, con queste, simili considerationi, s'accrosteranno alla Fenestrella à due à due, con la faccia coperta dal Velo, in maniera perr, che resti scoperta commodamente la bocca; accioche il Sacerdote possi, con ogni facilità, e senza pericolo d'alcun inconveniente, amminstrare il Sacramento'. *Constitutioni delle povere Capuccine Monache della prima Regola di s. Chiara del Monastero di s. Carlo di Piacenza* (Piacenza, 1683), p. 26.

121. Russo, *I Monasteri Femminili*, p. 88.

122. ASN, mon. sopp. Regina Coeli, 1975, fasc. 12 no. 10, unfoliated.

123. Undated document, ASN, Regina Coeli 1975, fasc. 12 n. 4, unfoliated. I think it dates from the 1640s to judge by its relative position, handwriting, etc.

124. This was in spite of attempts by Church authorities to limit such expenditure (e.g. *Lettera Circolare per li monasteri e conservatorii di questa Città di Palermo*, addressed to Reverend Mothers and other female superiors by the Sacra Congregatione dei regolari, published in Palermo in July 1708).

125. 'lautissima colazione di cose di zuccaro'. Quoted by Russo, *I Monasteri Femminili*, p. 110.

126. Such scandals prompted Archbishop Rubio of Palermo in 1658 to threaten conventual superiors with suspension and the friends and relations of nuns with excommunication if churches and parlours of convents continued to be used during feasts in unseemly ways. *Editto*, Palermo, June 1658, n.p.

127. Russo, *I Monasteri Femminili*, p. 101.

128. A splendid party for Maria of Austria, the wife of Ferdinand King of Hungary, was prepared by the nuns of SS. Trinità in their convent and garden. Russo, *I Monasteri Femminili*, p. 98.

129. That the Good Friday dinner was getting out of hand in this way is revealed from an edict issued by the Archbishop of Palermo in 1654: 'la Cena del Giovedi Santo si faccia con semplicità Religiosa senza forgio, ò apparati, ma in tutto si conformino con le rubriche, & ordinationi della Santa Chiesa'. *Editto*, Palermo, 1654, n.p.

130. 'li proibl nelle feste solenne delli titoli di monasteri non si facessero comiti di dame e cavalieri formandosi in chiesa più presto un abuso profano di festino sponsalizio che di devozione, con portarsi acqua concia, cose dolci tazze e mandili da paggi: era più presto chiasso che festa ecclesiastica'. Quoted by Russo, *I Monasteri Femminili*, p. 74.

131. Russo, *I Monasteri Femminili*, p. 93, n. 259.

132. 'stiano tutte le grade serrate acciò non siano vedute da persone esterne no se dia cosa veruna di zuccaro, ne altra cosa per smimil effetto'. *Editto*, Palermo, 1654, n.p.

133. 'una gran parte delli predetti zuccari va per l'esattioni delle entrate del monastero, e si fanno notabili presenti a diversi per havere il pagamento della Corte e Città, avendone il monastero 124,000 scudi di capitale. Di più parte de zuccari si da per le liti e ad altre persone che servano il monastero, come ad avvocati, procuratori, scrivani, officiali,

esattori, chierici, servitori del monasterio, Medici, chirugi, sagratori, ed altre persone simili'. ASN, Mon. sop., 4509. Quoted by Russo, *I Monasteri Femminili*, p. 94.

134. Ibid.

135. Caroline Walker Bynum has led the way in investigating women's relationship to food during the Middle Ages primarily in religious terms. For her suggestion that women tried to transform their body into food in order to resemble and incorporate themselves into Christ, see C.W. Bynum, *Holy Feast and Holy Fast: The Religious Significance of Food to Medieval Women* (Berkeley, 1988), pp. 260–9. Other scholars argue that manipulation of food is a rejection of societal expectations, an assertion of their autonomy (R. Bell, *Holy Anorexia* (Chicago, 1985)) and others see eating in sexual terms (e.g. A.J. Schutte, 'Inquisition and Female Autobiography: The Case of Cecilia Ferrazzi' in C. Monson (ed.), *The Crannied Wall* (Michigan, 1992), p. 110).

136. Russo, *I Monasteri Femminili*, p. 116.

137. 'Dal grande amour che serbò questa Vergine alla Purità, ebbe ancora l'origine la custodia gelosissima del suo Corpo, non permettendo, per quanto le fu possibile, che si scovrisse ad umane pupille parte alcuna di quello.' *Vita della Serva di Dio S[or]or Celestina Raineri Palermitana sorella professa nel Venerabile Monastero del Cancelliere di questa [. . .] Città di Palermo*, Palermo, 1734, 40.

138. *Regola e Constitutioni* (Turin, 1671), p. 33.

139. 'imperocché non può giovare a cosa veruna l'essere vedute dagli huomini'. Maggio, *Vita della Venerabile D. Maria Carafa* (1670), p. 452.

140. Maggio, *Vita*, p. 452.

141. Maggio, *Vita*, p. 455.

142. Maggio, *Vita*, p. 455.

143. Maggio, *Vita*, p. 456.

144. Maggio, *Vita*, p. 457.

145. Weddle, 'Enclosing Le Murate', p. 235.

146. 'la quale veste era la prerogativa che donava alle Monache la voce attiva, e passiva, e le faceva partecipi delli beni del Mon[aster]io'. ASN, mon. sop., S. Gregorio Armeno, 3435, f.126v.

147. 'Li giorni feriali s'ufficiava in choro con un manto negro, senza di cui non si posseva dire un piccolo verso in quel luogo.' ASN, mon. sop., S. Gregorio Armeno, 3435, 'Esemplare delle nobilii memorie . . .', f.126v.

148. Russo, *I Monasteri femminili*, p. 221. For plays performed in convents, see E. Weaver, 'The Convent Wall in Tuscan Convent Drama' in Monson (ed.), *The Crannied Wall*, pp. 73–83.

149. These were inveterate abuses which had been ruled against by Alfonso Carafa in 1564.

150. F. Vargas Macciucca, *Dissertazione intorno alla Riforma degli abusi*, (Naples, 1745), p. 76.

151. Russo, *I Monasteri Femminili*, p. 99.

152. The bill for brocade alone for decorating the church and atrium came to 22-2-10. ASN, Mon.Sop.3307, f.633r.

153. Families competed with each other in splendour to such an extent that the Church authorities attempted to curb expenditure. On 16 November 1629 the Sacra Congregazione dei Regolari of Rome wrote to the Vicar of Naples with nine new regulations to moderate expenditure on both dowries and monacation expenses. 'Copia di Lettera della Sacra Congregazione per la moderazione delle Spese da farsi nelle professioni delle Signore Monache indirizzata al Reverendissimo Monsignor Vicario, Napoli', ASN, Mon. Sop. S Francesco (Cappuccinelle a Pontecorvo) 4540, ff.3v–4r. Regulations included lifting the expenses of entrances, professions, and taking the veil, allowing 'only at the entry an honest voluntary recreation, which does not exceed in total the sum of 5 carlines for each nun'. 'solamente nell'ingresso un'onesta ricreazione volontaria, che non ecceda in tutto la somma di Carlini 5 per ciascuna monaca'. ASN, Mon. Sop. 4540, f.4r.

CHAPTER 5

GENDER AND THE ARCHITECT: WOMEN CLIENTS OF FRENCH ARCHITECTS DURING THE ENLIGHTENMENT

Tanis Hinchcliffe

I

This paper grew out of a general discontent on my part with the unremitting masculinity of architectural history, where both the content and the presentation seemed to leave no space for a female voice, let alone a female sensibility of any sort. It might seem perverse to expect architectural history to reflect in any significant sense the differences between the sexes. It has after all been constructed in similar vein to its close relative, the history of art, which had its origins in connoisseurship at the time when it was important to attribute to works of art identifiable artists through the stylistic characteristics of the works and their provenance. From this initial cataloguing activity came the interest in the careers of individual artists and their patrons. The history of art has become far more sophisticated in its analysis, but the basic framework remains. Architectural history also depends on a catalogue of buildings, their architects, and those people who commissioned them, so should questions of gender be any part of its business, especially when the architects and the great majority of patrons belonged to one sex? This is what I wanted to investigate, and rather perversely given the male domination of architecture, I set about looking for women in its practice.

Recently art history has looked for women as subject and object, that is as practitioners and as objects of representation.[1] Although architecture is often portrayed as a woman, it seemed unlikely that I would find in my area of interest, the French eighteenth century, any women who were recognizably 'architects'. I put it in those terms because current research is showing that architecture was practised by many people who would not necessarily describe themselves as architects.[2] To claim categorically that there were no female architects in the past is to apply our own notions of what the practice of architecture should be, and to subscribe to nineteenth-century professionalism to the exclusion of any other model. Nonetheless, it seemed that if I were to find women practising at this time, they would be both exceptional and on the margins.

To look for the female represented in buildings might seem more hopeful, especially as two of the five orders, the Ionic and Corinthian it was claimed, represented women and girls. However, there seemed little enlightenment to be had on that score in the available examples, such as the courtyard of Gondoin's

Ecole de Chirurgie in Paris where Ionic and Corinthian orders are present together in what was a building representative of the establishment of the 'male' profession of surgery.

Another possible area of female influence was in the familial circumstances of the architects themselves. Many of them benefited from financial assistance from their mothers or professional help from uncles on their mother's side. Architects also tended to marry the sisters of fellow architects, thus establishing networks which combined family and professional interests. None of these relationships seem to have any direct relationship to the design of buildings, fascinating as they might be as social history.[3] Therefore, I decided to look for female involvement among the architects' clients, where I knew I would find at least a few well identified women.

II

Once I had taken the decision to search for female clients in the second half of eighteenth-century France, I found myself plunged into what must be one of the few historic periods when women's involvement in architecture is visible. Initially my method was to take the text which has long been the authority on the architecture of France from the seventeenth to the nineteenth centuries, Louis Hautecœur's *Histoire de l'architecture classique en France*.[4] Hautecœur's work is encyclopaedic in its scope, and although the fate of classicism is the thread which holds his narrative together, his seven-volume work is a great compendium of French architecture. From the index I traced through the text those women he mentions and drew up my preliminary list of women clients.

Before I proceed further, I would like to say something about my sources, which are without exception secondary sources. Recent interest in eighteenth-century architecture, especially among the French, follows an interval of some years when no one much cared, and as a result texts often date from sixty or more years ago. Far from being gender blind, these texts seem to take a delight in the more sensational aspects of women's involvement in architecture, and I soon became aware that the discourse surrounding the social life of French women at the end of the Enlightenment would complicate my investigations. Even Hautecœur adopts a supercilious tone when he writes about women clients. This was not what I expected, and it became understandable only within the context of my growing awareness of the reconstruction of the eighteenth century by writers in the nineteenth century, particularly by the Goncourt brothers. In *La Femme au XVIIIe siècle* of 1862 the brothers sought to rehabilitate the century they claimed was the French century *par excellence*, and although their scheme was to produce three more volumes on men, the state and Paris, they began with 'the women' of whom they said, 'The woman in the eighteenth century is the principle which governs, the reason that directs, the voice which commands.'[5] What they wrote, however, is almost exclusively concerned with the private, the *chuchotement* of intimate life, whether at court, in the bourgeois home, or at the theatre and among the demi-monde. Sixty years later, another more scholarly study by Léon Abensour, *La*

Femme et le feminisme avant la Révolution of 1923, continued the historical fascination with eighteenth-century women,[6] and the influence of this work can be seen in, for example, Stern's *A l'Ombre de Sophie Arnould* (1930), where the life of the architect François-Joseph Belanger is bracketed by his relationships with volatile, but extremely useful actresses and opera singers.[7]

III

It was the construction of masculinity and femininity in the eighteenth century that provided the basis for the nineteenth century's fascination. In contrast to the bourgeois suppression of the feminine, it seemed that eighteenth-century women held sway in society in a way that excited male critics such as the Goncourts. More recently Michèle Cohen has shown that accepted wisdom and conduct books advised an ideal balance between the sexes in the public sphere of sociability where the rough edges of the male would be made smooth in the company of women, while the tendency for the female to excess would be curbed through male influence.[8] The balance was destabilized when viewed from the outside: for example, in English eyes at the end of the eighteenth century French men appeared effeminate becaused they talked too much, while women were considered mannish because they talked at all.[9]

Architects, it went without saying, were male with regard to their buildings and their clients, but could be regarded as 'female' by the builder on whom they relied to erect the building. This despite the fact that the builder dealt with the materiality of the building, which might have been expected to be associated with the female in opposition to the male spirit represented in the design.[10] In 1671 an Academy of Architecture had been formed in Paris by the king with the purpose of weakening the building trades guilds by giving official recognition to the architects. The means by which architects were to gain the advantage was through the classical style, knowledge of which depended on a certain sort of education different from the usual apprenticeship of the building trades, and closer to that of a gentleman. The curriculum of J.-F. Blondel's famous school of architecture, opened in 1742, included gentlemanly accomplishments such as dancing which would distinguish the aspiring architect from the builders and place him in the same social sphere as his clients.[11] Indeed a reading of the various treatises written since the fifteenth century and based on Vitruvius would suggest that the architect through his knowledge of theory and practice was able to assume the persona of the perfect client. By that I mean he had the knowledge not just of architecture, but of the world in general, which enabled him to empathize with the needs of the client, while the architect's understanding of building enabled the client to realize his or her desires. Chameleon-like, the architect put on his client's personality, whether male or female, with each job, and as Michael Dennis has pointed out in *Court and Garden*, 'Architects found fresh inspiration in the personalities of their clients, which led to great diversity in the simple format of the Neoclassical *hôtel*'.[12] We can now ask to what extent these clients were women.

IV

Of all the arts, architecture is the most expensive. Most really large buildings are paid for by corporate bodies, and only a relatively few individuals can afford to build their own houses. Of these even fewer are built by women since their access to wealth is extremely problematic. This was the case in eighteenth-century France, although the laws of property were not uniform throughout the country.[13] In the south the Roman code prevailed while in the north, common law was more prevalent. Usually women fared better under the Roman code, but laws also depended on local tradition, so that in Paris the inheritance laws did not exclude women as much as they did in the rest of the north. Basically the situation was similar to England under common law; women could own property if they were single or widowed, but once they married their property became their husbands. And since a woman remained a minor until she was 25, it was most likely that the only time she had any control over her own finances was when she was widowed, if she lived that long. The dowry was important in France, particularly for the less wealthy, and although the capital of this could not be touched by the husband, neither could it be used by the wife. On the other hand, the interest could be used by the husband, and he could borrow against it. The constraints on women owning property and wealth in their own right placed many women in a position of passivity whereby other people usually managed their affairs. When they did build it was most often a house for their own use or a building for a charitable institution.

V

The eighteenth-century women I discovered who had commissioned buildings themselves fell into a number of categories. First of all there were those at the top, that is those women around the king. In the case of Louis XV this meant his wife and daughters to a modest extent, but more especially his mistresses, Mme de Pompadour and Mme du Barry. Louis XVI's wife, Marie-Antoinette, carried on where her grandfather-in-law's mistresses had built before her, but on a reduced scale resulting from restraint on her budget. Faced with an absolute monarch, it is not surprising for us to find that the king's family and favourites should have the power to commission buildings. However, this activity also stretches to those connected to the king by birth, so that among the array of Bourbons, women were also engaged in building. Besides Louis XVI's immediate family there were his brothers, the Duc de Provence, the Duc d'Artois, and then there were the other branches of the Bourbon family such as the Condé and Conti, as well as the Orléans. A vast network of patronage flowed from this source which provided money and jobs for a good many people, including mistresses and their architects.

The deal with an absolute monarch is that if he is guaranteed an income through taxation, he will ensure the political stability of the country so that in the case of France mercantile capitalism could flourish. In order to keep the money flowing in, the feudal king had to make arrangements with the capitalists, which made him beholden to them, but which also locked them into the same system of patronage upholding the monarchy.[14] It has often been pointed out how entwined the aristocracy had become with the upper bourgeoisie, what with the purchase of office and even titles and the intermarriage between the two classes.[15] And yet just as important was the consolidation of a bourgeois class distinct from the aristocracy, which held enormous wealth and therefore power, although this was not always overt. It was this class perhaps more than the aristocracy which supported another group of women who built for themselves – the singers, dancers and actresses of the Opéra and the Comédie Française.

VI

From the point of view of where the money came from, the royal family and its circle are probably the least interesting as clients, but for the architects seeking patronage, they were the most satisfying. To become the architect of a member of the royal circle, even of the royal mistress, could open great possibilities, although by the second half of the eighteenth century the heroic age of royal building had passed. When Louis XV's queen, Marie Leczinska, the daughter of the Polish King of Lorraine, wanted to build a convent school in the town of Versailles, she sent for the architect who had been involved in rebuilding Nancy for her father, Richard Mique.[16] After her death, her unmarried daughters continued the patronage of Mique, with a request to build a chapel at the convent in St Denis where one of them became a nun. When Louis XVI came to the throne in 1774 he was little interested in building, but it pleased Marie Antoinette to arrange the grounds of Versailles around the Petit Trianon. Once again it was Mique who designed for the queen, and it was he who was responsible for the temple of love, the belvedere and the hameau.[17] Although Mique was lucky to have succeeded Gabriel as *architecte du roi*, he is now considered conservative and lightweight.

Gabriel was the architect of Mme de Pompadour's Petit Trianon, a pavilion ('pavillon') intended to be her private retreat from the formal life of the court. Mme de Pompadour has the reputation of having been a formidable patron of the arts, although this claim has been recently challenged.[18] She was the daughter of a financier, M. Poisson, an associate of Antoine Pâris, one of four brothers important in the banking world of the time. Having become the mistress of the king, Mme de Pompadour then pushed forward her brother, the Marquis de Marigny, until she succeeded in having him made the Intendant of Civil Building. This put Marigny in a position to commission architects to carry out the major works of the king, and his most ambitious project in Paris was the new church of Ste Geneviève (now the Panthéon) designed by Soufflot.[19] Mme de Pompadour is likely to have at least approved the selection of Soufflot as the architect of this prestigious commission, although at the time Gabriel was the architect to the king.

After Mme de Pompadour's death, the even more *déclassée* Mme du Barry became the king's mistress. Mme du Barry's contacts were with the Paris demi-monde and it may have been through the dancer, Mll Guimard, that she made the acquaintance of Ledoux, who became her architect.[20] Mme du Barry had been given the estate of Louveciennes to the west of Paris overlooking the Seine. Gabriel had renovated the chateau, but she asked Ledoux to design a pavilion for her. The house was intended to be used for entertaining and was of only one full storey, but what distinguishes the façade are four, free-standing Ionic columns, a feature we will return to again as significant in the battles over *convenance* or propriety (Figure 1). Mme du Barry was canny enough to support at court the Abbé Terray, the *contrôleur des finances*, who seems to have been an unlimited source of finance for her schemes. She asked Ledoux to redesign her chateau, but his grandiose scheme was never executed because on the death of Louis XV Mme du Barry fell out of favour, and although eventually she was allowed back to Louveciennes her building days were over. While she still had influence, the king's mistress was able to get Ledoux appointed as the inspector of the saltworks in the Franche-Comté, where he designed the saltworks at Arc et Senans.

VII

At the level of the throne it could be expected that women would have the chance to build, even if it was only the arrangements of their own apartments. We could express surprise that not more was built under their initiative, and during the last fifteen years of the *Ancien Régime* this was undoubtedly caused by the king's insistence on economy. Thus the royal women were constrained in their spending by the strings of the king's purse. The appetite to build was well established among the king's relatives, who were perhaps less restrained by public opinion. In 1781 the Comtesse de Provence, the wife of the king's brother, acquired property in Versailles, where she had a pavilion built for herself by the architect Chalgrin.[21] A central circular salon is flanked by four rooms, one octagonal, one oval and two hexagonal, forming the salon, the boudoir, the billiard and dining rooms. At this point Hautecœur says that having satisfied the wishes of his wife, the Comte de Provence wished to please his mistress, Anne de Caumont La Force, Comtesse de Balbi, who also wanted a pavilion in Versailles. He therefore acquired yet another piece of land on which Chalgrin built another pavilion.

It is worth pausing a moment to consider this apparently cosy domestic scenario. The Comtesse de Balbi had married the Comte who had a considerable fortune, but in the words of the *Biographie Universelle*, she did not make him at all happy.[22] When he discovered that she had been unfaithful, he wished to kill her and her lover, but her friends helped her to have him declared insane. The comtesse became lady-in-waiting to the wife of the Comte de Provence and acquired influence over her as well as winning the affections of the comte. She dissipated her husband's fortune and tried to recoup her losses by gambling and when she failed to win, she sent her bills to the Comte de Provence. Not only did the *Biographie* consider the Comtesse de Balbi a thoroughly bad lot, it claimed that she was not even good at political intrigue, and described her as 'a Pompadour with little feet'. Although the Comtesse de Balbi's career was rather spectacular, a number of upper-class women found themselves in a quasi-independent position after divesting themselves of their husbands.

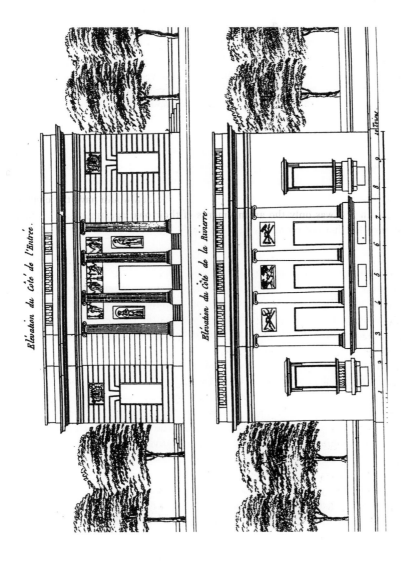

Élévation du Côté de l'Entrée.

Élévation du côté de la Rivière.

Figure 1 *Pavilion at Louveciennes for Mme du Barry by Ledoux. From J.C. Krafft and N. Ransonnette, Les Plus Belles Maisons de Paris, 2 vols, 1801–1812 (1992) II, pl. 1. Detail front and garden façades*

The Princess of Monaco, Catherine de Brignole, separated from her husband and formed a liaison with the Prince de Condé. The prince had inherited from his grandmother the Palais Bourbon (now the National Assembly) and when he took up residence he succeeded in buying up the property around the palace. In order to be close to the prince, the princess had the architect Brongniart design a house for her in the rue Dominique, part of the prince's domain[23] (Figure 2). This house was more than a pavilion, but nonetheless it was designed to accommodate the private needs of the princess and her lover by having the main bedroom on the ground floor to the left of the principal staircase while the salon was reached through two antechambers on the right.

The prince wished his unmarried daughter, Louise-Adélaïde, to live nearby, but she objected to his liaison with the princess and commissioned the same architect, Brongniart, to design a house for her in the rue Monsieur[24] (Figure 3). Mlle Condé is one of the few virtuous women who seemed to have been in a position to build, and Silvestre de Sacy in his book on Brongniart has said that the architect with delicate tact produced a design worthy to shelter a princess and young girl,[25] despite the fact that Louise-Adélaïde was twenty-five years old and presumably had reached the age when she could take control of her own fortune.

VIII

The wealth of the financiers and bankers at once supported the expenditure of the crown and its court, and destabilized its power. Enormous amounts of money came into the hands of the financiers and through judicious marriages that money became concentrated in a circle of families, such as the four Pâris brothers who have been mentioned already. The youngest of these, known as Pâris de Mont-martel, made his fortune through the slave trade.[26] He bought the title 'de Brunoy' and left his fortune to his son when he died in 1766. The Marquis de Brunoy had married the daughter of the aristocratic d'Escars family, an example of the union between money and birth. Unfortunately, the young man was unstable and spent large amounts of money on religious ceremonies. He spent 500,000 *livres* on one procession, and when his father died he draped all the trees on his estate in black and filled the fountains with ink. Eventually his relatives had him committed, and the marquise pursued her life independently.[27] In 1774 she asked Boullée to design a house for her which became known as the Temple of Flora (Figure 4). The words used by Braham to describe this house are 'fashionable luxury' and 'quasi-rural retreat', and this seems to have been a combination sought by most of the women who were in a position to build.[28] It may have had something to do with their ambivalent position in society, where although they had the wealth from whatever source to live independently, they may not have been completely socially accepted.

Mme de Thélusson, a rich widow, also required 'a house . . . half urban, half rustic, but rather with the air of a retreat than the appearance of a rich hotel'.[29] For this she went to Ledoux, and came to regret her choice of architect. Mme de Thélusson was widowed in 1776 at the age of forty when her banker husband died. Like many bankers in France at the time, he belonged to a Protestant family which

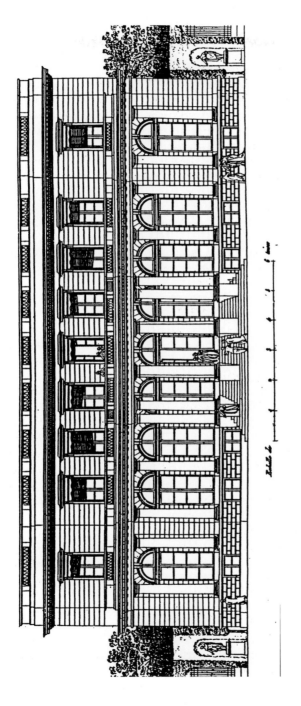

Figure 2   Hotel for the Princess of Monaco, Paris, by Brongiart. From Krafft and Ransonnette, I, pl. 69. Detail court façade

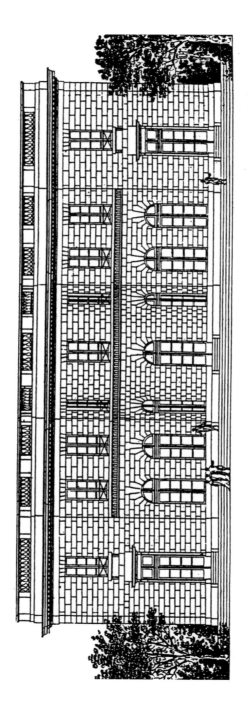

Figure 3 House for Mille Condé, Paris, by Brongniart. From Krafft and Ransonnette, I, pl. 61. Detail garden façade

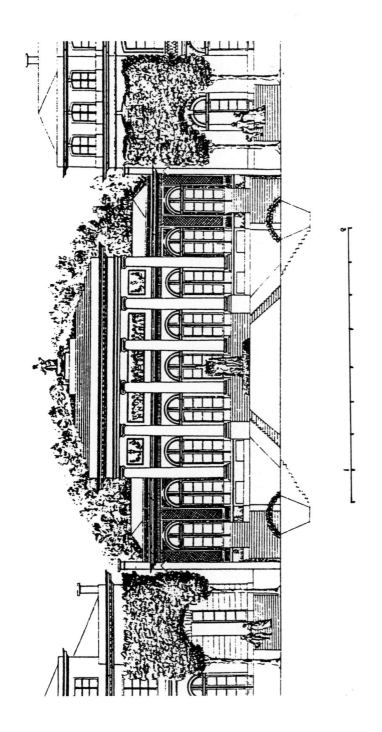

Figure 4 House for the Comtesse de Brunoy, Paris, by Boullée. From Krafft and Ransonnette, I, pl. 1. Detail garden façade

had gone to Switzerland on the revocation of the Edict of Nantes, but had returned to Paris in the eighteenth century. Mme de Thélusson was a woman of considerable fortune, a fact Ledoux was not slow to appreciate, and his design shows that he intended to make this house something out of the ordinary (Figures 5 and 6). The basic idea was to bring together classical forms in a natural setting. The front of the house was shielded from the street by a gaunt arch which led to a wilderness and grotto above which the central salon stood like a circular temple with Corinthian columns. There were two carriage ways that went into the grotto, under the house, emerging eventually into the courtyard at the rear. The entrance, which led to a very grand staircase, was to be found in the vestibule formed beneath the main reception rooms. It can be imagined how much all this cost. It was claimed that Mme de Thélusson had intended spending 400,000 *livres* on her house, but in 1781, the year of her death, with the work still unfinished the bill was already 2 million.[30] There is a suggestion that Ledoux was taking advantage of a susceptible client.

IX

Ledoux's house for Mme de Thélusson was criticized for its lack of *convenance* or propriety since it was on the scale and grandeur of a hotel suitable for a prince, not a common banker's widow, no matter how wealthy. This was not the first time that Ledoux had been accused of not keeping to the rules in his house design. All Paris was shocked by the house he had designed for the dancer, Mlle Guimard. Although many financiers sought to ally themselves with the aristocracy, many more seemed to be content to spend their money on the demi-monde.[31] This may be explained as part of the culture of patronage, since every dancer, singer and actor had to have wealthy friends in order to survive, and there was prestige to be had in supporting a successful performer. Le Camus de Mézières in *The Genius of Architecture*, after describing his ideal house room by room, defends its apparent prodigality by saying that 'A person, whose wealth inclines him toward splendour, will insist on this superabundance of space in which to live. An Actress or a lady of fashion will often go further.'[32]

A favourite place for these theatrical people to live were the new suburbs outside the old walls of Paris, the city's first boulevards. The area around the Prince de Condé's Palais Bourbon was a little too upmarket for them, as was the district opened by the Duc d'Orléans near the Faubourg St Honoré. But market gardens on property known as the Porcherons and owned by the religious order of the Mathurins were put up for sale as building land. A number of financiers became involved in speculation, among them Jean-Joseph Labord, an associate of Pâris de Montmartel and Thélusson, and architects such as Brongniart, Ledoux and Belanger took plots which they then sold on condition that they designed the houses.[33]

Mlle Guimard's house, designed in 1770 and built in the new neighbourhood, was known as the Temple of Terpsichore and was notorious for its four Ionic columns and sculpted group showing the muse of dance over the straight

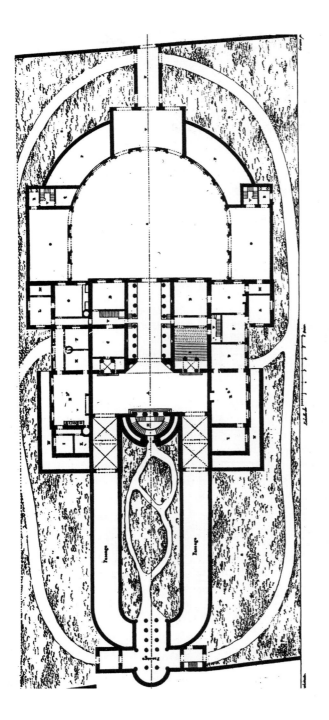

Figure 5 *Hotel for Mme de Thélusson, Paris, by Ledoux. From Krafft and Ransonnette, I, pl. 71. Detail plan of garden, gound floor of house, and court*

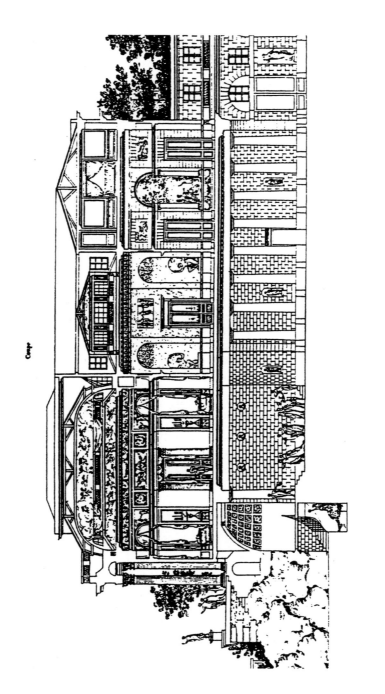

Figure 6   Hotel for Mme de Thélusson, Paris, by Ledoux. From Krafft and Ransonnette, I, pl. 72. Detail section of the house

entablature (Figures 7 and 8). Tongues clicked at the impropriety of providing such an inflated façade for a mere dancer. She had many lovers, both financiers and nobility, and it is believed that they provided the necessary funds for her house. When the Prince de Guéménée became bankrupt in 1786, Mlle Guimard was forced to sell her little temple.

Besides society, the architects had to withstand the criticism of the Academy, which condemned such a blatant flouting of the accepted social influence of the classical code. However, many performers were desirous to emulate Mlle Guimard and just as many patrons seemed to be willing to put forward the money for their houses. Daugny, the *fermier général*, installed his actress mistress, Mlle Baumenard, called Gogo, in a house in the neighbourhood, and the actress Mlle Dervieux had Brongniart construct a house for her in the rue Chatereine (Figure 9). Sophie Arnould, the popular opera singer, asked her lover and architect, Belanger, to design a house for her which would rival Mlle Guimard's, but in the end she was unable to afford it.[34] Mlle Dervieux also was nearly brought down by the bankruptcy of the Prince de Guéménée, since one of her patrons was the Prince de Soubise, the father-in-law of Guéménée. However, she took up with Lenoir, the lieutenant of Police, and went on to become involved in speculation in the area. Belanger, while retaining his affection for Sophie Arnould, became the lover and eventual husband of Mlle Dervieux as well as her associate in speculative building. He also designed for her additions to the house originally built by Brongniart.

It was not accidental that the theatrical world coincided with the financiers and architects in this new area of Paris. All of them were to a certain extent outside the rigid hierarchy of society and enjoying a mobility denied more respectable people. And there is a certain affinity between the architects and the actresses, since they too needed patronage. Those architects like Ledoux and Belanger who had a foot in the demi-monde were just those architects who had not proceeded in the direct path from the Academy School to the French School in Rome and then to established careers on their return. Another fact to consider is that actors and actresses lay outside the law in that they were unable to inherit property or to bequeath it, so that unless they repudiated their careers before they died, they were unable to pass on what they earned during their lives.[35] This may have lent a transitory character to whatever they built, and their architects may have felt freed from the obligation to produce the sort of monuments expected by the Academy.

X

Having identified women who built, the question must arise, so what? Did they build differently from men? The prevailing style during this period in France was already considered 'feminine' if not effeminate, and indeed during our period, the last decades of the eighteenth century, there were calls for a more masculine style of decoration, such as that provided by Ledoux in the Café Militaire.[36] One tangible result of women's involvement was the development of the 'pavillon', or detached house in its own garden. Although women were not the only ones to build these, the type suited the lifestyle of the woman alone, whether she lived on her

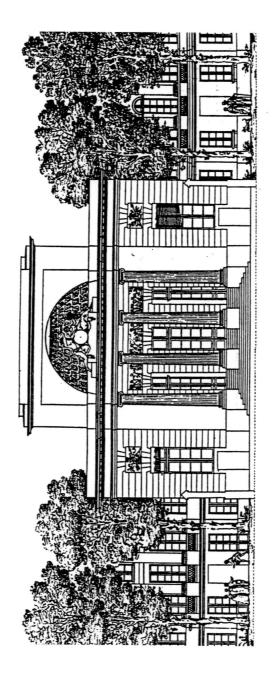

Figure 7 House for Mlle Guimard, Paris, by Ledoux. From Krafft and Ransonnette, I, pl. 49. Detail front façade

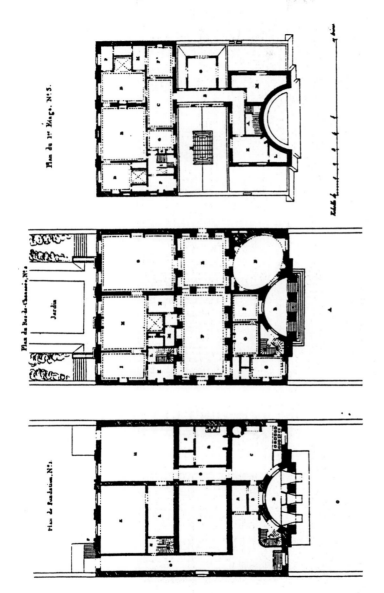

Figure 8 *House for Mlle Guimard, Paris, by Ledoux. From Krafft and Ransonnette, I, pl. 49. Detail plan of basement, ground floor, and first floor*

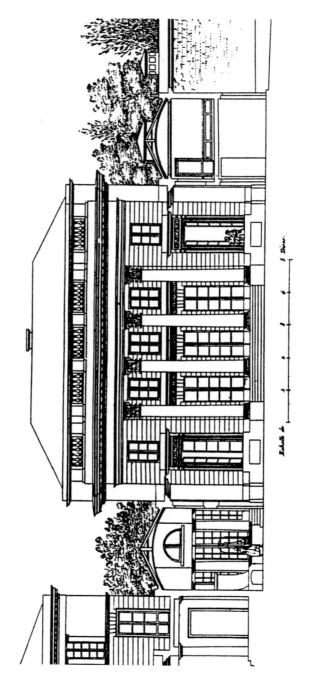

Figure 9 House for Mlle Dervieux, Paris, by Brongiart and Belanger. From Kraff and Ransonnette, 1, pl. 7. Detail court façade

own income or on that of a lover. Without a husband and a large entourage, but with an ambivalent position in society, the independent woman had her own requirements, which nonetheless gave priority to the private. In a comparable situation at the beginning of this century Alice T. Friedman has found that women building for themselves 'redefined domestic space to create room for a range of relationships that crossed boundaries prescribed by age, class, gender and sexuality'.[37] In addition, the speculation in the suburbs which enabled the proliferation of the 'pavillon' also allowed women, with their limited funds, to enter the property market as investors. It is interesting to note that the subsequent development during the nineteenth century in Paris swept away nearly all traces of these houses.

More generally women's involvement in building during the eighteenth century points to the position assumed by architecture in social life. The elaboration of sociability could almost be described as the main project of society at this time, with the introduction of every aspect of human life into the crucible of conversation.[38] Architecture, like so many other subjects, provided the occasion for men and women to communicate and this is illustrated in Blondel's novel, *L'Homme du monde éclairé par les arts*, when the Comtesse de Vaujeu makes the Comte de Saleran's letters of instruction in the arts an occasion for gathering her friends together to discuss what he has written.[39] Further, she organizes an outing for her friends to view the buildings mentioned by the comte in order to show them and her epistolary lover how well she has learned his lessons. Earlier he has pleaded with her to accept the instruction of the man of the world, since that is the basis of a sociability which benefits both men and women.

> The need for our lessons attaches us to them [women]; and if we know how to instruct them in a way that conforms to their delicate and supple natures, we inspire in them confidence, estime, and even love. Now, all that could not exist if, closed up in their cabinets, in order to be instructed by the Masters of Art, they succeed in having no more need of the men of the world; and thus so much good lost for us and for themselves. Equality would impoverish both sexes. . . .[40]

The comtesse proves rather more robust in her response and asks for 'more equality between you and me', but nonetheless continues the correspondence because she is determined to know more about the arts and architecture. An alternative to the letters from the comte was open to her in the form of the lectures organized by Blondel at his school of architecture for potential clients. Not only did he foster the sociability of architecture through the lessons in deportment for the aspiring architects mentioned before, but he also provided lessons in architecture for both building workers and clients.[41]

It is time to return to the relationship between architect and client. One thing that emerges from the examples we have reviewed is the variety of relationships between the architects and their women clients. Brongniart, it seems, took a paternal interest in Louise-Adélaïde and her house in the rue Monsieur; Ledoux appears to have exploited the vulnerable Mme de Thélusson; and Belanger developed a romantic attachment not just to one client but to two. Turned around the other way, we could ask what the client is expecting from the relationship, since she could just as well go to an experienced builder. We assume that the end product is the building, but is that the only 'product'? Is there, for example, something beyond the building which resides in the relationship between client and architect, and if so what could that be?

The architect has knowledge needed by the client, and this knowledge is not 'building' since that is vested in the builder. It must then be 'architecture', which depends on something other than building, what we call the 'design'. It can be asked, does the design issue from the architect alone, or does it come from a persona which is neither the architect nor the client, but somehow an amalgam of both? The architect has knowledge not claimed by the client, and most of the women we have considered would not have had the benefits of the education enjoyed by the men of their class. Nevertheless, the women were paying the bills, and they wanted at least what others in their social milieu had, even if they did not go as far as Sophie Arnould who took that desire to extremes by asking for a house that would have exactly the same dimensions as that of Mlle Guimard. Without generalizing about the relationship between the architects and their female clients, it would seem that sociability not only integrated architectural design into polite discourse, but that it also allowed women to collaborate with their architects to produce houses that satisfied their personal esteem as well as their practical needs.

CONCLUSION

Many of the people I have mentioned here perished during the Revolution and very few of the survivors seem to have made a successful transition to the world which came after. The women I have described could perhaps only have been allowed to exist in a society like that of France in the second half of the eighteenth century when a mature society was also in a state of flux. The anomalies created by mercantile capitalism and the absolute monarchy were breaking up the social order, but the institutions seemed so entrenched that a certain licence was allowed. Whether women took advantage of the situation to consolidate their material condition or simply to enjoy the moment, the instability of the period came to be blamed on women's love of luxury and pleasure. The lobby for a serious domestic role for women began to gain the upper hand to the extent that it easily became part of the Revolutionary ideology. Not that most women had had much of an option, even during the headiest days of the *Ancien Régime*, since only a handful of women had been in the position to act independently. Eventually the courtesans and the actresses returned and through the nineteenth century there was a dreary train of royalty and hangers-on who had houses built and renovated for themselves. But the energy of society had moved elsewhere to the development and perfection of bourgeois life. It is within the context of such a society that the relationship of nineteenth-century women and their architects must be considered. From the texts this looks like a much more difficult task than hunting out the women building in the eighteenth century. But I cannot believe that bourgeois women were completely without influence on the physical world in which they lived.

NOTES

1. See Whitney Chadwick, *Women, Art and Society* (London, 1990); Roszika Parker and Griselda Pollock, *Old Mistresses: Women, Art and Ideology* (London, 1981); and Linda Nochlin, *Women, Art and Power and Other Essays* (London, 1989).
2. Lynne Walker, 'Women Architects' in Judy Attfield and Pat Kirkham (eds), *A View from the Interior, Women and Design* (London, 1989), pp. 90–105.
3. This information comes from the observation of many biographies of architects.
4. Louis Hautecœur, *Histoire de l'architecture classique en France*, vols I–VII (Paris, 1943–1957).
5. Edmond and Jules de Goncourt, *La Femme au dix-huitième siècle*, ed. E. Badinter (Paris, 1982).
6. Léon Abensour, *La Femme et le féminisme avant la Révolution* (Paris, 1923).
7. Jean Stern, *A l'Ombre de Sophie Arnould, François-Joseph Belanger Architecte des Menus Plaisirs*, 2 vols (Paris, 1930). The Goncourts had published a work on Sophie Arnould in 1857.
8. Michèle Cohen, *Fashioning Masculinity: National Identity and Language in the Eighteenth Century* (London, 1996).
9. Ibid., and Katharine M. Rogers, 'The View from England' in Samia Spencer (ed.), *French Women and the Age of Enlightenment* (Bloomington, Indiana, 1984), pp. 357–68.
10. See Naomi Schor, *Reading in Detail, Aesthetics and the Feminine* (London, 1987); and Adrian Forty, 'Masculine, Feminine or Neuter?' in Katerina Ruedi, Sarah Wigglesworth and Duncan McCorquodale (eds), *Desiring Practices, Architecture, Gender and the Interdisciplinary* (London, 1996), pp. 141–55.
11. J.-F. Blondel, *Cours d'architecture*, vols 1–7 (Paris, 1771–1777).
12. Michael Dennis, *Court and Garden, From the French Hôtel to the City of Modern Architecture* (Cambridge, MA, 1992), p. 152.
13. Vera Lee, *The Reign of Women in Eighteenth-century France* (Cambridge, MA, 1975).
14. Elizabeth Fox-Genovese and Eugene D. Genovese, *Fruits of Merchant Capital, Slavery and Bourgeois Property in the Rise and Expansion of Capitalism* (Oxford, 1983).
15. Yves Durand, *Finance et Mécénat, les fermiers généraux au XVIIIe siècle* (Paris, 1976), p. 33.
16. Hautecœur, *Histoire*, vol. IV, p. 77.
17. Ibid., pp. 84–5, 88.
18. Katie Scott, *The Rococo Interior, Decoration and Social Spaces in Early Eighteenth-Century Paris* (New Haven and London, 1995), p. 264.
19. Allan Braham, *The Architecture of the French Enlightenment* (London, 1980), p. 33.
20. Anthony Vidler, *Claude-Nicolas Ledoux, Architecture and Social Reform at the End of the Ancien Regime* (Cambridge, MA, 1990), p. 54.
21. Hautecœur, *Histoire*, vol. IV, pp. 103–4.
22. *Biographie Universelle*, vols 1–45 (Paris, 1843). This publication tends to make moral judgements which reflect the time it was written.
23. Hautecœur, *Histoire*, vol. IV, pp. 115–16.
24. Ibid.
25. Jacques Silvestre de Sacy, *Alexandre-Théodore Brongniart, 1739–1813. Sa vie – son œuvre* (Paris, n.d.), p. 57.
26. *Biographie Universelle*.
27. Ibid.
28. Braham, *Architecture of the French Enlightenment*, p. 115.
29. Ibid., p. 187.
30. Ibid., p. 189.
31. Durand, *Finance et Mécénat*, p. 144.
32. Nicolas Le Camus de Mézières, *The Genius of Architecture or the Analogy of this Art with our Sensations*, 1780, trans. by David Britt (Santa Monica, 1992), p. 106.

33. Durand, *Finance et Mécénat*, p. 214.
34. 'Cette maison devoit être construite à côté de celle de Mlle Guimard, dans les mêmes dimensions.' Stern, *A l'Ombre de Sophie Arnould*, p. 41.
35. Barbara G. Mittman, 'Women and the Theatre Arts' in Spencer (ed.), *French Women*, p. 160.
36. Vidler, *Claude-Nicolas Ledoux*, p. 22.
37. Alice T. Friedman, *Women and the Making of the Modern House* (New York, 1998), p. 17.
38. Lawrence E. Klein, 'Gender, conversation and the public sphere in early eighteenth-century England' in Judith Still and Michael Worton (eds), *Textuality and Sexuality, Reading Theories and Practices* (Manchester, 1993).
39. J.-F. Blondel, *L'Homme du monde éclairé par les arts*, vol. I, letter XXXV (Paris, 1774).
40. Ibid., vol. I, letter XII.
41. Richard Cleary, 'Romancing the Tome; or an Academician's Pursuit of a Popular Audience in 18th-Century France', *Journal of the Society of Architectural Historians*, XLVIII (June 1989), (139–149) 140.

Chapter 6

Ramblers and Cyprians: Mobility, Visuality and the Gendering of Architectural Space

Jane Rendell

Despite disciplinary differences, feminist analysis of gender and space has tended to focus on critiquing the paradigm of the separate spheres (the binary system which describes gendered space as oppositional and hierarchical with two mutually exclusive categories – the dominant male public realm of the city and the subordinate female private realm of the home). This paradigm is problematic because as a patriarchal and capitalist ideological device, it perpetuates certain assumptions regarding sex, gender and space, and prioritizes the relation of men to the city. This chapter argues that the binary parameters of the separate spheres represent a patriarchal appropriation of the public sphere, and instead follows feminist critiques or 'deconstructions' of this binary. It suggests that the gendering of space can be reconceptualized through feminist theory, specifically the work of Luce Irigaray. By looking at rambling, an urban movement which represents early nineteenth-century London as a series of gendered spaces, I argue that the gendering of space can be understood as a form of choreography, a series of performed movements between men and women, both real and ideal, material and metaphoric, which are constructed and represented through social relations of looking and moving – exchanging, consuming and displaying.

The early nineteenth century is an important historical period for contemporary feminists investigating gender and space. This period precedes the patriarchal 'fixing' of the separate spheres as the most pervasive ideology of gender and space in the mid nineteenth century. But although I consider an examination of the early stages of articulation of an ideology important in order to grasp its workings, it is not my intention here to explain why the separate spheres came into being; rather I am interested in looking at how issues of gender were raised in connection with the public spaces of the city.

In the early nineteenth century increasing urbanization and the expansion of capitalism resulted in the rising cultural importance of certain social spaces of leisure, consumption, display and exchange. These were the site of conflicting concerns, those of public patriarchs seeking to control female occupation of the city, worried that their female property – mothers, wives and daughters – would be visually and sexually available to other men, and those of consumer capitalists aiming to extend the roles of women as cheap workers and consumers in the city. In order to examine the gendering of space in early nineteenth-century London, this chapter looks at rambling as a mode of movement which celebrates the public spaces of the city and the excitement of urban life from a masculine perspective.

The rambler visits sites of leisure, pleasure, consumption, exchange and display in early nineteenth-century London: the theatre, opera house, pleasure garden, park, club, sporting venue and bazaar. By traversing the city, looking in its open and its interior spaces for adventure and entertainment, the rambler creates a conceptual and physical map of the city. Rambling rethinks London as a series of spaces of flows of movement rather than a series of discrete architectural elements. I argue that the ramble represents such spaces as gendered in a number of ways: through the exclusion of women, in taverns, sporting venues and clubs; and through the establishment of male dominance in spaces occupied by men and women. The perpetual movement of the ramble places urban locations in sequential relation, framing social events, activities and rituals in time and space. Gender differences are articulated spatially, through relations of movement and vision: moving and being-moved, viewing and being-viewed, consuming and being-consumed, exchanging and being-exchanged, displaying and being-on-display.

THE PURSUIT OF PLEASURE: RAMBLERS AND CYPRIANS

Pleasure was the word – *Gaiety* the pursuit.[1]

The verb 'to ramble' describes incoherent movement, 'to wander in discourse (spoken or written), to write or talk incoherently or without natural sequence of ideas'. As a mode of movement, rambling is unrestrained, random and distracted: 'a walk (formerly any excursion or journey) without any definite route or pleasure'.[2] In the early nineteenth century, the verb specifically described the exploration of urban space: 'This day has been wholly devoted to a ramble about London, to look at curiosities.'[3] Rambling was concerned with the physical and conceptual pursuit of pleasure, specifically sexual pleasure – 'to go about in search of sex'.[4] Closely related activities were 'ranging' or 'rangling' or 'intriguing with a variety of women'.[5]

The rambling genre has its origins in texts published from the sixteenth century onwards, which delved further into the London underworld, pretending to be authentic and using sensational tales as their framework, but revealing no more than graphic detail. These texts, partly moralizing, partly titillating, were aimed at 'Johnny Raws' from the country, and both tempted the reader with the excitement of urban life, but also warned against the corrupting influence and sophisticated criminals of the city. Such texts may be distinguished by their structure and take the form of 'spy' tales – journeys through the city.[6] Spy tales tell of various country gentlemen's initiations to the adventures of city life under the guidance of a street-wise urban relative, wise to the delights and entertainments, as well as the tricks and frauds, of the urban realm. The tradition continued into the eighteenth century, focusing on the seamy side of metropolitan life, with stories and pictures of crime, robbery and prostitution.[7]

The term ramble appeared alongside spy in the eighteenth century; although the terms were often used in an interchangeable way, their emphasis differed

Figure 1 *George and Robert Cruikshank, 'An INTRODUCTION – Gay Moments of* Logic, Jerry, Tom *and* Corinthian Kate', *Pierce Egan,* Life in London; or, the day and night scenes of Jerry Hawthorn, Esq., and his elegant friend Corinthian Tom, accompanied by Bob Logic, the Oxonian, in their Rambles and Sprees through the Metropolis *(London: Sherwood, Neely and Jones, 1820–1821), p. 250*

slightly. Spy texts were fascinated with the darker aspects of urban life, while rambles were involved with excitement in the form of fun and pleasure. By the first decades of the nineteenth century, some publications continued to follow earlier models and focus on the detection and exposure of criminal codes, but a number of publications including *Real Life in London*,[8] Pierce Egan's *Life in London*,[9] William Heath's *Fashion and Folly*[10] and Bernard Blackmantle's *The English Spy*,[11] differed from the earlier texts in a number of ways.

Unlike the earlier primarily scripted descriptions which included only a few black and white woodcuts, the new rambles were highly visual documents, with coloured lithographs, engravings and etchings. Instead of addressing themselves to the country visitor, these new rambles provided a place for urban dwellers to look at themselves. The 'look' of the urban explorer changed, from the secretive spy looking but not wanting to be looked at, to the fashionable rambler of the 1820s, a self-conscious man demanding to be visually appreciated. In the shift from the spy to the rambler, the importance of urban exploration and knowledge was retained, but the emphasis on the excitement of revealing secret activities was replaced by a new attention to fashion, display and spectacle. In the decade following the Napoleonic Wars, this attention to display coincided historically with the return of military men from Europe, especially Paris, bringing with them new French fashions and a flamboyant style of military dress. The early nineteenth-century rambler was a highly visible figure, pro-active in his occupation of space.

In their intention to inform the reader about the city, rambling texts could be described as guidebooks to the city. But unlike traditional guidebooks, spy tales and rambles were only semi-documentary. The intention of the ramble was sensational – to excite and produce a pleasurable response in the reader. The places selected were real, but their choice was highly subjective, only those places deemed to attract pleasure seekers were featured. Such sites were described, not as objects, but in terms of the activities going on within them. Rambles were also unlike guidebooks in the organization of the material. Rather than describe districts or relate sites by location or type, places were linked through time, as part of a journey, more like the accounts of London in the diaries of contemporary visitors. Rambles could be described as 'spatial stories'.[12] But although the ramblers generate urban adventures, there is no plot or 'story', and characters are not developed; instead the spatial motivation of intentions are emphasized – to move through the city in the pursuit of pleasure. The ramble develops pleasure in the reader visually, contrasting reality and fantasy and juxtaposing image and written text.

This chapter focuses primarily on *Life in London*, one of the most popular of these early nineteenth-century rambling texts. The author was Pierce Egan (1772–1849) and the illustrators George Cruikshank (1792–1878) and Robert Cruikshank (1789–1856). *Life in London* describes the rambles of three young males as they explore London in 1821. The three men are: Corinthian Tom, a young Londoner, bachelor, member of the aristocracy, with an inheritance and a London residence – Corinthian House; Robert Logic, Tom's drinking companion, an Oxford student, also with an inheritance, living at the Albany chambers for bachelors; and Tom's cousin, Jerry Hawthorn, a fine sportsman and drinker, who comes from the same class background, but lacks credibility as a male due to his rural origin. Through rambles around London, involving various drinking and sporting activities, *Life In London* tells of Jerry's initiation into urban lifestyle and manhood.

Rambling played an integral part in producing a public display of heterosexual, upper-class masculinity. The rambler represented the shared features of a new kind of urban masculinity – the mobility, visuality and urbanity of a young, heterosexual, middle- to upper-class male consumer. But there were also contrasts; the male 'type' of the rambler was contradicted by and reinforced through other urban masculinities: specifically, the corinthian, or upper-class sporting gentleman; the bruiser, or working-class boxer; and the dandy, or aspiring man of fashion. Different masculine identities were articulated through various cultural codes of display and consumption, the rambler, corinthian, bruiser and dandy all adopted specific modes of dressing, talking and walking.

MOBILITY: THE RAMBLER AS CORINTHIAN

CORINTHIAN TOM'S unceasing Anxiety to mix with the World uncontrolled.[13]

In contemporary urban discourse, we are increasingly obsessed by figures who traverse space – flâneur, spy, detective and prostitute. For the rambler, mobility was a critical aspect of his masculinity and public urban identity. His mobility was both social and spatial – his dominant class position allowed him to mix with a variety of social classes and to move freely between the exclusive clubs, opera houses, assembly rooms in the west of London and working-class taverns and other leisure spaces in Covent Garden's Holy Land and further east in East Smithfield. The juxtaposition of the scene in Allmax, a tavern in the east, and Almack's exclusive assembly rooms in the west represents the rambler's mobility – the ability to experience both sides of the city – the prerogative of the dominant upper- or middle-class male.

In *Life in London* the idealized figure of the corinthian represents the mobility of the rambler. Corinthian Tom was the archetypal corinthian, a gentleman with property in the form of land and money, known for his elegant manner, fashionable clothes and sportsmanship.[14] In social rank, the corinthian was 'the highest order of swell', where swell refers to a 'well-dressed' man.[15] This hierarchy, like 'the supereminence of that order of architecture', was determined by decoration, 'superlative articles of dress'.[16] But unlike the swell whose identity was determined only by dress, a crucial aspect of the corinthian's identity was his class. Class defined the corinthian's leisure time and gentlemanly attitude, as well as his character, politeness, generosity, good humour and, most importantly, his sportsmanship. Corinthians were 'sporting men of rank and fashion' – first class boxers, fencers, hunters and drivers.[17]

Sport represented the possibility for male bonding within a class society. Boxing, in particular, by prioritizing the ideal qualities of English manhood and creating patriotic unity, appeared to cut across class and political boundaries. Boxing publications were accompanied by images of the stylized heads and torsos of working-class bruisers, whose sporting physiques were compared to the celebrated beauty of the classical Greek hero.[18] But as well as representing idealized physical attributes, pugilism also promoted admirable social aspects of masculinity – sportsmanship, courage, gallantry, calmness, tolerance, fair-play and honour. For men of different classes, sport and associated leisure activities, such as drinking, offered opportunities for male bonding.[19]

Sporting societies, such as the Pugilistic Society and the Four-in-Hand coaching club, established shared social codes, including sporting rules, dress, language and manners.[20] Such codes, although adopted by upper-class men as an essential aspect of fashionable sporting masculinity, originated as integral parts of lower-class culture. A contemporary etching described how 'a modern man of fashion' should 'dress like a coachman', 'study boxing and bull baiting' and 'speak the slang language fluently'.[21] The flash lingo or 'the canting or slang language' was the language of working-class criminals.[22] However, given its close links to cockney or vernacular London language, its use represented urban identity, and flash dictionaries, rambling tales and boxing treatises often published by the same publishers, sometimes as two-volume sets,[23] were aimed at upper-class men, students and sporting men.[24]

The corinthian represented an idealized version of the rambler, as an upper-class male, who mixed with different classes through socializing, while retaining his own hierarchical relation. The Corinthian column in the frontispiece of *Life in London* represents this ideal social order (Figure 2). At the top of the column are the 'ups' or 'the flowers of society', the King and the nobles, next are the merchants or 'respectables', and at the bottom are the 'downs' or 'the mechanicals, the

Figure 2 *George and Robert Cruikshank, 'The Corinthian Capital', Pierce Egan,* Life in London; or, the day and night scenes of Jerry Hawthorn, Esq. and his elegant friend Corinthian Tom, accompanied by Bob Logic, the Oxonian, in their Rambles and Sprees through the Metropolis *(London: Sherwood, Neely and Jones, 1820–1821), frontispiece*

humble labourers and the human vegetables'. The ramblers, Tom, Jerry and Logic, are positioned at the centre of the column, drinking.[25]

Structured around social and spatial contrasts, the ramble represents a culturally diverse journey ranging from high culture to popular culture, from grand interiors to dark streets. The most striking juxtapositions are between the east and the west, represented as two different class zones. From the seventeenth century onwards, the city and the eastern districts surrounding it were commercial and industrial zones, inhabited by the working class mostly in slums, including a large number of immigrants, most numerously the Irish. The west was populated by members of the aristocracy, nobility and wealthy bourgeois class who moved out of the city westwards to new residential squares, first to Covent Garden and Soho and later to St James and Piccadilly. In search of pleasure, the ramblers moved freely between the clubs, opera houses, theatres and arcades in the west of London and the places where 'real' life was to be found – the leisure spaces of the working class, from Covent Garden's Holy Land to the taverns of St Giles and East Smithfield. The rambler's desire and ability to mix with a variety of social classes and experience both the west and east of the city represented an important part of his urban identity – his social and spatial mobility.

In the eighteenth and nineteenth centuries, as London developed into an important centre of consumption, the role of streets became increasingly important as zones of trade, commerce, administration and entertainment. A number of improvements in lighting, paving and drainage facilitated the movement of people and goods and also provided a social space for visual display and consumption.[26] John Nash's work in the first decades of the nineteenth century in the fashionable, commercial and residential areas around Piccadilly focused on celebrating urban movement.[27] His urban designs combined classical and romantic elements of town-planning, treating urban elements, streets, buildings and the flow of traffic, like landscapes.[28] Regent Street, designed with promenading and walking in mind, was nicknamed 'Corinthian Path', indicating its high class and fashionable status. The amount of traffic on streets, both vehicular and pedestrian, created a need for adopting distinctive styles of public urban behaviour, such as the fast and aggressive driving of wheeled vehicles or walking on the right-hand side of the street.[29]

MOBILITY: THE CYPRIAN AS FEMALE RAMBLER

> We have already taken a promiscuous ramble from the West towards the East, and it has afforded some amusement; but our stock is abundant, and many objects of curiosity are still in view.[30]

The rambler's mobility represents an attempt to establish the public realm of the city as a place for men. The rambler's aim was to partake in a world of pleasure, heterosexual sexual pleasure. Contemporary magazines concerned with sex and whoring described themselves in terms of rambling.[31] The pursuit of women was an important aspect of rambling. All the women the rambler encountered in the public spaces of the city were represented in terms of their sexuality and described

Figure 3 *George and Robert Cruikshank, 'Tom getting the best of a Charley', Pierce Egan,* Life in London; or, the day and night scenes of Jerry Hawthorn, Esq., and his elegant friend Corinthian Tom, accompanied by Bob Logic, the Oxonian, in their Rambles and Sprees through the Metropolis *(London: Sherwood, Neely and Jones, 1820–1821), p. 232*

as 'cyprians'. The word is defined as 'belonging to Cyprus, an island in the eastern Mediterranean, famous in ancient times for the worship of Aphrodite or Venus', goddess of love, as 'licentious, lewd', and, in the eighteenth and nineteenth centuries, 'applied to prostitutes'.[32] The term cyprian described women occupying public space as prostitutes, whether or not they were exchanging sex for financial benefit. Cyprians were stimuli to the ramble; the rambler's desire for, and pursuit of, these female sexual commodities defined his urban masculinity and hetero-sexuality.

The language of prostitution used words derived from, or sounding like, Greek – such as nymph, cyprian, paphian and corinthian, in order to subvert codes of decency through the innuendo of double meanings. For example, the term corin-thian could mean noble or licentious. For the Roman architectural historian Vitruvius, the Corinthian architectural order was distinguished by its decorative capital. In the early nineteenth century, the term 'corinthian trimming' referred to the decorative borders of dresses.[33] Corinthian Tom as a nobleman was an ornament of society – decorated, refined and well-balanced. But in slang terms, the term 'corinth' also meant brothel, making reference to the Greek view of the ancient city of Corinth as a wealthy place of debauchery.[34] Corinthians were 'frequenters of brothels',[35] but in *Life in London*, although Tom pursued, flirted, drank with cyprians and spent the 'weight of his purse' on them,[36] his rambles never took him to a brothel.

The term corinthian also had a double meaning in relation to women. For Vitruvius, the order was a feminine one, distinguished from the more matronly Ionic by being slender and girl-like. Corinthian represented virginal qualities but also the licentiousness of a city such as Corinth, whose patron was Aphrodite. Aphrodite, goddess of love in Greek mythology, originated in the east, in Cyprus or Cytherea, which added an erotic and an exotic element to the term.[37] The cyprian was a spectacle – an object of display – her body was the site of the ramblers' desire and gaze. Corinthian Tom's partner in *Life in London* was the alluring and beautiful cyprian, Corinthian Kate. When describing women, corinthian also implied a high order of decoration, but used interchangeably with the term cyprian, the association with Aphrodite suggested an enticing aspect to the decor.

Moving was also a defining feature of the cyprian. Cyprians were described as 'lady birds' having 'lightness and mobility of spirit' or 'energy of body and spirit'. The names of cyprians spotted by ramblers in the park corresponded to birds, such as the Sparrow Hawk and the White Crow.[38] Their mobility defined in terms of lightness and flightiness referred to their moral constitution – their 'moral frailty' – as well as their ability to move. Movement for women held moral connotations. For example, although female magazines encouraged their readers to walk as a suitable form of female exercise, it was only under certain controlled conditions: moderately, in the early morning, with company. Walking in the public streets, especially lingering rather than hurrying, and wearing revealing or conspicuous clothes, was suggestive of a woman's immorality.[39]

The cyprian was an urban peripatetic – a nymph of the pavé.[40] Her mobility in the public places of the city was a cause of concern. Her link to the street, as streetwalker or nightwalker, associated her with the lowest class of prostitute. Whereas the movement of the rambler, his active engagement in the constant pursuit of pleasure, was celebrated as urban exploration, the mobility of the cyprian was represented as the cause of her eventual destruction. Her movement was transgressive, blurring the boundaries between public and private, suggesting the uncontrollability of women in the city. The cyprian body was perceived as disorderly, because as a moving female public body, it flouted patriarchal rules for women's occupation of space.

Irigaray's conception of woman-as-commodity – the object of physical and metaphorical exchange among men – is critical to understanding the gendering of space through movement.[41] In patriarchy, men are distinguished from women through their relationship to space. In terms of ownership, men own space and women as property, whereas women are owned as property, confined as and in space. In patriarchal relations of exchange, men move through space as subjects of exchange; whereas women are moved through space between men as sexual commodities – as objects of exchange.

In Irigaray's work, by taking herself to market and exchanging herself, the prostitute mimics male discourse; in so doing, she disrupts the male economy, exposing the exchange of women at its foundation. For some critics, it is the 'ambiguous unity in the prostitute of use and exchange value which positions her as a speaking subject'.[42] Motivated by the desire to sell herself, the cyprian's position as a self-perpetuating, moving subject establishes her as a threat to patriarchal ideologies concerning the circulation of women among men. In patriarchy the ownership and exchange of property is controlled by defining boundaries and identifying thresholds which are permanent, closed and fixed around women. Female subjects and spaces which operate within, but also escape, the controlling mechanisms of private property and ownership in patriarchal capitalism are represented in terms of spatial metaphors of disorder.

Architectural spaces, such as arcades, colonnades and quadrants, which promoted mobility or movement were considered problematic when associated with women and described as places of prostitution.[43] The thresholds of buildings other than family homes, known to be occupied by women, such as shops, brothels and theatres, were represented as sites of danger and intrigue. The threshold – the place where the boundary is pierced – where passage occurs from outside to inside is both a material transition from exterior to interior, from known public territory to unknown private territory, but also a metaphor of sexual penetration.

In particular, the threshold of the brothel was connected with suspicion. It was because entrances to brothels were hidden or tucked away, rather than on display, that men could be accosted, decoyed or lured inside. The presence of cyprians at the entrance lured men over the threshold to take a 'peep at the *Curiosities*' within.[44] The procuress, on the other hand, was represented as a repulsive figure at 'the mouth of her cavern',[45] guarding the entrance, using various deceits to entrap innocent people. If the threshold to the brothel, the place which allowed movement in and out, was considered problematic, a covered hole, a trap or snare, in a similar way, so was the cyprian body. In pornographic rambling tales, the spatial metaphors of 'closet', 'slit' and 'catacomb' were used as forms of titillation,[46] but the terms 'hole', 'pit' and 'ditch' were also used to describe the sexually immoral or public woman in religious tracts.[47] The more promiscuous the woman, the deeper and more open the hole.[48] The cyprian body was perceived as an open body occupying the public realm. Punctured, but not necessarily exposed, it created a treacherous topography, a trap one could fall into – 'a serpentine allurement'.[49]

The seduced or penetrated body of the cyprian was an open and disorderly one requiring regulation. The two laws which indirectly controlled prostitution in public space did so through the ordering of disorderly spaces and disorderly bodies. The Disorderly Houses Act of 1752, still not updated in the early nineteenth century, and used to prosecute brothel owners, expressed concern for unregulated public spaces – disorderliness here was the source of 'irregularity and crime'.[50] Women's movement on the street was controlled through the Vagrancy Acts, updated in 1822 and 1824, which defined 'prostitutes' and 'nightwalkers' 'wandering in public streets' as 'idle and disorderly'.[51] Disorderly spaces and bodies were also associated with class trouble, fear of revolution and disputes over property ownership. Such concerns were represented through the various solutions mooted to control prostitution, which invariably involved the incarceration of the female body in places for punishment and/or rehabilitation.

The figure of the male rambler has been discussed as a new kind of urban identity – that of the young, single, heterosexual and upper-class man – a man of leisure, fashion and sport. The rambler represented an attempt to establish the public realm of the city as a place for men. The rambler's social and spatial mobility, and his desire for, and pursuit of, cyprians – female sexual commodities – defined his urban masculinity and heterosexuality. Moving was also a defining feature of the cyprian, but whereas the movement of the rambler was celebrated as the pursuit of pleasure, the mobility of the cyprian was a cause for concern and control.

VISUALITY: THE RAMBLER AS DANDY

The Dandy – swell of the Bon Ton.[52]

Scopophilia, what Sigmund Freud called the desire to look, is stimulated by structures of voyeurism and narcissism which both derive pleasure in looking. Voyeurism is a controlling and distanced way of looking in which pleasure is derived from looking at a figure as an object. Narcissistic pleasure is produced by identification with the image and can be considered analogous to Jacques Lacan's mirror stage – just as a child forms his/her ego by identifying with the perfect mirror image, so the spectator derives pleasure from identification with the perfect image of themselves in others.

Laura Mulvey has argued that various kinds of visual pleasure are constructed through relations of sexual difference, structured by the gendered unconscious rather than the conscious. For example, in the work of Freud, the fear and anxiety of castration which arise in the boy child as a result of looking, cause him to invent fetish objects to stand in for the mother's lack of phallus. Here looking is active and gendered masculine, being-looked-at is passive and feminized. This model of the male gaze and the female spectacle, although binary in nature and over simplified, provides a useful starting point for thinking about the gendering of space through looking.[53] In the first instance, it positions the rambler as an active 'looking' male subject. Representations of the male gaze are integral to the construction of urban masculinity. The rambler's precedent, the London spy, is represented as a voyeur, and his successor, the Parisian flâneur, associated with a 'mobile, free, eroticized and avaricious gaze'.[54] Rambling is connected with visual pleasure, with narcissism and voyeurism, with the desire to look.

For the rambler, looking was connected to exploring and to knowing. *Life in London* provided a 'complete cyclopedia' – a new kind of book for a new kind of city – a text which allowed readers to 'see life'.[55] By adopting a 'camera obscura' view of the city, Egan's rambler became a voyeur, possessing 'the invaluable advantages of SEEING and not being seen'.[56] The camera obscura position allowed the viewer to gain visionary control, to frame the object like a picture. On a visit to a low life tavern, a site of potential danger, the ramblers donned disguises which served to distance them from the scene in a voyeuristic manner.[57] On a visit to Newgate, the reality of the scene – prisoners preparing to die – was suppressed by adopting a panoramic and distancing view, tending towards a surveillant and categorizing gaze.[58] Similar elements of spectacular and detached observation

Figure 4   *Robert Cruikshank, 'Exterior of Fishmongers-Hall, St James's Street, with a view of a Regular Break down', showing 'Portraits of the Master-Fishmonger and many well known Greeks and Pigeons', Bernard Blackmantle, The English Spy (London: Sherwood, Jones and Co., 1825), vol. 1, p. 373, plate 24*

were created at this time in other cultural forms, such John Nash's schemes for urban improvement, panoramas and dioramas as new popular forms of entertainment, and the social caricatures of graphic artists.

The rambler and other figures in the ramble, such as the dandy, also demanded visual reciprocity. The rambler as a dandy had a narcissistic body – one associated with its own surface – a surface which made social position apparent through body position and gesture, and the display of materials or ornaments.[59] Fashion played an essential role in the construction of male urban identity in the early nineteenth century. Rambling tales strongly stressed the difference between town and country through ways of dressing.[60] In the eighteenth century, court hierarchies of dressing had been rejected in favour of simple and practical styles, derived from the dress of the sporting country gentleman. The John Bull outfit consisted of everyday riding clothes – a top hat, a simple neckcloth, a small coat (cut away in the front), a waistcoat, breeches fitting into riding boots and a stick, later modified to suit urban lifestyles and a city aesthetic.[61] In *Life in London*, on arrival in the metropolis, Jerry, the country relative, undergoes an 'elegant metamorphose', discarding his 'rustic habit' for fashionable top-boots, white cord breeches, a green coat with brass buttons and a neat waistcoat.[62]

The adoption of simple styles made it possible to obscure social rank through dress, and so increasingly subtle codes were used to establish exclusivity. Beau Brummel, the archetypal dandy, rejected finery for a sparse and precise style of dress and an obsessive attention to detail – cleanliness, cut and fit.[63] The socially aspiring attitude of the dandy who, in order to reject bourgeois notions of thrift and hard work, sought to emulate the leisured life of the aristocracy, posed a class threat. By representing his interest in fashion and display as ridiculous, the dandy was marginalized as a 'fashionable non-descript[s]'.[64] His attention to surface effect, a characteristic usually associated with the feminine, was considered unmanly and his appearance was described in terms of exaggerated female forms, such as waists pinched-in with stays.[65] Alternatively, in relation to the highly decorated masculinities preceding him, the dandy's sleek and unadorned appearance has also been interpreted as a highly erotic version of 'unpainted masculinity'.[66]

The social ritual of dressing in the correct urban fashion was an important first step in the process of initiation for new ramblers. This set of activities took place in the chambers of the urban bachelor with a tailor in attendance. Dressing was followed by an afternoon parade around St James's to purchase new commodities and display self and possessions.[67] Bond Street and St James's Street catered for the male consumer, with gun shops, booksellers, theatre ticket agents, sporting prints exhibitions, hatters, tailors, cravat makers, hairdressers, perfumers, jewellers and other expensive tradesmen.[68] Other urban locations visited by ramblers within St James's included chambers, hotels, sporting venues, coffee houses, clubs and taverns, all of which played an integral part in producing a public display of heterosexual, upper-class masculinity. The narcissistic aspects of the rambler, represented through the dandy, reflected an intense preoccupation with developing an urban aesthetic and style which opposed those of the corinthian. For the corinthian, fashion was displayed through social mobility, whereas the dandy's most renowned social art was one of exclusivity, 'cutting' or ignoring acquaintances in the street.[69] Unlike the corinthian, who mixed with both classes and moved from east to west in search of pleasure, the dandy's social exclusivity required him to remain in the west.[70]

The rambler, as a narcissistic spectator, derived pleasure from identifying the perfect image of himself in others and required sites for looking at other men. The rambler also desired spaces to display his leisure time and money, his 'conspicuous consumption', to other men and women. Possibly the most fashionable places of display for upper-class young men were the ground floor bow windows of the clubs on St James's Street. Membership to these clubs was extremely select and the famous 'Bow Window at Whites', built out over the entrance steps in the centre of the front facade in 1811, was inhabited as a space of high fashion by a circle of dandies, including Beau Brummel.[71] From the bow windows, men could show off their exclusivity to those in the surrounding rival clubs and display status and leisure time to the street. When Crockford's club opened in 1828, the ground floor rooms also possessed windows. These were carefully distinguished as 'bay' windows or observatories, from which to 'look out' and 'survey' the street, in distinction to White's 'bow' window, a place in which to be looked at.[72] The bow window was a place for dandies and ramblers to look out and to be looked at.

VISUALITY: THE CYPRIAN AS FEMALE SPECTACLE

The Rambler in the public streets,
Admires at everything he meets [. . .]
Ladies you'll find of every class,
In shape, just like the hour glass [. . .][73]

Although we have seen that 'looking' and 'being-looked-at' are, in certain cases, reciprocal positions which can both be adopted by one sex, psychoanalytic theories of the male gaze and the female spectacle tend to allow us to consider women only as looked at objects on display. The cyprian body was the site of the ramblers' desire and gaze – an object of display in the public spaces in the city. Rambling texts represented female identity in terms of surface display.

The displayed surface of the body is composed of a close relationship between clothes and the fleshy body. In the early nineteenth century, the issue of 'covering' was connected with a number of gendered themes around decency. A correct amount and kind of covering represented feminine decency in terms of honesty and modesty, whereas an incorrect covering represented indecency in terms of dishonesty and immodesty. Clothing was expected to be neither too revealing nor too obscuring of the body that lay beneath. To cover too little was immodest, to cover too much was dishonest. Both transgressions were connected with excess, extravagance and with prostitution. An excess of flesh represented exposure and wantonness, and an excess of clothing in the form of decoration represented artifice and vanity.

Strict rules governing the appropriate amount and kind of covering to be worn were recorded as 'fashion' in women's magazines.[74] Fashionable clothing for women of the upper classes in England in the first two decades of the nineteenth century was a highly minimal costume adopted from post-revolutionary Paris, inspired by the democratic politics of Greek culture. The gowns were full length, of a semi-transparent white fabric, worn with minimal undergarments and stockings. Sparse, revealing and décolleté, the waist was raised to draw attention to the breasts. The material was dampened so that it clung to the body like drapery, representing the body as a sculptural form.[75] But fear of French politics meant that by the end of the second decade of the nineteenth century, nakedness was connected with political radicalism. The exposure of the breast and the transparency of the gown were considered immoral.[76]

In rambles, cyprians were associated with surface value and considered to be kept rather for '*empty shew* than real use'.[77] In *Life in London*, the display of breasts by females in the street and in the theatre and assembly rooms represented them as cyprians.[78] Cyprians were also distinguished by the excessive display of gaudy dresses and decorative headwear and jewellery. Cyprians were believed to be motivated by 'allure',[79] 'principles of lust, idleness, or avarice'.[80] Their desire to 'dress-up' above their class in order to attract rich clients connected them with wearing deceitful coverings. Similarly, since their occupation could often not be distinguished through their surface appearance, cyprians' clothes also represented deceitfulness. Evidence that some cyprians, dress-lodgers, did not own their clothes but rented them from brothels,[81] and that others would pawn their clothes in hard times, substantiated suspicions concerning the dishonest quality of cyprian dress.[82]

In rambling texts associations were made between the pleasures of viewing the city through the controlling and framing techniques of the camera obscura and viewing the female body. Associations were made between the surface of buildings and femininity as 'to-be-looked-at-ness'. The connection between gambling and deceptive appearance featured in descriptions of Crockford's club as a common gaming house 'masquerading' as a respectable subscription house in order to create an aura of respectability.[83] The extravagance of the interior decoration, the use of glass, mirrors and chandeliers, was considered to be falsely seductive and interpreted by anti-gamblers as part of a plan to seduce the gambler and encourage the play of unrealistically large sums of money.[84] Gambling halls were described as: 'temple[s] of ruin, indolence, and guile' and gambling as: 'an abandoned prostitution of every principle of hallow and virtue'.[85]

The issue of display took on a special relevance in relation to the role of actresses and dancers whose bodies were uncovered/exposed on public stages.[86] On stage, the aspects a woman usually kept private were made visible, and such visibility, in terms of the overlapping of public and private, was connected to indecency and immorality.[87] Madame Vestris, a performer best known for her travesty roles, provided a focused example of public display. Playing male figures, dressed in breeches and skintight trousers, she displayed to the audience her legs, buttocks, hips and thighs.[88] For audiences largely consisting of young men; the display of Vestris' legs was the focus of attention.[89] The leg of the travesty dancer provided a metaphor for the transgressive eliding of public and private spheres in terms of covering and display, where the display of a female leg on a public stage was read as an act of exposure and wantonness.

The omnibus boxes on stage at the Italian Opera House in St James's formed a focus for the visual pleasure of the male ramblers and patrons of the ballet, providing privileged vantage points for the close scrutiny of the predominantly women dancers and singers. In these boxes, as in the foyers of theatres, men were represented holding spy glasses to their eyes.[90] In an etching of the green room at the Italian Opera House in a rambling text, the focus was also on visual display (Figure 5). Here the ramblers represented were engaged in watching and sketching the dancers, using eye glasses; while the dancers surveyed their own bodies and dancing techniques in the large mirrors.[91]

Two other public female figures encountered by the rambler, conflated with cyprians, and associated with surface and display, were female shoppers and shopgirls. Through their 'conspicuous consumption' – the items bought, the clothes worn and the amount of leisure time spent shopping – the female shopper was a visual indication of male wealth and status.[92] But the commonly held male view of the female shopper was that she was overly concerned with her appearance and therefore trivial, superfluous, overindulgent and extravagant – a 'dollymop' or amateur prostitute.[93] Shopgirls were also considered to be obsessed with their appearance and to have a desire for 'finery' beyond their means. Such women were assumed to supplement their incomes with prostitution – to be 'slygirls'.[94] The connection of shopgirls and female shoppers with cyprians was closely bound up with issues of surface display, where inappropriate covering, in this case excessive covering, represented through a fascination with dress and decoration, was considered deceitful. Such surfaces were represented as immoral in their ability to mask what lay beneath, in this case class difference.

If we take traditional models of psychoanalysis where the gaze is constructed through the development of the male subject, it is only possible for a female spectator 'to look' if she is identified with an active male, or to consider the

Figure 5   *Robert Cruikshank, 'The Green Room of the King's Theatre, or Noble Amateurs viewing Foreign Curiosities' (Portraits of ten noble and distinguished patrons of the opera, with those certain daughters of Terpsichore), Bernard Blackmantle,* The English Spy *(London: Sherwood, Jones and Co., 1825), vol. 1, p. 225, plate 11*

construction of female identity in relation to being looked at. For Joan Rivière, woman *is* masquerade, the display or performance of femininity,[95] but for other feminists masquerade theorized this way is an alienated or false version of femininity.[96] Irigaray's work utilizes the operations of masquerade and mimicry as conscious subversive, destabilizing and defamiliarizing strategies for flaunting spectacle and speech. Irigaray suggests that by deliberately assuming the feminine style assigned to them, women can uncover the mechanisms which exploit them.[97]

In emerging discourses around the threat of female presence in public space, male ambivalence (simultaneous feelings of fear and desire towards female sexuality) placed emphasis on the looked-at nature of the surface, on the tension between display, what was being revealed, and secrecy, what remained hidden. Places occupied by women, such as the bow windows of shopping arcades, the boxes of the opera, as well as carriages in the park, were represented as sites of intrigue and deceit. The problem with such deviant spaces was that, being occupied by women indicated that they might be owned by women thus subverting patriarchal codes about property ownership.

From the late eighteenth century, the great majority of opera box subscribers were women, and opera boxes provided women with contained spaces from which to display themselves and entertain visitors.[98] Opera boxes were associated with female competition, jealousy and rivalry,[99] represented as sites of infidelity where wives were unfaithful to their husbands,[100] and connected with cyprian display.[101] The arcade shop was another private space also connected with sexual intrigue and prostitution. The boundary between 'shop' and 'street', created by bow windows allowed a view of the interior but not direct access, setting up a tantalizing tension between inside and outside, between what could be seen but not touched.[102] Shopowners and shopgirls occupying bow windows could be looked at, as objects on display, but their presence could also be interpreted as a display of female property-owning status to the street. The representation of both opera box and shop bow window, frequently the property of women, as sites of intrigue indicated patriarchal fears of women as property owners.

A critical aspect of gendered identity is played out through spatial relations of movement and vision. Men and women represent their social and gendered relations of equivalence and dominance through positions as spectators and objects of sight, and through free movement and viewed containment in public arenas. The rambler and the cyprian, precursors to the Parisian flâneur and prostitute, are gendered representations of urban space in early nineteenth-century London. Thinking about the dialectical relation between identities and spaces, representations and constructions, allows an analysis which pays greater attention to the complexity and fluidity of gendered space. By paying greater attention to the fluidity of urban movement, the figures and spaces of the ramble are a starting point for considering the gendering of public space through the pursuit of pleasure. It is through this complex series of gendered looks and moves that relations of consumption, display and exchange are played out, and the patterning of gendered space is far more complicated than the continuing debate around the separate spheres suggests.

Notes

1. Pierce Egan, *Life in London* (London: Sherwood, Neely and Jones, 1820–1822), p. 75.
2. *Oxford English Dictionary*, CD ROM, 2nd edn (1989).
3. Nathaniel S. Wheaton, *A Journal of a Residence During Several Months in London* (Hartford: H. and F.J. Huntingdoton, 1830), p. 119.
4. Eric Partridge, *A Dictionary of Slang and Unconventional English* (London: Routledge and Kegan Paul, 1964), p. 958.
5. Francis Grose, *A Classical Dictionary of the Vulgar Tongue* (London: S. Hooper, 1788), n.p.
6. The semi-narrative structure first appears in Edward Ward, *The London Spy* (London: J. Nutt and J. How, 1698–1699).
7. See, for example, R. King, *The Complete London Spy for the present year 1781* (London: Alex Hogg, 1781).
8. Amateur, *Real Life in London* (London: Jones and Co., 1821–1822).
9. Egan, *Life*.
10. William Heath, *Fashion and Folly: or the Buck's Pilgrimage* (London: William Sams, 1822).
11. Bernard Blackmantle, *The English Spy* (London: Sherwood, Jones and Co., 1825).
12. Michel de Certeau, *The Practice of Everyday Life* (Berkeley: University of California Press, 1988), pp. 115–22.
13. Egan, *Life*, p. 72.
14. Egan, *Life*, Chapters 3 and 4, pp. 43 and 53.
15. Pierce Egan, *Grose's Classical Dictionary of the Vulgar Tongue* (London: Sherwood, Neely and Jones, 1823), n.p.
16. John Badcock, *Slang: a Dictionary of the Turf* (London: T. Hughes, 1823), p. 57.

17. Charles Hindley, *The True History of Tom and Jerry* (London: C. Hindley, 1890).
18. See, for example, Pierce Egan, *Boxiana* (New Series), (London: George Virtue, 1828–1829).
19. Among the accoutrements every rambler should own is a flagon. See Egan, *Life*, title page.
20. Egan, *Boxiana* (1818), p. 28 and Jacob Larwood, *The Story of the London Parks*, vol. 8 (London: Francis Harvey, 1872), pp. 282–4.
21. See T. Rowlandson, 'Three Principal Requisites to form a Modern Man of Fashion' (London: n.d.).
22. Francis Grose, *A Classical Dictionary of the Vulgar Tongue* (London: S. Hooper, 1788), n.p.
23. See, for example, George Andrewes, *The Stranger's Guide* (London: J. Bailey, 1808); George Andrewes, *A Dictionary of the Slang* (London: G. Smeeton, 1809); Badcock, *Slang*; John Badcock, *A Living Picture of London, for 1823* (London: W. Clarke, 1828); Egan, *Boxiana*; Egan, *Grose's*; Egan, *Life*; Smeeton, *Flash*; Smeeton, *The Art of Boxing* and George Smeeton, *Doings in London* (London: Smeeton, 1828).
24. See Egan, *Grose's*, title page and preface, pp. xxv–xxviii.
25. Egan, *Life*, pp. xiii–xiv and 22–4.
26. The London Lighting Act of 1761 and the Westminster Paving Acts of 1761 systematized street lighting and paving to a certain extent.
27. See, for example, Hemione Hobhouse, *A History of Regent Street* (London: Queen Anne Press, 1975), pp. 72–3.
28. See, for example, John Summerson, *John Nash: Architect to King George IV* (London: George Allen and Unwin, 1935), pp. 204–5.
29. Badcock, *Living*, pp. 47–8.
30. Amateur, *Real*, pp. 198–9.
31. See, for example, *The Rambler's Magazine* (London: R. Randall, 1783–1789); *The Ranger's Magazine* (London: J. Sudbury, 1795); *The Rambler's Magazine* (London: J. Mitford, 1820); *The Rambler's Magazine* (London: Benbow, 1822); *The Rambler* (London: T. Holt, 1824) and *The Rambler's Magazine* (London: J. Mitford, 1828).
32. *OED*; Partridge, *Dictionary*, p. 284.
33. *La Belle Assemblée* (London: J. Bell, 1819), (February 1819), p. 85.
34. See Egan, *Grose's*, n.p. and Partridge, *Dictionary*, p. 151.
35. Grose, *Classical* (1788), n.p.
36. Egan, *Life*, pp. 48–9.
37. Joseph Rykwert, *The Dancing Column: on Order in Architecture* (London: The MIT Press, 1996), pp. 317 and 320.
38. Blackmantle, *Spy*, vol. 2, pp. 18–19.
39. *Belle* (July 1806), p. 314.
40. Smeeton, *Doings*, p. 91.
41. Luce Irigaray, *This Sex which is Not One* (Ithaca: Cornell University Press, 1985), pp. 170–91.
42. Shannon Bell, *Reading, Writing and Rewriting the Prostitute Body* (Bloomington and Indianapolis: Indiana University Press, 1994), p. 91.
43. Anon. (K. Griffenhoofe), *Memoirs of the Life Public and Private Adventures of Madame Vestris* (London: John Duncombe, 1836), p. 126; and *Rambler's*, 1: 5 (1828) 245.
44. Egan, *Life*, p. 167.
45. Amateur, *Real*, vol. 1, p. 524.
46. *Rambler's Magazine* (London: J. Mitford, 1828), 1: 1, 32 and 2: 1, 212.
47. Guardian Society, *Report of the Provisional Committee of the Guardian Society for the Preservation of Public Morals providing Temporary Asylums for Prostitutes* (London: James Low, 1816), p. 33.
48. *A Letter to the Right Rev. the Lord Bishop of London containing a statement of the Immoral and Disgraceful scenes which are every evening Exhibited in the Public*

Streets by Crowds of half Naked and Unfortunate Prostitutes (London: Williams and Smith, 1808), pp. 12–13.

49. William Hale, *Considerations on the Causes and the Prevalence of Female Prostitution* (London: E. Justing, 1812), p. 35.

50. See 'An Act for the Better preventing Thefts and Robberies, and for regulating Places of Publick Entertainment, and Punishing Persons Keeping Disorderly Houses', 25 George II, cap. 36, n. 4, (1752), *Statutes at Large, 23 George II – 26 George II, (1750–2)*, vol. 20 (Cambridge: Charles Bathurst, 1765), pp. 375–80.

51. See 'An Act for Consolidating into one Act and Amending the Laws relating to Idle and Disorderly Persons, Rogues and Vagabonds, Incorrigible Rogues and other Vagrants in England', 3 George IV, cap. 40, (1822), *Statutes at Large, 3 George IV, (1822)*, vol. 62 (London: His Majesty's Statute and Law Printers, 1822), pp. 133–42 and 'An Act for the Punishment of Idle and Disorderly Persons, and Rogues and Vagabonds, in that part of Great Britain called England', 5 George IV, cap. 83, (1824), *Statutes at Large, 5 George IV, (1824)*, vol. 64 (London: His Majesty's Printers, 1839, pp. 281–9.

52. Badcock, *Slang*, p. 54.

53. See, for example, Laura Mulvey, 'Visual Pleasure and Narrative Cinema' in Laura Mulvey (ed.), *Visual and Other Pleasures* (London: Macmillan, 1989), pp. 14–26.

54. See, for example, Janet Wolff, 'The Invisible Flâneuse: Women and the Literature of Modernity', *Theory, Culture and Society*, 2: 3 (1985) 36–46 and Griselda Pollock, *Vision and Difference: Femininity, Feminism and the Histories of Art* (London: Routledge, 1988), p. 79.

55. Egan, *Life*, pp. 23–4.

56. See Chapter 2 entitled 'A Camera-Obscura View of the Metropolis, the Light and Shade attached to "seeing Life"', Egan, *Life*, p. 18.

57. See 'TOM and JERRY *"masquerading* it" among the cadgers in the *Back Slums* in the Holy Land', Egan, *Life*, p. 346.

58. Egan, *Life*, p. 282.

59. Arthur W. Frank, 'For a Sociology of the Body: An Analytic Overview' in Mike Featherstone, Mike Hepworth and Bryan S. Turner (eds), *The Body: Social Process and Cultural Theory* (London: Sage Publications, 1991), pp. 36–102, pp. 63 and 67 and Pierre Bourdieu, *Distinction: a Social Critique of the Judgement of Taste* (London: Routledge and Kegan Paul, 1984), p. 190.

60. Amateur, *Real*, vol. 1, p. 102.

61. James Laver, *Dandies* (London: Weidenfield and Nicolson, 1968), pp. 10 and 153.

62. Egan, *Life*, pp. 145–8.

63. Faired Chevianne, *A History of Men's Fashion* (Paris: Flammarian, 1993), p. 9.

64. Egan, *Grose's*, n.p.

65. See, for example, Robert Cruikshank, 'Dandies Dressing' (1818); Richard Dighton, 'The Dandy Club' (1818); George Cruikshank, 'The Dandies Coat of Arms' (1819) and George Cruikshank, 'Monstrosities' (1822).

66. Elizabeth Wilson, *Adorned in Dreams* (London: Virago Press, 1985), p. 180.

67. See, for example, Amateur, *Real*, vol. 1, p. 102; Blackmantle, *Spy*, vol. 2, p. 253; Egan, *Life*, p. 213; Captain Gronow, *Reminiscences* (London: Smith Elder and Co., 1862), pp. 74–9; Heath, *Fashion*, plate 14; and Felix MacDonogh, 'A Morning Ride in a Noble-Man's Curricle', *The Hermit in London*, vol. 2 (London: Henry Colburn, 1819) (pp. 35–42), pp. 40–1.

68. Captain Gronow, *Recollections and Anecdotes* (London: Smith, Elder and Co., 1863), pp. 136–7.

69. See, for example, M. Egerton, 'The Cut Celestial', 'The Cut Infernal' and 'The Cut Direct' (1827).

70. The dandy, Beau Brummel, once apologized for having been seen as far east as Charing Cross. See Eileen Moers, *The Dandy: Brummel to Beerbohm* (Lincoln: University of Nebraska Press, 1978), p. 66.

71. Gronow, *Reminiscences* (1862), pp. 46 and 62.

72. See Robert Cruikshank, 'Exterior of Fishmongers-Hall, St James's Street, with a view of a Regular Break down', showing "Portraits of the Master-Fishmonger and many well known Greeks and Pigeons"', Blackmantle, *English*, vol. 1, p. 373, plate 24.

73. *Rambler's*, 1: 3 (March 1822) 109.

74. *Belle* (July 1806), p. 231 and *Belle* (July 1809), p. 43.

75. *Belle* (February 1806), p. 64.

76. *Belle* (February 1806), pp. 16 and 20.

77. *Rambler's*, 1: 4 (April 1822) 161.

78. Egan, *Life*, p. 173.

79. Mary Wilson, *The Whore's Catechism* (London: Sarah Brown, 1830), p. 76.

80. Hale, *Considerations* p. 4.

81. Amateur, *Real*, vol. 1, p. 571.

82. Amateur, *Real*, vol. 1, pp. 566–7.

83. Deale, *Crockfords or Life in the West*, vol. 1 (London: Saunders and Otley, 1828), p. 72.

84. Deale, *Crockfords*, vol. 2, p. 253.

85. Heath, *Fashion*, plate 21.

86. Anon. *Memoirs* (1836), pp. 7–8.

87. Tracy C. Davis, 'Private Women and the Public Realm', *Theatre Survey*, 35: 1 (May 1994) 65–71; 67–8 and 71.

88. The *Drama or Theatrical Pocket Magazine* 3: 7 (December 1822) 316, King's Theatre Archives, (1826), Theatre Museum, London.

89. Anon. *Memoirs of the Life of Madame Vestris* (London: Privately Printed, 1830), p. 63.

90. Gronow, *Reminiscences* (1862), p. 179.

91. See Robert Cruikshank, 'The Green Room of the King's Theatre, or Noble Amateurs viewing Foreign Curiosities', Blackmantle, *English*, vol. 1, p. 225, plate 11 and pp. 208–9.

92. Thorstein Veblen, *The Theory of the Leisure Class* (London: Penguin, 1979).

93. Hilary Evans, *The Oldest Profession* (London: David and Charles, 1979), p. 116.

94. Dorothy Davis, *A History of Shopping* (London: Routledge and Kegan Paul, 1966), p. 125.

95. Joan Rivière, 'Womanliness as Masquerade', *International Journal of Psychoanalysis*, 10 (1929) 303–13.

96. See, for example, Mary Ann Doane, 'Film and the Masquerade: Theorising the Female Spectator', *Screen*, 23: 2–4 (September–October 1982) 74–87.

97. Luce Irigaray, *The Speculum of the Other Woman* (Ithaca: Cornell University Press, 1985), pp. 113–17 and Irigaray, *This Sex*, p. 84.

98. See Box 2482, King's Theatre Archives, Theatre Museum, London.

99. Blackmantle, *English*, vol. 1, p. 226 and Marguerite Gardiner, *The Magic Lantern or Sketches of Scenes in the Metropolis* (London: Longman, Hurst, Rees, Orme and Brown, 1823), pp. 84, 87 and 90–1.

100. Gardiner, *Magic*, pp. 84–90.

101. Blackmantle, *English*, vol. 1, p. 228 and J. Britton and A. Pugin, *Illustrations of the Public Buildings of London*, vol. 1, 2nd edn (London: John Wedle, 1838), p. 282.

102. Fanny Burney, *The Wanderer* (1816) (Oxford: Oxford University Press, 1991), p. 452.

CHAPTER 7

La Donna è Mobile

Esther da Costa Meyer

'La donna è mobile
Qual piuma al vento. . .'
Verdi, *Rigoletto*

This paper will focus on the appearance of agoraphobia, and the imbrication of women, urban space and pathology.[1] Since this neurosis straddles the fault line between public and private, and affects women in particular, it seems to be a relevant subject of study for us today. Even though agoraphobia cannot be generalized as reflecting the situation of women today, like other urban pathologies, it tells us something about the way space is constitutive of personality. Pathology, Freud reminds us, always sheds light on human development: 'An unbroken chain bridges the gap between the neuroses in all their manifestations and normality.'[2] I wish to explore different theories of agoraphobia – sociological, psychological, psychoanalytic, feminist, New Historicist – to discover what each of these has to say about this most spatially confining of anxiety disorders, and its relation to women.

Agoraphobia is most commonly defined as the fear of, or in, open spaces, or more literally, the fear of the marketplace. First coined by Dr Carl Westphal in 1871, the term did not gain common currency until relatively recently.[3] Different authors used *Platzscheu* or *Platzfurcht* (fear of public squares), *Platzschwindel* (dizziness in public squares), *Strassenangst* (fear of streets), *Raumangst* (fear of space) and *Topophobie*. With time, fear of urban spaces came to be identified more correctly with situations located in the public realm: not only streets and squares, but more specifically crowds, shopping, trains, bridges, tunnels, elevators, and so forth.

In recent years, the incidence of agoraphobia has increased exponentially, and currently constitutes over 50% of all patients with phobic or psychoneurotic disorders.[4] Its connection to women is beyond dispute: around 85% of agoraphobes in the USA are women,[5] and although the vast majority of these are white and affluent, we simply do not know enough about the extent of the disease and the forms it takes in other ethnic groups which have no access to psychiatry and lack the economic resources to stay at home.

Combating the Symptoms

One of the first to deal with agoraphobia was the Viennese architect and urbanist, Camillo Sitte. Sitte fell back on a literal interpretation of agoraphobia – the fear of open space. Or perhaps it is more fair to say that he was primarily concerned with agoraphobia as a sociological rather than a pathological phenomenon. Always attuned to psychological questions, Sitte noticed that many of his contemporaries either scuttled uneasily across large city squares, or engaged in long detours skirting the walls of surrounding buildings.[6] As he wrote in 1889, 'Recently a unique nervous disorder has been diagnosed – "agoraphobia". Numerous people are said to suffer from it, always experiencing a certain anxiety or discomfort whenever they have to walk across a vast empty place.'[7] According to Sitte, only small-scale, enclosed squares took account of what he liked to call 'our natural craving for protection from the flank'.[8]

Sitte had particular reason to be concerned with agoraphobia. Vienna's old ramparts, which had for centuries served as a psychological and architectural boundary that enclosed the old city, had been torn down to make way for the Ringstrasse, a vast boulevard 190 feet wide, whose width was out of scale with the historic fabric. But perhaps unconscious class fears had something to do with the tensions attaching to the Ringstrasse as well. From time immemorial the old city had been the seat of the court, the aristocracy, the wealthy bourgeoisie, and their servants, while the proletariat was housed in the featureless urban sprawl beyond the walls. The destruction of the ramparts implied the erasure of the main spatial divide that separated the affluent from the Habsburg empire's ethnic minorities and from the poor.

Sitte redesigned parts of the Ringstrasse, adding infill architecture to produce small, protective city squares of the sort he had seen in Tuscany and Umbria (Figure 1). His projects, which were not carried out, represent a nostalgic, petit bourgeois protest against the inevitable transformation of Vienna into a metropolis. To be sure, they would have helped dispel the malaise of the small-town dweller, inured to the shelter and comfort of the capillary street network, but only at the expense of future traffic. Although his insights were based on an incomplete formulation of the complex social issues involved, his sensitive reading of the intricacies of urban space remains a valuable tool for town planning even today. And his emphasis on the emotional importance of walls is most perceptive, though it misses the psychosexual connotations that other scholars were later to identify and analyse.

Pathologizing Women

For Sitte's contemporary and fellow citizen Sigmund Freud, who focused on the clinical picture, the fear of urban space was a symptom, not a cause, of aberrant behaviour. In Freud's view, anxiety neuroses such as agoraphobia were due to repressed, unconscious fears or wishes masquerading as spatial ones, and were connected not with empty space but with *urban* – that is, social – space, above all streets. Streets were threatening to those, like affluent or middle-class women, who led a sheltered or repressed life, because they held out promises of temptation, sexual fulfilment, and escape from home.[9] This freedom of choice was a source of great anxiety for the agoraphobe who experienced unconscious guilt for

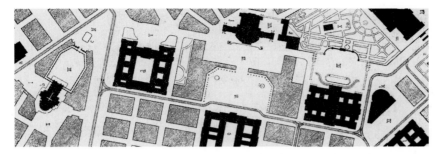

Figure 1 *Camillo Sitte's plan for the Ringstrasse. The Roman numerals designate the close-knit squares created by his infill blocks. Reproduced from Camillo Sitte,* Der Städtebau nach seinen künstlerischen Grundsätzen *(Vienna: Karl Gruber, 1922)*

what were in fact unconscious desires, and thus felt the need for a restraining influence, like the walls of the house or a companion to walk with.[10]

Freud thus linked the aetiology of agoraphobia to repressed sexual desire and theorized it largely as a female malady, at least in his early writings on the subject. As he put it rather crudely in a draft entitled, appropriately enough, 'The Architecture of Hysteria' (1897), 'Agoraphobia seems to depend on a romance of prostitution.'[11] Yet the first three known patients for whom Westphal named the disease were, in fact, men, as were the overwhelming majority of cases reported in the medical literature of the day.[12] Freud himself had treated one case of male agoraphobia in 1893 and two in 1895. And though he did not know it at the time, his most important experience with agoraphobic patients was to revolve around a five-year-old boy – the celebrated case of Little Hans.[13] This was an unusual case, as Freud rarely analysed children and tried, rather, to reconstruct the child in the adult. He only saw Little Hans once, and analysed him by proxy: the child's father, a physician, was an early follower of Freud. Not surprisingly, the mother plays a shadowy role in this tale of two fathers. Significantly, this is the only one of Freud's case histories where he makes use of urban plans, however schematic (Figures 2 and 3).

When Little Hans developed a fear of going out into the streets and squares of Vienna, including the sheltering ones so admired by Sitte, Freud correctly saw that space *per se* was incidental to the disease, and incapable of causing trauma. In the case of agoraphobia, buildings and squares have no intrinsic architectural meaning, but are convenient 'symbolic substitutes' for repressed feelings.[14] Desire, thwarted by prohibition, transfers itself by metonymy to a nearby object. Urban and architectural space become eroticized through displacement – the final resting place of the repressed and overdetermined signified, at the end of a long metonymic chain. Freud later explained the mechanism and the secondary gains it affords:

> In the case of phobias one can see clearly how this internal danger is transformed into an external one . . . the agoraphobiac is always afraid of his impulses in connection with temptations aroused in him by meeting people in the street. In his phobia he

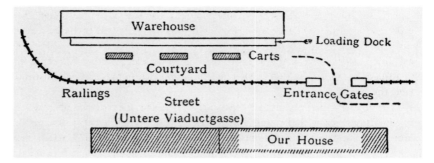

Figure 2 *Freud's diagram showing the location of Little Hans's house. Sigmund Freud, 'Analysis of a Phobia in a Five-Year-Old Boy'. Reproduced with permission from the Standard Edition of Complete Psychological Works of Sigmund Freud, by the Hogarth Press and the Institute of Psychoanalysis, London*

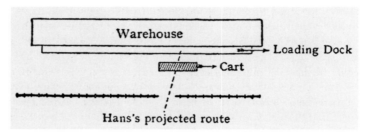

Figure 3 *Freud's diagram showing Hans's projected route. Sigmund Freud, 'Analysis of a Phobia in a Five-Year-Old Boy'. Reproduced with permission from the Standard Edition of Complete Psychological Works of Sigmund Freud, by the Hogarth Press and the Institute of Psychoanalysis, London*

> makes a displacement and is now afraid of an external situation. What he gains thereby is obvious; it is that he feels he can protect himself better in that way. One can rescue oneself from an external danger by flight, whereas an attempt to fly from an internal danger is a difficult undertaking.[15]

For Freud there was no easy fit between the urban or architectural signifier and the referent, which is always overdetermined, and thus partly unavailable. In this sense, one might say that he was a post-structuralist *avant la lettre*: 'In the process of the formation of a phobia from the unconscious thoughts underlying it, condensation takes place; and for that reason the course of the analysis can never follow that of the development of the neurosis.'[16] Like all phobias, the story of Little Hans can be broken down into different issues that never exhaust the whole picture: his fear of the streets had to do with, among other things, zoophobia (in his case, a fear of horses). One of Hans's playmates had fallen down while both children were playing horses, and he had also seen a horse fall down in the street. He wished his father too would fall down and hurt himself: the Oedipal triangle would thus happily resolve itself around Little Hans and his mother. Had Hans limited himself to feelings of love for his mother and ambivalent feelings towards his father he would not be phobic. 'What made it a neurosis,' wrote Freud, 'was one thing alone: the replacement of his father by a horse. It is this displacement, then, which has a claim to be called a symptom.'[17] Displacement – a form of censorship – permitted Little Hans to overcome the ambiguity of his emotions with respect to his father by transferring the aggressive impulses to a substitute object, the horse.

Freud later changed his mind with regard to the origin of agoraphobia in one very important aspect. Reflecting on the case of Little Hans from a distance of several years, he began to revise his earlier view according to which anxiety was the *result* of repressed material. Anxiety, he now believed, was the *cause* of repression: 'the majority of phobias go back to an anxiety of this kind felt by the ego in regard to the demands of the libido. It is always the ego's attitude of anxiety which is the primary thing and which sets repression going. Anxiety never arises from repressed libido.'[18] What agoraphobes fear is the outbreak of their anxiety attacks.

Be that as it may, Freud successfully isolated the main components of the symptomatology of agoraphobia – the underlying sexual symbolism, the mechanisms of condensation and displacement, and the bipolar world of the patient, torn between a fear of obscure forces transferred to urban space, and a home which could be far from nurturing even in the case of affluent women. Though Freud knew better than to mythologize the home as a benign, sheltering cocoon, he nevertheless underestimated the extent to which even placid, happy homes could be confining to women, and not only those with intellectual proclivities. By concentrating on individual cases, which were seen as unique occurrences, he also avoided any correlation between pathology and society. Today, psychoanalysis has moved far beyond its own initial sexist and essentialist explanations which focused primarily on *women* agoraphobics, and disregarded the cultural construction of gender in the pathogenesis of mental illness. Today, agoraphobia is considered as much a social problem as it is an individual affliction – at least by those, male or female, who have done research on the subject with an eye to women's issues.

CAPITALISM, CONSUMPTION AND AGORAPHOBIA

The synchronicity of the appearance of agoraphobia with the rise of the metropolis also anchors it firmly within capitalism. The Industrial Revolution entailed, among other things, the sexual division of labour which separated dwelling from workplace. As a result, the social identities of men and women came to be constituted differently. Yet the doctrine of the separate spheres – a male public sphere and a female private one – cannot be accepted today except as ideology. Numerous historians have underscored the continued presence of women in the public realm throughout the centuries.[19] It was only to men that they had been invisible. And several scholars have shown that in the USA, non-Caucasian women often spent more time in the public realm than men. The relentless focus on the private realm betrayed an exclusively white middle-class conception of domesticity.[20]

But the Industrial Revolution also radically altered the class structure and its inscription in the urban fabric. With zoning, the proletariat, often split up into ethnic subgroups, was more often than not driven out of the historical city with tragic consequences, particularly for working-class women: 'the slogan "woman's place is in the home" took on a certain aggressiveness and shrillness precisely at the time when increasing numbers of poorer women *left* their homes to become factory workers.'[21] Only affluent white housewives could afford to lead shuttered lives secluded in suburbia.

Class plays a powerful role in the geopolitical distribution of this neurosis over urban space. Just as the equation of obesity with lower-income groups plays a role, however subliminal, in the rise of anorexia,[22] so too one must ask to what extent the isolation, if not the suburbanization, of the agoraphobic in the USA – her spatial segregation from other social and ethnic groups – may be linked to class fears.[23] Are we dealing with a pathological pastorale, if we can be permitted the oxymoron? Is the agoraphobic's attempt to reterritorialize urban space unwillingly complicit with some form of societal discrimination? It seems clear that the semiotics of this anxiety disorder include powerful markers of class and ethnicity, as well as gender. The correlation of urban space and social class is not incidental to the emergence of phobias. Personality evolves in response to specific economic, social and cultural opportunities made possible in and through the urban environment. According to David Harvey, 'assignment of place within a social-spatial structure indicates distinctive roles, capacities for action, and access to power within the social order'.[24] Positionality, one might say, is destiny.

Agoraphobia must, I think, be theorized in relation to capitalism. But we must remember too that what we call the public sphere has to do not only with gender, but with social class and ethnicity, issues that vary from culture to culture, and are articulated differently in terms of space. As Susan Bordo notes, 'Agoraphobia and anorexia are, after all, chiefly disorders of middle- and upper middle-class women – women for whom the anxieties of *possibility* have arisen, women who have the social and material resources to carry the language of femininity to symbolic excess.'[25]

If gender is the product of social practices and institutions (disciplines), we must contextualize agoraphobia, not just pathologize it. Several scholars have done just that, relating cultural factors – as well as psychological ones – to the genesis of psychological disorders.[26] Going back to the etymology of agoraphobia, Gillian Brown has reinterpreted it as the fear of the marketplace or *agora*, that is, the fear of consumption. In her view, agoraphobia epitomizes the plight of the individual in a market economy and can thus also be seen as a painful and pathological attempt to circumvent the consumerist role assigned to middle-class women in affluent societies.[27]

However, withdrawal from the marketplace is no longer feasible: the two realms have become consubstantial. This desperate attempt to reprivatize the home and wrest it from commercialism was doomed to failure from the start. With the advent of industrialization, economic pressures caused severe strains in the traditional value system of American society. The transformation of the home from a place of production to one of consumption had great impact on women's personalities and led to a drastic change from the Protestant values of thrift and self-denial to those of self-indulgence and self-fashioning. The spread of consumer ideology eroded the tenuous boundary between house and marketplace.[28]

Furthermore, the early literature on the issue does show a strong connection between agoraphobia and consumption, but not according to the scenario suggested by the New Historicists. Westphal had already noted that his first agoraphobic patient was overtaken by fear whenever 'he needs to walk along walls and extended buildings or through streets on Holidays, Sundays, or evenings and nights when the shops are closed'.[29] A second patient had the same problem: 'It is altogether impossible for him to cross open spaces, yes even in the highest degree, disagreeable to move in streets, namely on Sundays when the shops are closed.'[30] A few years later, the first French psychiatrist to write on agoraphobia notes the same connection to space and shops: 'Fear of space,' noted Henri Legrand Du Saulle in 1889, 'can also occur in streets without shops or where the shops are closed, in churches, concerts, theatres, in the presence of long walls, of smooth and monumental façades, of vanishing perspectives, [or] bridges with numerous arches.'[31] And Freud himself mentions a young patient (female, in this case) who could not go into the streets alone because of an incident that occurred in a shop when she was a young girl.[32] It would be a mistake, however, to interpret these early recorded cases in simplistic gendered terms: men seeking, and women avoiding, stores and shopping. Rather, one should remember that shops, and in particular department stores, are places where desire is manipulated, and where commodities are staged so that they are eroticized by metonymy – that is, by their calculated proximity to mannequins, advertisements, or any other prop that can heighten their allure. 'Urban civilizations,' wrote Louis Chevalier, 'are erotic: not only do they develop sexual needs, but they also receive from sexuality an incitation that is imparted to all domains – economic, social, cultural.'[33] Not surprisingly, victims of anxiety disorders displace their fears and desires to this architectural typology as a whole.

While agoraphobia is generally linked to the fear of public, that is urban, space, there is some evidence that it may have moved into the house. Legrand du Saulle found a very interesting case of a 43-year-old woman, Mme B, who was perfectly capable of crossing the Champs-Elysées, or any other broad street or square in Paris. Her home, however, was a different matter: 'All the rooms of her apartment are literally crammed with furniture, paintings, statuettes, and old tapestries. *She lives in a veritable bazaar*, and thus does not find herself isolated; and [she] manages on occasion to endure the absence of her [kin]. The void alone terrifies her.'[34] Significantly, a similar situation appears a few years later in Proust's *Remembrance of Things Past*, when the narrator compares Charlus's faltering entrance into the salon of the hateful Verdurin clan to that of 'a young painter, brought up by a saintly protestant female relative . . . head bent and trembling, eyes tipped heavenward, hands tugging an invisible sleeve'. Only the relative's 'remembered image and real and tutelary presence will help the intimidated artist to cross without agoraphobia the space cleft by chasms that goes from the antechamber to the *salon*'.[35] Proust's blinding insight, borne out by recent work, is remarkable. The supposedly lithic, Cartesian world of architecture is read, or transliterated, by agoraphobes in terms of landscape. Not just landscape, but

Romantic landscapes in particular: Charlus's 'space cleft by chasms' ('l'espace creusé d'abîmes') resonates with intimations of the sublime. Hence the acrophobic fear of heights, dizziness, etc.

THE PRODUCTION OF AGORAPHOBIA

Agoraphobia can also be said to allegorize the sexual division of labour and the inscription of social as well as sexual difference in urban space. It speaks, after all, the same symbolic language as patriarchal society: the gendered antinomy between interior and exterior space reasserts the economic (active) function of the male, and the 'non-productive' (passive) one of the middle-class female. Agoraphobia represents a virtual parody of twentieth-century constructions of femininity.[36]

The parodic femininity of agoraphobia is based on a literal interpretation of domesticity as immobility, helplessness and infantilization, according to the main stereotype fabricated in the West as a role model for affluent women.[37] Significantly, the vast majority of cases of agoraphobia develops *after* marriage.[38] And it is the only phobia known to appear when the patient is an adult.[39] The transition from a state of total dependency on the parents to one of expected independence reactivates fears of separation and may precipitate a crisis resulting in agoraphobia. Obviously, an anxiety neurosis as complex as this is always overdetermined. But in light of the escalating number of cases, we cannot be satisfied with purely psychological explanations. The very fact that most cases appear after marriage should alert us to the socio-economic connotations of a disease that keeps women out of the labour force and reiterates their role as housekeepers for their husbands.[40] Agoraphobia is known, to no one's surprise, as 'housewives' disease'.[41]

Sadly enough, it is just the fragile and ultimately illusory frontier between domestic and urban space that agoraphobes hang on to – the nerve-racked, angst-ridden threshold behind which they retrench themselves. Perhaps the most tragic aspect of this disorder lies in the fact that the home to which all agoraphobics are inexorably chained is not a shelter.[42] It is, rather, the place from which they unconsciously struggle to escape.

In recent years, feminist scholars on both sides of the Atlantic have produced a steady stream of challenging literature that treats gender-specific types of neurosis as outlets of resistance to patriarchy: Luce Irigaray, Hélène Cixous, Catherine Clément and Michèle Montrelay in France, and in the USA, Carroll Smith-Rosenberg and Elaine Showalter, among others. For these scholars, psychopathology is a form of protest: the hysteric's repressed impulses are articulated symbolically through the body – a fact which implies, from a Lacanian point of view, a refusal of the phallocentric power anchored in language.

Studies on agoraphobia have followed the same trend. Like other forms of psychopathology, it is a language with a syntax of its own. Robert Seidenberg and Karen DeCrow, for example, see agoraphobia as a strategy of opposition to what one might call the ethic of renunciation usually demanded of married women.[43] It is precisely the somatization of the symptoms that permits the victim to express feelings which she finds unacceptable. The agoraphobic, say Seidenberg and DeCrow, is 'a living and acting metaphor'.[44] Conversely, agoraphobics avoid situations that give (unconscious) symbolic expression to their hidden fears or wishes: trains (the wish to flee), elevators and tunnels (fear of being trapped in unhappy marriages), and so forth.[45]

The notion that agoraphobia is 'body talk' is crucial also for Julia Kristeva, who comes to a similar conclusion from a different perspective. Drawing on the work of Lacan, she sees phobia as a failure of the subject's 'signifying system'.[46] The [agora]phobic personality, she writes in her analysis of Little Hans's case study, is 'incapable of producing metaphors by means of signs alone . . . the only rhetoric of which he is capable is that of affect, and it is projected, as often as not, by means of *images*'.[47] But – and here she departs radically from the others – symbolicity is cathected by a drive that has nothing to do with object choice, and thus bypasses sexual difference.[48]

Years ago, Roman Jakobson called attention to the bipolar structure of semiotic systems or forms of language in his path-breaking article on aphasia.[49] Metaphor and metonymy, he concluded, are equally present in language (literature) as well as in pathology (aphasia). While space perception depends on mastering institutionalized signs, agoraphobes tend to read them figuratively. Both the places they avoid and those they designate as shelters have to do with distinct typologies which are metaphors for situations they fear or desire. Their spatial codes are personal and hermetic rather than socialized.

There can be no doubt that agoraphobia is a coherent signifying system. Its victims stand to gain something from their extreme stance, and are prepared to pay exorbitant prices for it. As Freud points out, illness of this kind ends in compromise: Little Hans's fear of going out into the streets served as a ruse for keeping him at home with his beloved mother.[50] Susan Bordo, however, has underscored the self-defeating nature of the agoraphobic protest and its ultimate unwilling and unconscious collusion with the system.[51] Non-discursive, symbolic protest through the body ends up by subserving the hated establishment and reproduces the sexual division of labour by keeping women at home – which is to say, it reproduces capitalism.[52] Neuroses, as Freud was fond of pointing out, often seem to do the bidding of the more conservative forces of society: they are, after all, the result of repression of vital instincts.

While psychoanalysts and clinical psychologists interpret fear of the built environment as 'merely symbolic of interpersonal issues' and ignore the socio-political dimension, environmental psychologists see it in purely ecological terms, insisting on the connection between place and pathology.[53] Choosing one or the other of these two opposing conceptions carries serious implications for the victims of agoraphobia. From a psychoanalytical point of view, the notion of cure is highly problematic. Recovery is not frequent, and is marked by relapses even when it occurs.[54] The psychoanalysts' pessimistic prognosis helps explain the popularity of the behaviourist approach which nowadays tends to dominate the field. Behaviourists teach the patients to revisit the threatening sites or typologies, often with the help of antidepressants. In dealing exclusively with the symptoms, they deny the metaphoric nature of agoraphobia and hence overlook its causes.[55]

THE SEMANTICS OF THE SPATIAL SIGNIFIER

But whether one sides with psychoanalysts or with behaviourists, the persistence of architectural imagery in this gender-specific disease raises several issues. Are the buildings and urban space just empty husks to which repressed pathological behaviour attaches itself? Are they, in other words, simply neutral signifiers? Or is there not some underlying reason that leads victims of agoraphobia to cast their scenarios of fear and foreboding in architectural terms? If architecture is eroticized through metonymy which depends on propinquity, why is the garden, for example, not an equally powerful source of affect?

Helène Deutsch, the first woman psychoanalyst to study agoraphobia, was also the first to analyse the architectural imagery of the house. According to her studies, the act of leaving the protective walls of the home, and finding oneself 'outside' is associated by many agoraphobics with the act of giving birth.[56] For some psychoanalysts this would explain the high rate of agoraphobia among women. Lest this be taken for an essentialist claim, I hasten to add that agoraphobia is one of the rare phobias in which the association of crossing the threshold with parturition occurs also in male agoraphobes: it is not linked to biological sex but to gender. The equation of home and womb would thus seem to be so profoundly ingrained that it has the power to feminize male patients. There is a surplus of sigification at work here: in their regression to intrauterine memories, the agoraphobes' *Lebensraum* shrinks to this tautological condensation of home and womb. But it is not just space that contracts. By choosing to stress the ontological priority of the maternal body over the home what is implied is also a rejection of temporality. The agoraphobe's inspired misreading of domestic space is revelatory: after all, 'everyone's first environment is a woman'.[57] Agoraphobes are thus at odds with Filarete's definition of the architect as 'mother' to the building as soon as it is born.[58] It is the building that is the perennial mother to the architect and to the human being in general.

But architecture has reasons of its own that inflect the slippery referentiality of the word 'home'. Size, scale and the anthropomorphic resonances encoded in the articulation of architectural form all conspire to give it a strong presence in the urban environment. As Denis Hollier writes, 'Architecture is society's authorized superego; there is no architecture that is not the Commendatore's.'[59] And he quotes Lacan to this effect: 'This edifice [Lacan was speaking metaphorically of the psychoanalytic building] is appealing to us. For, metaphoric though this may be, it is perfectly constructed to remind us of what distinguished architecture from building: that is, a logical power organizing architecture beyond anything the building supports in terms of possible use. Moreover no building, unless reduced to a shack, can do without this order allying it with discourse.'[60] As we can see, the different ways in which agoraphobes interpellate space shed light on the elusive and overdetermined signifiers of urban and domestic space, not just on the equally intractable referents.

To conclude, agoraphobia was engendered by Western culture even before it was first diagnosed. Femininity, construed as planned helplessness, has still not disappeared from our society. Until relatively recently, buildings also figured prominently in children's books where girls were often shown immobilized in the house, behind the protection of windows, fences, porches, while boys were shown actively exploring the environment.[61] Although today women are no longer inexorably trapped in this circularity that culturally constitutes them through images, even the most emancipated ones come up against a major obstacle that retains them behind walls. When one woman out of every four is raped in the USA (or one every ten minutes), agoraphobia – the fear of *public* spaces – takes on a different coloration altogether. In the case of rape victims, public space as such does not exist except as part of a topology of fear. And time, not just space, is also a constituent element of agoraphobia: at night, in most cities, *all* women are agoraphobic.

Neither the appearance of agoraphobia nor the escalating number of victims is accidental. Psychopathologies that emerge within a given society, as Susan Bordo has forcefully demonstrated, far from being exceptions to the rule are in fact products of that culture.[62] Agoraphobia is not easy to categorize: it cannot be reduced to a cultural stereotype (its victims suffer intensely) nor to a purely psychological or individual phenomenon, given the growing incidence of cases. Most important, due to the circumscribed nature of its social distribution, it cannot be universalized: it does not represent the female condition. After all, the Duke in *Rigoletto* was literally correct: even though his famous definition of women was meant sarcastically – women are inconstant, fickle, changeable – today, at least, and against all odds, *la donna è mobile*.

ACKNOWLEDGEMENTS

I wish to thank John Goodman and George Hersey for their suggestions and helpful readings of the manuscript.

NOTES

1. An earlier, and slightly shorter version of this paper, was published in *Assemblage*, 28 (1996) 6–15, and again in Diana Agrest, Patricia Conway and Leslie Kanes Weisman (eds), *The Sex of Architecture* (New York: Harry N. Abrams, 1996), pp. 141–56.
2. Sigmund Freud, *Three Essays on the Theory of Sexuality*, trans. James Strachey (New York: Basic Books, 1995), p. 37.
3. Carl F.O. Westphal, 'Die Agoraphobie: eine neuropathische Erscheinung', *Archiv für Psychiatrie und Nervenkrankheiten*, 3 (1872) 138–61. Westphal himself lists 1871 as the date of the first appearance of his paper, which was apparently published separately: this publication has never been traced. All quotations are from the American edition, *Westphal's 'Die Agoraphobie' with Commentary: the Beginnings of Agoraphobia*, commentary by Terry J. Knapp, trans. Michael T. Schumacher (Lanham, MD: University Press of America Books, 1988).
4. Isaac M. Marks, 'Agoraphobic Syndrome', *Archives of General Psychiatry*, 23 (December 1970) 539.
5. Iris Goldstein Fodor, 'The Phobic Syndrome in Women: Implications for Treatment' in V. Franks and V. Burtle (eds), *Women in Therapy: New Psychotherapies for a Changing Society* (New York: Brunner/Mazel, 1974), p. 151.

6. Sitte seems to have been familiar with Westphal's work, although there is no proof. According to Westphal, one of his patients could not cross the Dohnhofsplatz in Berlin because the further he got from the encircling houses, 'the less the feeling of safety'. Another felt intense fear when crossing empty spaces, but felt better 'merely approaching houses again'. Westphal's 'Die Agoraphobie', pp. 60 and 70, respectively.

7. George R. Collins and Christiane C. Collins, *Camillo Sitte: The Birth of Modern City Planning* (New York: Rizzoli, 1986), p. 183.

8. Ibid., p. 233.

9. 'Where there is no shame (as in a male person), or where no morality comes about (as in the lower classes of society), or where disgust is blunted by the conditions of life (as in the country), there too no repression and therefore no neurosis will result from sexual stimulation in infancy.' Sigmund Freud, *The Standard Edition of the Complete Psychological Works of Sigmund Freud*, vol. 1, 1886–1899, trans. Alix Strachey (London: The Hogarth Press, 1966), p. 222.

10. Muriel Frampton, *Agoraphobia* (Bodmin, Cornwall: Thorsons Publishing Group, 1990), p. 36.

11. Jeffrey Moussaieff Masson, *The Complete Letters of Sigmund Freud to Wilhelm Fliess, 1887–1904* (Cambridge, MA: Belknap Press of Harvard University Press, 1985), p. 248. On this passage and on urban pathology in general, see the illuminating article by Anthony Vidler, 'Bodies in Space/Subjects in the City: Psychopathologies of Modern Urbanism', *differences* 5: 3 (Fall 1993) 31–51.

12. Terry J. Knapp, 'Introduction', *Westphal's 'Die Agoraphobie'*, p. 34. See also pp. 28ff.

13. 'Analysis of a Phobia in a Five-Year-Old Boy' (1909), *The Standard Edition of the Complete Psychological Works of Sigmund Freud*, vol. 10, trans. James Strachey (London: The Hogarth Press, 1973), pp. 3–149.

14. Ibid., p. 48.

15. *New Introductory Lectures on Psycho-Analysis* (1933), trans. W.J.H. Sprott (London: The Hogarth Press, 1949), pp. 111–12.

16. Freud, 'Analysis of a Phobia', p. 83.

17. Sigmund Freud, *Inhibitions, Symptoms and Anxiety* (1926), trans. Alix Strachey (New York: W.W. Norton, 1989), p. 25.

18. Ibid., p. 32. See also Jacques Derrida, 'To Speculate – on Freud', now in *A Derrida Reader*, ed. Peggy Kamuf (New York: Columbia University Press, 1991), p. 523.

19. See Linda K. Kerber, 'Separate Spheres, Female Worlds, Woman's Place: The Rhetoric of Women's History', *Journal of American History*, 75: 1 (June 1988) 9–39; Nancy Fraser, 'Rethinking the Public Sphere: A Contribution to the Critique of Actually Existing Democracy', *Social Text*, 25/26 (1990) 56–80; Mary Ryan, *Women in Public: Between Banners and Ballots, 1825–1880* (Baltimore: The Johns Hopkins University Press, 1990); Glenna Matthews, *The Rise of Public Woman: Woman's Power and Woman's Place in the United States, 1630–1970* (New York: Oxford University Press, 1992).

20. Patricia Hill Collins, *Black Feminist Thought: Knowledge, Consciousness, and the Politics of Empowerment* (Boston: Unwin Hyman, 1990), pp. 46–7. See also Gillian Rose, *Feminism and Geography* (Minneapolis: University of Minnesota Press, 1993), pp. 125–6.

21. Gerda Lerner, quoted in Kerber, 'Separate Spheres', p. 12 (emphasis in the original).

22. Noelle Caskey, 'Interpreting Anorexia Nervosa', in Susan Suleiman (ed.), *The Female Body in Western Culture* (Cambridge, MA: Harvard University Press, 1986), p. 178.

23. The literature is not altogether unanimous on this score. Although Marks claims that agoraphobia cannot be correlated with class, virtually all the case histories discussed in the literature clearly have to do with relatively affluent women. Cf. I.M. Marks, *Fears and Phobias* (New York: Academic Press, 1969) and Fodor, 'The Phobic Syndrome in Women', p. 136.

24. Quoted in Gillian Rose, *Feminism and Geography*, p. 18. Space, according to many modern geographers, is not an environment *in which* social life takes place but 'a

medium through which social life is produced and reproduced'. Ibid., p. 19 (emphasis in the original).

25. Bordo, 'The Body and the Reproduction of Femininity: A Feminist Appropriation of Foucault', in Alison M. Jaggar and Susan R. Bordo (eds), *Gender/Body/Knowledge* (New Brunswick, NJ: Rutgers University Press, 1989), p. 22 (emphasis hers). Denis Hollier also calls attention to the class component of agoraphobia in the fear of crowds expressed by nineteenth-century writers. See Denis Hollier, *Against Architecture: The Writings of Georges Bataille*, trans. Betsy Wing (Cambridge, MA: MIT Press, 1989), p. xix.

26. Particularly the New Historicists: see Gillian Brown, 'The Empire of Agoraphobia', *Representations*, 20 (Fall 1987) 134–57, and Walter Benn Michaels, *The Gold Standard and the Logic of Naturalism* (Berkeley: University of California Press, 1987), pp. 3–28. But see also Susan R. Bordo, 'Anorexia nervosa: Psychopathology as the Crystallization of Culture' in Irene Diamond and Lee Quinby (eds), *Feminism and Foucault: Reflections on Resistance* (Boston: Northeastern University Press, 1988), pp. 87–117.

27. Gillian Brown, 'The Empire of Agoraphobia', passim.

28. Jürgen Habermas, *The Structural Transformation of the Public Sphere*, trans. Thomas Burger (Cambridge, MA: MIT Press, 1993), and Brown, 'The Empire of Agoraphobia', p. 142.

29. Westphal, *Westphal's 'Die Agoraphobie'*, p. 60.

30. Ibid., p. 65.

31. Henri Legrand Du Saulle, *Etude clinique sur la peur des espaces (Agoraphobie, des allemands)* (Paris: V. Adrien Delahaye, 1878), p. 7 (transl. mine): 'La peur des espaces se produit également dans des rues sans boutiques ou dont les boutiques sont fermées, à l'église, au concert, au théâtre, en présence de longues murailles, d'une façade monumentale et lisse, d'une perspective fuyante, d'un pont aux arches nombreuses.' In the rest of the passage, however, he cites the tingling feeling in the legs which Freud linked to the sexual aetiology of agoraphobia.

32. Sigmund Freud, 'Psychopathology of Hysteria: Hysterical Compulsion', *The Standard Edition of the Complete Psychological Works of Sigmund Freud*, vol. 1, 1886–1899, trans. Alix Strachey (London: The Hogarth Press, 1966), p. 353. This was actually an example of *Nachträglichkeit*: the incident remembered by the patient, led to the reinterpretation of an earlier visit to a shop during childhood. See also Milton Miller, 'On Street Fear', *International Journal of Psycho-analysis*, 34 (1953) 238.

33. Louis Chevalier, *Classes laborieuses et classes dangereuses* (Paris: Hachette, 1984), pp. 60–1: 'Les civilisations urbaines,' wrote Louis Chevalier, 'sont érotiques: non seulement elles développent les besoins sexuels, mais elles reçoivent de la sexualité une incitation qui se traduit en tous les domaines, économiques, sociaux, culturels.'

34. Legrand Du Saulle, *Etude clinique sur la peur des espaces*, p. 10: 'Toutes les pièces de son appartement sont littéralement surchargées de meubles, de tableaux, de statuettes et de vieilles tapisseries. *Elle vit dans un véritable bazar*, ne se trouve point isolée ainsi et supporte très-bien à l'occasion l'absence des siens. Le vide seul l'effraye.' (Emphasis mine.) One is reminded of Benjamin's analysis of the *horror vacui* of French late nineteenth-century interiors: 'The interior was not only the private citizen's universe, it was also his casing. Living means leaving traces. In the interior, these were stressed. Coverings and antimacassars, boxes and casings, were devised in abundance, in which the traces of everyday objects were moulded.' Walter Benjamin, *Charles Baudelaire: A Lyric Poet in the Era of High Capitalism* (London, 1973), p. 169.

35. 'Tel jeune peintre, élevé par une sainte cousine protestante, entrera la tête oblique et chévrotante, les yeux au ciel, les mains cramponnées à un manchon invisible, dont la forme évoquée et la présence réelle et tutélaire aideront l'artiste intimidé à franchir sans agoraphobie l'espace creusé d'abîmes qui va de l'antichambre au petit salon.' Marcel Proust, *Sodome et Gomorrhe* (Paris: Gallimard, 1989), p. 299 (translation mine). For Proust's allusion to agoraphobia, see Anthony Vidler, 'Bodies in Space/Subjects in the City: Psychopathologies of Modern Urbanism', *Differences*, 5 (Fall 1993) 35–6.

36. Bordo, 'The Body and the Reproduction of Femininity', p. 17.
37. See Alexandra Symonds, 'Phobias After Marriage, Women's Declaration of Dependence', in Jean Baker Miller (ed.), *Psychoanalysis and Women* (New York: Brunner/Mazel, 1973), p. 297.
38. Kathleen Brehony, 'Women and Agoraphobia: A Case for the Etiological Significance of the Feminine Sex-Role Stereotype', in Violet Franks and Esther Rothblum (eds), *The Stereotyping of Women* (New York: Springer, 1983), p. 115.
39. Marjorie Gelfond, 'Agoraphobia and Personal Crisis' in Carol Malatesta and Carroll Izard (eds), *Emotion in Adult Development* (London: Sage, 1984), p. 126.
40. We might also add fashion to the strategies that kept women homebound and immobile. In the nineteenth century the middle-class housewife was, so to speak, tethered to the home. Thorstein Veblen's acid pen described the economic function of female fashion – the wasp waist produced by the corset – as 'mutilation, undergone for the purpose of lowering the subject's vitality and rendering her permanently and obviously unfit for work'. Quoted in Bordo, 'Anorexia Nervosa', p. 107.
41. Dianne L. Chambless and Alan J. Goldstein, 'Anxieties: Agoraphobia and Hysteria', in Annette M. Brodskey and Rachel T. Hare-Mustin (eds), *Women and Psychotherapy* (New York: Guilford Press, 1980), p. 123.
42. Wilfried De Moor, 'The Topography of Agoraphobia', *American Journal of Psychotherapy*, XXXVIX: 3 (July 1985) 375.
43. Robert Seidenberg and Karen DeCrow, *Women Who Marry Houses: Panic and Protest in Agoraphobia* (New York: McGraw-Hill, 1983), p. 31.
44. Ibid., p. 209. The authors point out that while Susan Sontag lamented, with reason, the way illness was treated as metaphor (*Illness as Metaphor* (New York: Farrar, Straus, and Giroux, 1977)), in the case of agoraphobia 'metaphors are being treated as diseases' with equally disastrous results.
45. Chambless and Goldstein, 'Anxieties', pp. 116 and 126.
46. Julia Kristeva, *Powers of Horror* (New York: Columbia University Press, 1982), p. 35.
47. Ibid., p. 37 (emphasis in the original).
48. Ibid., p. 45.
49. 'Two Aspects of Language and Two Types of Aphasic Disturbances', in Roman Jakobson and Morris Halle (eds), *Fundamentals of Language* (The Hague: Mouton, 1980), pp. 67–96. It is not, perhaps, accidental that several students of Westphal, such as Carl Wernicke and Arnold Pike, were specialists on aphasia. See *Westphal's 'Die Agoraphobie'*, p. 15.
50. Freud, 'Analysis of a Phobia', p. 139.
51. 'On the symbolic level, too, the protest dimension collapses into its opposite and proclaims the utter defeat and capitulation of the subject to the contracted female world' (Bordo, 'The Body and the Reproduction of Femininity', p. 21).
52. 'In focusing on the association of agoraphobia with consumerism, I do not mean to suggest a market determinism, but rather to trace one internalization of market capitalism that is neither simply a commodity nor a site of resistance to commodification. The agoraphobic imagination both produces and is produced by capitalism. Like any commodity, it might also serve other purposes – such as feminist resistance to domesticity' (Brown, 'The Empire of Agoraphobia', p. 154, n. 25).
53. Marjorie Gelfond, 'Agoraphobia in Women and the Meaning of Home', *Proceedings of the Annual Environmental Design Research Association Conference* 13 (Raleigh, NC, c. 1982), p. 349.
54. The average duration of agoraphobia is about 19 years. See Brehony, 'Women and Agoraphobia', p. 114.
55. Until the 1970s, there were several cases of 'treatment' by lobotomy in Great Britain. See I.M. Marks, J.L.T. Birley and M.G. Gelder, 'Modified Leucotomy in Severe Agoraphobia: A Controlled Serial Inquiry', *British Journal of Psychiatry*, 112 (August 1966) 757–69. Of the 22 patients so treated in this particular experiment, 18 were women.

56. Helène Deutsch, 'The Genesis of Agoraphobia', *International Journal of Psycho-analysis*, X (1929) 69; see also Miller, 'On Street Fear', p. 238.
57. Ruth Perry, 'Engendering Environmental Thinking: A Feminist Analysis of the Present Crisis', *Yale Journal of Criticism*, 6 (Fall, 1993) 13. Freud himself suffered from a mild case of travel phobia until it was dispelled by analysis when he was in his mid-forties. He discovered, not surprisingly, that it stemmed from his fear of leaving home, which he associated with the maternal breast/body. See Ernest Jones, *The Life and Work of Sigmund Freud*, ed. Lionel Trilling and Steven Markus (New York: Basic Books, 1961), p. 11.
58. For the citation on Filarete, see Anthony Vidler, 'The Body in Pain: The Body and Architecture in Post-Modern Culture', *AA Files* (Spring 1990), p. 4.
59. Hollier, *Against Architecture*, p. ix.
60. Ibid., pp. 32–3.
61. Fodor, 'The Phobic Syndrome in Women, p. 143.
62. Bordo, 'Anorexia nervosa', p. 89. See also Bordo, *Unbearable Weight: Feminism, Western Culture, and the Body* (Berkeley: University of California Press, 1993).

CHAPTER 8

HAREMS AND HOTELS: SEGREGATED CITY SPACES AND NARRATIVES OF IDENTITY IN THE WORK OF ORIENTAL WOMEN WRITERS

Reina Lewis

This paper is concerned with narratives of space and identity. It takes the interaction between architecture and gender as a starting point for a discussion of how spaces can be experienced as differently socializing and racializing by the various bodies that inhabit them. Specifically it is concerned with how Oriental and Occidental women represent their experience of gender and racialized segregation in Istanbul and in Europe. I shall be looking at English-language writings by Oriental women whose work challenges Western stereotypes about the segregated space of the harem at the same time as they contribute to local debates about female and national emancipation. Writing back to the West from the position of the racialized 'other', these sources show how their experience of Oriental locations is transformed not only by their own experience of travel (to Europe and the USA) but by their awareness of how their Occidental readers understand Oriental spaces. All the Oriental women I am discussing were Ottoman subjects: Demetra Vaka Brown was a Greek Ottoman, raised in Istanbul before emigrating to the United States in 1894, and wrote three volumes of memoirs/travel writing and several novels; Halide Edib Adivar was a Muslim Turk whose radical nationalism included involvement in the formation of the Republic with Mustapha Kemal Ataturk, and who published two volumes of autobiography in 1926 and 1928, several novels and much journalism; Zeyneb Hanum was also a Muslim Turk who, with her sister Melek Hanum, inspired Pierre Loti's novel *Les Désenchantées*, and who wrote a book about their travels in Europe. This was edited by the English feminist Grace Ellison, whose own account of her visit to Turkey I shall also be discussing.

Before I proceed I want briefly to explain how I am using the term 'Oriental'. Although this is the label by which the Ottoman writers identify themselves, I want to argue that it must be understood as a constructed, relative term, not simply as one of neutral, geographic description. Oriental, then, can be considered as a classification for one who has been Orientalized; that is, racialized in the specific terms of an Orientalist discourse, which is also, of course, gendered.

These sources present a series of movements from West to East, from East to West, and back again, all of them animated by a concern with bodies and the spaces they occupy. I want to think about how the experience of travel and the textual self-inscription of transculturated writing subjects is formative of identifications that are racialized, sexualized, gendered and classed in both local and international terms. If we think of space as productive of, and produced by, social relations rather than as transparent and pre-existent (Lefebvre 1991), then we can begin to trace how the segregated spatializing practices of Istanbul and the differently gendering spatial relations of Europe are experienced by this range of racialized female subjects as they negotiate their positioning in public and private realms around the world.

The space on which all these women focus is the Oriental female space of the harem, against which are contrasted the public and private spaces of Europe and the United States and the newly desegregating spaces of the modernizing Ottoman empire. Implicit and explicit in their accounts is a challenge to dominant Orientalist stereotypes of the harem. I want to argue that we should see the harem as both an actual space, the segregated space of women and children in elite Muslim households, and an imaginary space – an isolated, sexual prison in which the many wives of the Oriental despot are incarcerated to await his sexual pleasure. Though architectural and sartorial mechanisms of seclusion were a prevalent feature of Middle Eastern Islamic life over several centuries (Keddie 1991), the division of household space into men's and women's quarters, like the use of the veil, was generally a privilege of the wealthy and often the urban. Indeed, harem, meaning sacred or forbidden, operated as a seclusionary activity to protect status not simply gender. As Leslie Peirce has discussed, the Sultan as ruler and caliph was secluded from all but the smallest number of strangers by the spatial organization of the imperial palace and, when he ventured abroad, by the symbolic cordon provided by a large retinue (Peirce 1993).[1] So when we consider the way the harem is represented in these sources and read by the West we are dealing with a form of spatial division experienced mainly by a small elite,[2] from which strata my sources are drawn, but one whose symbolic importance for the West defines all Oriental domestic relations and therefore impacts on nearly all Orientals who encounter Western attitudes. Similarly, even though polygamy was very rare by the start of the twentieth century – Duben and Behar (1991, pp. 148–50) find that under 3% of men in Istanbul were involved in polygamous marriages between 1885 and 1907 – the harem was inevitably understood by the West as polygamous. But the experience of space as segregated did not only apply to those women rich enough to live in the large mansions or *konaks*:[3] most women were bound by imperial regulations about female dress in public; respectable women were reluctant to be seen, even veiled, in many public spaces; and upper-class women often lived in houses arranged around the concept of harem even if they were not in a polygamous family (harems as spaces of women and children would also be the domicile of sisters, mother-in-laws, visiting female relatives, aunts etc.). But, for the West, the image of the harem remained a delightfully shocking one of polygamy and sequestration.

In the imagary of what we might call dominant Orientalist discourse the harem figures as a polygamous space animated by different forms of tyranny (from despot to women, from eunuchs to women, from mistress to slave, from favourite to rival), of excess (the multitude of women, the opulence of the interior, the passions of the despot), and of perversion (the barbarity of polygamy, the violence of castration, the sapphism of the women locked up without 'real' men, the illicit affairs carried out behind the despot's back). All these things are found deplorable and enticing by turn. In this well-known and endlessly rehearsed knowledge about the Oriental harem, the stereotype of the actual imperial seraglio (the biggest, most hierarchical and richest of Ottoman harems) comes to stand in as a signifier for all harems: dominant Orientalist discourse can talk of 'the' harem with a clear sense of what it means and of the spatial relations it enacts.

PRODUCING GENDER AND RACE: DOMESTIC SPACES

That the effects of these spatial relations are understood in specifically sexualized terms is highlighted by Grace Ellison, whose 1915 book, *An Englishwoman in a Turkish Harem*, sets out to challenge the Orientalist reification of the harem (Ellison 1915).

> I asked Halide-Hanum, perhaps the most active and best known of modern Turkish women, in the name of one of our prominent suffrage societies, how we English women could help the Turkish women in their advancement. 'Ask them,' she said, 'to delete for ever that misunderstood word "harem", and speak of us in our Turkish "homes". Ask them to try and dispel the nasty atmosphere which a wrong meaning of that word has cast over our lives. Tell them what our existence really is.' (Ellison 1915, p. 17)

So, both Turkish and English feminists are aware of the runaway signification of the term harem. Halide demonstrates an awareness of the gap between harem as a local denotation of a social and spatial organization and its international connotations within Orientalist codes of knowledge. Her attempt to recode the space as a home rather than harem is not an assertion that the two are interchangeable: the insertion of the qualifier 'Turkish' indicates that homes are not the same the world over and will produce specific spatial relations, an oscillation between being like and not like the Occident common to all these sources. What are the equivalencies between Occidental and Oriental domestic and segregated spaces and what different forms of experience and identification do they produce for the bodies which inhabit them?

As the title of Ellison's book underlines, her gender gives her a privileged access to the harem. This was a major selling point for her work – though associating oneself with this sexualized realm was also risky. Ellison was quite aware that some of her Western readers would be determined to think the worst:

> When I said I had actually stayed in an harem, I could see the male portion of my audience, as it were, passing round the wink. 'You must not put the word "harem" in the title of your lecture,' said the secretary of a certain society. 'Many who might come to hear you would stay away for fear of hearing improper revelations, and others would come hoping to hear those revelations and go away disappointed.' (Ellison, introduction to Zeyneb Hanum 1913, p. xvi)

> To the Western ear, to be staying in a Turkish harem sounds alarming, and not a little
> – yes, let us confess it – improper . . . [In England] I was accused of 'advocating
> polygamy', for to the uninitiated the word 'harem' means a collection of wives legiti-
> mate or otherwise, and even the initiated prefers to pretend he knows no other
> meaning. (Ellison 1915, p. 2)

On the one hand, European women can add value to their accounts because they can report first hand on the forbidden spaces of the harem. But on the other hand, those very codes of authenticity locate them as gendered *participants* in a stereo-typically immoral realm. As Billie Melman has argued in relation to the nineteenth century, it was difficult for European women to adopt the mode of detached scientific neutrality now cultivated by ethnography and anthropology when they risked being contaminated by too great a proximity to their object of study (Melman 1992; see also Mills 1991).

European women writers developed a number of strategies for avoiding this contamination. Notably, as Melman argues, they demystified the harem by domesticating and particularizing it; representing it as a domestic space akin to the European drawing room and using detail to establish the differences between individual harems and the generic fantasy harem of the Orientalist stereotype. Ellison follows this alternative tradition pointing out that:

> [t]he Turkish home in which I am staying at present has little in common with the
> harem described by most Western writers, and no doubt those readers accustomed to
> the *usual* notions of harem life will consider my surroundings disappointingly
> Western. (Ellison 1915, p. 19, original emphasis)

The spaces in which she resides are directly contrasted to the imperial harem which she also visits. Pictured as an opulent place of ritual and state function rather than a regular domestic home, Ellison encounters the imperial harem during a highly formal court audience and admits that this:

> . . . remains the harem in the real sense of the word, the harem about which Western
> readers expect to hear . . . This is the first time since I have been back in Turkey that
> I have felt myself really within a harem. Even when I wear a veil, even when I forget I
> am not in England and try to push back the fixed lattice windows [even when I sit
> down to dinner] where not even the master of the house may be present, I do not
> realize the atmosphere of the harem. But within the palace, amidst its curious
> assembly of slaves and eunuchs, and in spite of its wide corridors and immense
> salons, there is a most uncomfortable feeling of bondage which would turn me into a
> raving lunatic at the end of a week. (Ellison 1915, pp. 36–7)

The distinction she sets up between the imperial harem and the elite harems in which she has been living offers an eye-witness and womanly challenge to the generalizations of Orientalist knowledge. But more than this, it also marks out as different and as healthier the domestic spaces which she depicts herself inhabiting. Thus, by emphasizing the particularity of the imperial seraglio, she is able to restrict the most negative and potentially morally contaminating elements of the harem myth (which she knows inform her readers' minds) to a space other than those in which she dwells in relative happiness. This splitting allows her to linger on the luxuries and hospitality of the elite Turkish home which, whilst evidently a source of great pleasure to her personally, will also provide some of the expected pleasures of Orientalism for her readers.

> In no other land have I met with such lavish hospitality – hospitality even that makes one feel a little uncomfortable, especially when one realizes how little one has done to deserve it. The courtesy, also, is almost overwhelming. Every time I go in or out of the room the assembled company, men and women, stand, and every time coffee, cigarettes, and sweets are brought by the slaves for the guests, my hostess rises to serve me herself. Always, too, I sit in the place of honour, as far away from the door as possible, and sometimes right in the draught of the window.

> It is the custom, too, for the master of the house to pay all the visitor's bills. That I should have proposed to stamp my own letters hurt my friend. The result is that, nowadays, I write no letters and buy practically nothing. I feel almost guilty when I accept what I do and give nothing in return, and always I have before me the haunting fear of the terrible disappointment my friend will have when she visits my country, for our hospitality cannot be compared to this. (Ellison 1915, p. 22)

The luxury of Oriental homes emerges as a defining crucial characteristic and as key to her potential pleasure in the experience of segregated Oriental space. At times Ellison positively delights in the elevated position she enjoys as a result of her incorporation into Oriental spatial relations where the privilege of her national identity and status as foreign guest allows her to accede to a social status far above that to which she is accustomed. Her anxiety about Fatima's reception should she visit England is not just a reflection on the different customs of hospitality in England and Turkey. It also reveals the extent to which specific spaces can modify a subject's gendered, classed and racialized position within social relations. Clearly, for Ellison, to be contaminated by her presence in the Oriental female space is as often pleasurable as it is bewildering or frustrating.

I have found it useful here to think about what Emily Apter (1996) in her work on French colonial literature describes as a haremization effect: a product of the harem experience which challenges the normative phallocentric ordering of Western colonial desire. For Western writers, both male and female, Apter argues, the relentless intrusion of a sapphic subtext into harem narratives reveals as only ever partial the presumed power and sexual omnipotence of the sultan, producing an 'other' eroticism which transcends the limitations of the harem regime and hints at forms of pleasure (*jouissance* in Apter's Lacanian scenario), outside of a Western libidinal economy.[4] The haremization effect re-presents and makes strange to itself European subjectivity and sexuality. Apter discusses how in a story by Guy de Teramond (*Schmam'ha*, 1901) set in North Africa, a French woman is engaged in adulterous sex when she notices that her Kabylian maid is still in the room waiting to be dismissed. At this moment, the Oriental gaze that spectates on the French woman in her performance of abandon becomes a 'voyeurism [that] 'haremizes' European eroticism by rendering it self-conscious, strange to itself' (Apter 1996, p. 213). This combination of sequestered female spaces, cultural voyeurism and fantasies of visual control can then 'make strange' both the stereotype of the fantasy harem and the experience of Western subjectivities.

Vaka Brown is keen to identify herself as an Oriental woman, but after living in the USA for six years she too finds herself being newly overtaken by the harem-izing experience of Oriental female spaces. Her ambivalence about the pleasures and dangers of contamination comes through most clearly at the end of the book when she writes:

> [a]fter six years of hurrying, of striving as if life counted only the amount of work done, of knowledge acquired, I was back again in the calm leisure of Turkey, where eternity reigned, and no one hurried. Not to stay, for I fear that he who tastes of American bustle can never again live for long without it. Yet as I stood at my window I was happy – happy to have nothing to do – happy merely to live for the pleasure of living . . . Among the Orientals I am always overwhelmed by a curious feeling of resigned happiness, such as the West can hardly conceive of. (Vaka Brown 1909, p. 221)

Vaka Brown uses her identification as Oriental to establish her authority, relying on the value-added currency of being not only a female reporter on the harem but also a nearly-native informant (though remember she is Ottoman but not Muslim). But she also finds herself undercutting her very claim to power and knowledge:

> Orientalism was a like a labyrinth: the more I advanced in it, the more entangled I became. One woman after another was confronting me with a new problem . . . and I felt stupid and incapable of understanding them. It hurt my vanity, too, to find how small I was in comparison with them. (Vaka Brown 1909, p. 127)

The depiction of life à la turque is made more difficult for Vaka Brown because she has to present herself as sufficiently American to be a reliable witness for her readers but remain sufficiently Oriental to be a credible insider informant. We see in her work a continual oscillation between being like and not like the Muslim Ottoman women she studies. This produces a hybrid identification whose authority is sometimes directly contested. Halide Edib Adivar, for example, explicitly challenges the right of the Greek Christian Vaka Brown to represent Muslim life accurately (Adivar 1926, p. 144), though Vaka Brown anticipates such criticism by regularly including quotes from Turkish women who attest that she is one of the few who can really understand them and represent them fairly for the West (Vaka Brown 1923, pp. 60–5). We can see how the movement from Turkey to the USA and back again registers in her accounts. In her first volume in 1909 the Orient figures as something familiar made newly strange by her now partially-Americanized eyes. It is only later once she has established sales and an authorial reputation and, more importantly, firmed up a suitably acculturated (i.e. not too immigrant) Ottoman-American identification (Kalogeras 1989) that she can write about the dislocating experience of travel to America (Vaka Brown 1915). At this stage, in 1909, the terms of her hybrid and authorial identity are still dangerously unstable and so she is at pains not to be merged with the harem and its women.

For Grace Ellison, whose identification as an 'Englishwoman' in a Turkish harem is so emphatically signalled, the contradictions about closeness to the object of study are less acute. For her, the haremization effect is clearly produced by the Oriental organization of domestic space. It is this and the interpersonal relations it fosters which impedes her ability to operate in her normal mode as a modern professional European woman.

> [T]he greatest obstacle to one's writing, setting aside the atmosphere, is the lack of solitude . . . as we understand it in the West, i.e. one's own self within one's own room, and the door locked . . . Several times I have escaped to my room to write. But my maid . . . follows me . . . and runs to fetch my hostess. She too, fails to understand why I go to my bedroom to write in solitude when I could write at a big desk in the salon with the other ladies to keep me company. (Ellison 1915, pp. 9–10)

Of course she will not find privacy in the Ottoman house since privacy, as Lefebvre points out, is a historically contingent (Occidental) concept, the spatial conditions for the emergence of which did not develop in Europe until the rising bourgeoisie adapted and changed the previously prevalent aristocratic form of residential space (Lefebvre 1991, pp. 314–15). The concept and behaviours of privacy so central to early twentieth-century European feminists (witness Virginia Woolf's room of one's own) are not a characteristic of Islamic cultures of the Middle East.[5] European women travellers regularly complain about the lack of privacy especially, as Melman discusses, since they see privacy as a prerequisite for their treasured habit of journal-keeping, a 'private and highly individual activity of the self [that is] a statement of Western, middle-class identity' (Melman 1992, p. 154). Ellison experiences obedience to the spatial relations demanded by Oriental architecture as acutely alienating, having internalized other forms of spatial compliance:

> I cannot master Turkish architecture – at least, this funny place [Zeyneb Hanum's house] has entirely upset my calculations . . . A hateful idea it is, to have rooms with more than one door; it's like having people with eyes in the back of their heads, and I wonder whether there isn't also a door under my bed and one in the ceiling. It's rather uncanny too, for in a country where doors have not locks and would not lock if they had, everyone flits unheard into one another's room. (Ellison 1915, p. 188)

If for Vaka Brown the American way wins in the end, Grace Ellison is far more sorely tempted to prefer the Oriental, despite its deleterious effect on her literary ambitions.

> The diary of my existence as a Turkish woman, which in England I imagined could be written in a very short while, lies day after day in the form of a pencil and exercise book, untouched in the little mother-of-pearl table in the most comfortable corner of my large bedroom. 'To-morrow,' I say, like a true Turkish woman . . . (Ellison 1915, pp. 3–4)

Note that both women are overtaken by this 'curious resigned happiness', a passivity in the face of destiny that is frequently identified as characteristic of Oriental attitudes, especially women's. For Ellison Turkey is experienced as a refuge of calm and quiet after the noise and the rush of 'what we in the West call pleasures of society' (Ellison 1915, p. 2), making her ambivalent about her Orientalized loss of motivation: 'if we in the West posses what is known as the "joy of liberty" have not so many of us been denied the blessing of protection?' (Ellison 1915, p. 196). She is torn between wanting to defend the Turks by presenting them as modern and modernizing and her nostalgia for elegant Oriental conventions. But the distinctive Turkish traditions which she describes in such loving detail become exasperating when they thwart her ethnographic and scopophilic desire to gather photographic evidence.

> Before I leave this house I hope to get some photos of the interesting persons it contains, but in undertaking to photograph a Turkish household I had forgotten first that the windows are dimmed by the inevitable lattice-work, . . . and when the sun shines it shines through the lattices, throwing on to the furniture all around large lozenge-shaped reflections. But there is another and greater difficulty, and this, photography is forbidden by the Moslem religion. My friend would certainly let me photograph the house if I asked her. The sacred law of hospitality is part of her religion . . . But Fatima has to deal with a most fanatical entourage, the women much more than the men . . . (Ellison 1915, pp. 27–8)

But even when she manages to takes photographs they are not always acceptable to the West.

> Had I been able, as I hoped, to send some photographs of the interior of my friend's house, those photographs would probably be considered 'fakes', or perhaps even they might be returned (as they were returned to me when I last stayed in Turkey five years ago) with the comment 'This is not a Turkish harem.' (Ellison 1915, p. 19)

The presence of thirteen photographs proudly announced on the fly sheet attest to the significance attached to photographic documentation and to Ellison's determination. Clearly photography was not as strongly prohibited as Ellison suggests, although like all Western goods and technologies their consumption would have been uneven (Çizgen 1987). Ellison's photographs reveal the double bind of representing Oriental domestic space: the photographs' production and circulation are hampered by both an allegiance to the old and Oriental (religious interdiction) and the problematic signification of the new and Occidental (too much modern furniture). One of Ellison's rejected photographs ('A corner of a Turkish harem of today, Figure 1) was reproduced in Zeyneb Hanum's book in 1913. Its caption reads, 'this photograph was taken expressly for a London paper. It was returned with this comment: "The British public would not accept this as a picture of a Turkish Harem." As a matter of fact, in the smartest Turkish houses European furniture is much in evidence' (Zeyneb Hanum 1913, p. 192). Ellison's book, then, treads a delicate line between offering the expected pleasures of recognizable Orientalness and challenging Orientalist stereotypes. These contradictory attitudes structure her experience of Turkey: she wants to show that Turkish homes are not what Europe imagines them to be, but are in fact modern, respectable domiciles full of European furniture but she also loves participating in old Turkish customs and dressing up in Turkish clothes. In recognition of Ellison's desire for an authentic Turkish environment, her hostess starts shopping for 'antiquated' Turkish goods in order to furnish a proper 'Turkish room' for Ellison's next visit, buying in the bazaar 'those quaint and delightful souvenirs of the Turkey of the past, in much the same way as we English who can afford it indulge our tastes for the furniture and porcelain of a century that is gone' (Ellison 1915, p. 20).

Figure 1 *A corner of a Turkish harem of today. In Zeyneb Hanoum (1913)* A Turkish Woman's European Impressions, *Ellison, G. (ed.) (London: Seeley, Service Co.)*

PRODUCING GENDER AND RACE: PUBLIC SPACES

References to shopping in the bazaar take us outside the harem and point to the changing nature of women's interaction with public spaces.[6] For both Ellison and Vaka Brown, in her second book about Istanbul (*The Unveiled Ladies of Stamboul*, 1923), it is women's occupation of public spaces that is the most conspicuous sign of change in Ottoman society during the period of the Second Constitution (1908–1918) and leading up to the republic in 1923. In 1915 Grace Ellison describes the early effects of Turkish women's increased presence in public spaces:

> Five years ago we never walked a step; now we not only saunter through the bazaar, but go to a big dressmaker's in Pera, whilst formerly all our goods had to be purchased from Greek merchants and Paris dressmakers who came with their goods to the harem. But not only in the bazaar do we walk; we have walked in the magnificent newly laid-out park, where women are allowed for the first time to walk in a park where there are men. The men I must say, have not yet grown accustomed to the new

and extraordinary state of things, and vie with the Levantine 'mashers' in their desire to see the features under the veil. It is not a very comfortable experience for the Turkish woman, but it is the darkness before the dawn. (Ellison 1915, pp. 31–2)

This reconfiguring of public and previously masculinized spaces is seen by many as a turbulent and challenging experience (Duben and Behar 1991). The use of Western goods and the behaviours associated with them inevitably had political overtones (Coçek 1996) and were unevenly adopted by different sections of the population where they were used in conjunction with conventional products and spatial relations in a variety of ways. Even those few households which considered themselves extensively Westernized would still be operating a mix of traditional and newly formulated habits in their homes. Fatima's home, for example, which is furnished in the best European Empire style, is still policed by 'fanatical' old women whose adherence to conventional gendered uses of space curtails her activities in her home and her husband's desire to allow her more liberty of movement outside it.

Ellison's reference to Pera, the foreign quarter of Istanbul, and the new European-style park[7] indicates that the role of veiling is being altered by the new hybrid spaces of the modernizing city. Though there was a long tradition of illicit meetings between men and women in boats and on the banks of the Sweet Waters of the Bosphorus, where groups of women would make ostensibly single-sex excursions, these public interactions were without sanction. In contrast, the new spaces like the park were designed to permit a mixed gender social life.[8] But walking in unsegregated public spaces nonetheless attracts attention since such changes to the conception of public space raised all sorts of anxiety about gender and morality. Ellison and Fatima's presence in the park occurs in a new space whose social etiquettes are not yet mapped out and where Turkish men also engage in hybrid behaviours.

When Vaka Brown returns to Istanbul to report again in 1921 she signals at once the significance of women's changing occupation of public space by titling her book *The Unveiled Ladies of Stamboul* (Stamboul being the old Turkish quarter of the city). She includes a photograph (Figure 2) of a man and a woman talking together in the street with the legend 'A sight that would have been impossible ten years ago'. The assumption that what is remarkable in the picture needs no further interpretation shows how prevalent was the stereotype of Turkish women as secluded and passive. The photograph, with its almost totemic invocation of the empty space which would have preceded this scene, emphasizes the startling insertion of Muslim Turkish women into a mixed public space. But though the caption suggests an absolute reversal, implying that this interaction would have been 'impossible' in the past, the continuation of traditional sartorial signs of seclusion (the headscarf and overcoat or *feredge*) suggests instead how the transition was inevitably conducted in hybrid terms. Even those women who passionately embraced all that is Western as a sign of modernity and progress found that their personal allegiances to traditional ways could not easily be overcome. Halide Adivar writes of how in 1908, even as she was writing for the constitutionalist newspaper *Tanine*, she was still 'not emancipated enough to go to

Figure 2 *A sight that would have been impossible ten years ago. In Demetra Vaka Brown (1923)* The Unveiled Ladies of Stamboul *(Boston: Houghton Mifflin). By permission of The British Library (shelfmark 08415 i 49)*

the newspaper office' and knew only those men who were the 'most intimate friends' of her husband and father (Adivar 1926, p. 265).

Writing a few years after this episode, Ellison describes Fatima's fearless incursion into the previously forbidden space of her hotel:

> She came at one to see me at an hotel. A Turkish woman visiting me at an hotel! Was it possible? Five years ago what would not have been her punishment for such reckless *license*? The customs of the country do not yet, however, allow women to visit hotels, and in taking every step forward she has to run the risk of offending the ignorant and fanatical mob.

> Fatima did not come in by the front entrance. Quite recently a restaurant for 'ladies only' has been opened by the same management as the hotel where I stayed and is, to some extent, a rendezvous for Turkish women. It is their first step towards a 'fashionable' club, and to me, the newcomer, another big step towards freedom. Let those Western critics [who take a stand against the new government] take into consideration such details . . . It is part of a great scheme of reform, and everything is going on in proportion. In 1908 more than two men sitting at a café together were 'suspect' and reported at headquarters; in 1913 Turkish *women* meet in a restaurant and discuss political subjects – certainly this is not the Turkey I expected to see. (Ellison 1915, p. 5, original emphasis)

Access to different spaces has clearly captured the imagination of the elite secluded Turkish woman. Fatima had long been fascinated by the forbidden space of the hotel and is thrilled at her own audacity, arriving 'thickly veiled' and smuggling herself in unseen by a side door, when 'five years ago the zenith of [her] longing was to be taken up in a hotel lift' (Ellison 1915, p. 6). The liberties promised by the hotel and its exciting Western technologies are not only important for women: Ellison is careful to put Fatima's visit in the context of the general change in politicized spatial relations. The constitutional period made freedom of movement and of association more available to the whole population although, of course, women's access to these new civil liberties always operated on a gendered axis. It is clear that the occupation of newly gender-liberated spaces is not homogeneous or neutral: not all women are equally able to assume spatial rights though they may at times assert both traditional and unconventional spatial behaviours as political statements. When Vaka Brown visits in 1921 she travels through a city still partially occupied by foreign troops and frequently has to position herself vis-à-vis the much-resented American and European imperialism being played out in the streets of the city. Although she often identifies herself as Oriental, her Western dress leads passers-by to assume she is Occidental:

> The tram gave a jerk, a throb, and stopped [then] started again on its course toward old, sunlit Stamboul. The passenger who had caused the stop was a solitary Turkish woman. Carefully balancing herself on her excessively high heels, she came in by the front end, and scanned the 'harem' end of the car for a vacant seat. There was none.
>
> For a second she stood poised, taking in the fact that all the seats in the women's compartment were occupied. Through the opening in the curtains she could equally discern that beyond them were empty seats in the men's end. Her black lustrous eyes – so piquantly opposed to the gold of her hair – turned back from the men's compartment, and scanned the faces of such Christian women as were seated in the women's end. Then she advanced to where I sat, and with a motion of her small, white-gloved hand said in French:
>
> 'There is room for *you* in there.'
>
> She was within her rights. I yielded my place to her, and changed to one beyond the curtains. Yet the tone in which she had ordered me to give her my seat disturbed me. It was something new to me in Turkish women. Losing no sight of the fact that she had a perfect right to ask a European woman to go into the other end of the car when there were places available there, I yet wondered at her doing so. That right I had never seen them exercise before. And the tone she had used had nothing to do with rights. It smacked of hatred. It was as if she said: 'This opportunity I take to enforce in our capital that which belongs to us Turks.' (Vaka Brown 1923, pp. 122–3)

The woman, to whom Vaka Brown later makes sure to talk, is driven by a fierce hatred of the occupying European forces (marvellously expressed by marrying a Frenchman to whom she denies herself, despite her passion for him, thus torturing them both!). In the context of the annexation of the city's space by the armies of occupation (Vaka Brown's respondent meets her husband when he is sent to requisition her house for billets), Vaka Brown finds herself more and more positioned as either Euro-American or Greek (in the context of Turkey's war with Greece). By asserting her right to the gender-segregated space at the front of the bus, the Turkish woman reactivates the nationalizing and racializing dynamic inherent in the bus's gendered spatial relations and the city through which it travels. Vaka Brown's surprise at encountering a Turkish woman so uncharacter-istically haughty indicates some of the new ways of being that emerge with the different spatialities of the changing city. If we follow McDowell and Sharpe (1997) in using the term spatiality to emphasize the active agency of space, we can see how the multiple subject positions made possible for individuals by different socio-spatial relations can be experienced, and at times consciously enacted, in over-lapping and contradictory ways. Whilst Halide Adivar represents as frustrating her inability to brave the newspaper office, this woman is depicted as manipulating codes of seclusion to make a political point: the inference being that her aversion is not so much to sitting in the mixed section of the bus as it is to the visible presence of foreigners in the bus *qua* the city. The political and personal slippage between local minority populations (Christians) and foreign interlopers is suggested later in Vaka Brown's account when she watches her board another tram where 'several vacant seats in the women's end robbed her of the pleasure of ordering a Christian woman out'. The switch between Europeans and Christians is indicative of how changes in spatial ordering reformulate previous social relations: not only the space of the bus and the relative control of that domain by the Muslim woman[9] vis-à-vis non-Muslims but also of course the relative control over domains of the city by the occupying foreign powers. As typified in many national liberation struggles, her assertive enactment of 'traditional' religious spatial rights[10] is used as a sign of her anti-imperialist allegiances, even at the same time as many of her compatriots are arguing against the veil and other mechanisms of seclusion in the name of national progress and modernity.

CONCLUSION: EUROPEAN HAREMS

Two women who have such an aversion to Oriental seclusion that they flee for a 'free' life in Europe are Zeyneb Hanum and Melek Hanum. Unable to recognize the signs of Western freedom as truly valuable (they cannot get over the pointlessness of sport as a leisure pursuit or the crazy pace of a Paris Season) they look with eyes which are both haremized and haremizing and find the harem in Europe. Zeyneb Hanum stays in a 'Ladies Club' in London and is not impressed with the experience:

> What a curious harem! and what a difference from the one in which you are living at present [she is writing to Ellison in Istanbul].

> The first time I dined there I ordered the vegetarian dinner, expecting to have one of those delicious meals which you are enjoying (you lucky woman!), which consists of everything that is good. But alas! the food in this harem has been a disappointment to me . . . In the reading room, where I spend my evening, I met . . . people, who spoke in whispers, wrote letters, and read the daily papers. The silence of the room was

restful, there was an atmosphere almost of peace, but it is not the peace which follows strife, it is the peace of apathy. Is this, then, what the Turkish women dream of becoming one day? Is this their ideal of independence and liberty? . . . What I do feel, though, is that a Ladies' Club is not a big enough reward for having broken away from an Eastern harem and all the suffering that has been the consequence of that action. A club, as I said before, is after all another kind of harem, but it has none of the mystery and charm of the Harem of the East. (Zeyneb Hanum 1913, pp. 182–6)

Like the Kabylian servant in Teramond's story, Zeyneb Hanum exerts a haremizing gaze on the West that makes strange its familiar division of space and organization of sexuality. It is notable that at these points in her book, Zeyneb Hanum breaks off to address directly her respondent Grace Ellison – an exchange of opinions in which the usually silenced Oriental woman speaks back with her observations on both Eastern and Western life. Zeyneb Hanum's haremization effect is very particular. When she writes about the Eastern harem she uses her experience of harem life to challenge its sexualization and to domesticate it into a home (Melman 1992). But having removed the excesses of sexualization and privation from the Orient, Zeyneb Hanum reattributes them to the Occident, implicitly challenging the Orientalist sexualization of Oriental female space and behaviours. Her sarcasm knows no bounds when she visits the Houses of Parliament.

But, my dear, why have you never told me that the Ladies' Gallery is a harem? A harem with its latticed windows! The harem of the Government! No wonder the women cried through the windows of that harem that they wanted to be free! I felt inclined to shout too. 'Is it in Free England that you dare to have a harem? How inconsistent are you English! You send your women out unprotected all over the world, and here in the workshop where your laws are made, you cover them with a symbol of protection.' (Zeyneb Hanum 1913, p. 194)

Positioning the Western and Eastern women's spaces in conjunction to each other, Zeyneb Hanum haremizes in reverse. She specifically reassigns the sexualized projections of indolence and apathy back to their Western point of origin, the spectacular lack of luxury in the London 'harem' (with its grotesquely inedible food and unfriendly apathy) paradoxically serving to emphasize the domestication of the Istanbul harem. Her knowing gaze – 'my dear, why have you never told me?' – sees in the West what the West tries to project onto the East. But in Zeyneb Hanum's account neither the Oriental nor the Occidental spaces of female sequestration are highly sexualized. Rather than create an alternative erotics, Zeyneb Hanum's account emphasizes the similarities between East and West whilst simultaneously criticizing the limitations of both. Though the limitations of the Oriental harem were not for her, the European alternatives are neither sufficiently better nor sufficiently *different*.

I want to close by looking at two photographs of Zeyneb Hanum in Paris ('Zeyneb in her Paris drawing-room', Figure 3 and 'Zeyneb in her Western drawing-room', Figure 4). Despite their different titles both figures show the same room. But in the first, which forms the frontispiece to the book, Zeyneb Hanum wears a yashmak despite being in her own room in the European capital. Surprisingly in a book about their travels in Europe the sisters appear in Turkish dress in all but one

Figure 3 *Zeyneb in her Paris drawing-room. In Zeyneb Hanoum (1913)* A Turkish Woman's European Impressions, *Ellison, G. (ed.) (London: Seeley, Service Co.)*

of the illustrations. Accompanied by pseudo-ethnographic captions these images serve, I think, to authenticate their Turkish identity despite their evident acculturation to European social mores.[11] The staging of the Orient in the West produces an ersatz authenticity, if I can use such a phrase, whose attempt to perform the two geographical categorizations signalled by the captions suggests the instability of both. That she wears a yashmak in Figure 3 can only be for reasons of

Figure 4 *Zeyneb in her Western drawing-room. In Zeyneb Hanoum (1913)* A Turkish Woman's European Impressions, *Ellison, G. (ed.) (London: Seeley, Service Co.)*

publication since she is no advocate of the veil. But this transparent performance of the marker of racialized identity par excellence (the veil being the most easily decodable sign for the West of Oriental womanhood) ends up destabilizing the potential authenticity of the Turkish room. Like the Turkish textiles that do not quite cover the striped walllpaper and floral border of the Paris decoration in their attempt to Turkify the room, her cross-cultural musical behaviours[12] suggest a diasporic hybridity. The personal and social relations of this transculturated identification are difficult for the book to contain since its sales are premised on her lived experience as a 'real' Turkish woman. Whilst Zeyneb Hanum's book is intended in part as an attack on the worst of Western stereotypes, the engraving on the front cover of a woman in a yashmak suggests the pervasive power of the exotic to which it must also appeal.

If, by the turn of the century, objects signifying the 'authentic' Turkish past are already being recommodified as of quaint historic interest by the Turks (for both the domestic and souvenir market) what forms of Oriental spatial behaviour should Zeyneb Hanum be trying to enact in Paris? The gap between what is legible to her Occidental audience and personally meaningful to the expatriate Turk in a period of personal and social upheaval remains tantalizingly open in these visuals. Her hasty and clandestine departure gave little opportunity for arranging much luggage (Melek Hanum 1926) and it would certainly seem unlikely that they had furniture shipped to France, so these photographs also suggest the circulation of Oriental (though not necessarily Turkish) goods in Europe.[13] The market for Oriental goods in Europe takes on a different meaning when these signs of the covetably exotic are used by a woman for whom they are mundane if outdated signs of a traditional set of domestic behaviours.

I hope I have shown through my analysis of these sources how spaces and the objects and people within them are experienced, represented and interpreted in ways which are culturally as well as gender specific. Bricks and mortar, wooden structures, spaces of congregation and of legislation, of hospitality and of seclusion, of respite and of labour are felt as both instinctively 'right' and familiar and as strange and unnerving. Though travel and transculturation may reveal the non-naturalness of spatial relations most acutely, the reorganization of space as seen, for example, in early twentieth-century Istanbul, can also make strange conventional behaviours and illuminate for the city's inhabitants and visitors the social and psychic productivity of the spaces at home and abroad which frame their lives.

NOTES

1. Fatima Mernissi's analysis of Muslim conceptualizations of space sees the seclusion of women as a method to protect the purity of the *umma*, the community of believers in which women only exceptionally had a justifiable place. Restricting contact between the sexes – men were not encouraged to linger in the domestic spaces categorized as female – helps to avoid the dangers of *fitna*, the chaos and disorder threatened by illicit sexual thoughts and/or relations which could be sparked by the seductive presence or visibility of women (Mernissi 1985).
2. Although poorer families might screen women from the gaze of non-familial men this was more likely to be achieved by keeping such social interactions outside the home than by the actual architectural division of household space.
3. Konaks were the old large, often wooden, houses of the Istanbul elite which came to typify the most complex, multiple-family living arrangements of the old order. By the first three decades of the twentieth century commentary on the end of the konak lifestyle signalled the shift to modern, Western-model nuclear families and affective rather than arranged marriages (Duben and Behar 1991).
4. On the sapphic subtext of my sources, see Lewis (1999a).
5. Nor was the separation of production into the public as opposed to the private as accentuated as it is often pictured as being in Europe. On the household as unit of family production and women's role in the developing industrial base, see Quartaert (1991).
6. For a reconsideration of the categories public and private in relation to women's role as cultural consumers, see Micklewright (1999).
7. On the remodelling of the city, see Çelik (1986).
8. Loti records secret assignations with Melek Hanum and Zeyneb Hanum at the Sweet Waters. I wish to thank Nancy Micklewright for her discussion of this point with me.
9. It is evident from other references in the book that non-Muslim women generally sat in the 'harem' compartment in trams so one wonders what dynamics were at play as public transport moved towards formal de-segregation with the advent of the republic in 1923.
10. Although it seems from Vaka Brown's comment that this custom had fallen into disuse.
11. For a further discussion of the role of dress and the veil in the performance of racialized gender identities, see Lewis (1999b).
12. The caption to Figure 4 reads 'Although Turkish woman are now good pianists and fond of Western music, they generally like to play the oute [described as the 'Turkish guitar'] at least once a day'.
13. On the contemporary European vogue for Oriental and Oriental-style dress and decor, see Wollen (1987).

REFERENCES

Adivar, H. Edip (1926) *Memoirs of Halide Edip*. London, John Murray.

Apter, E. (1992) 'Female trouble in the Colonial Harem'. *Differences: A Journal of Feminist Cultural Studies*, 4(1): 205–24.

Berkes, N. (1964) *The Development of Secularism in Turkey*. Montreal: McGill University Press.

Çelik, Z. (1986) *The Remaking of Istanbul: Portrait of an Ottoman City in the Nineteenth Century*. Seattle: University of Washington Press.

Çizgen, E. (1987) *Photography in the Ottoman Empire 1839–1919*. Istanbul: Haset Kitalevi.

Duben, A. and Behar, C. (1991) *Istanbul Households: Marriage, Family and Fertility, 1880–1940*. Cambridge: Cambridge University Press.

Ellison, G. (1915) *An Englishwoman in a Turkish Harem*. London: Methuen.

Kalogeras, Y.D. (1989) A child of the Orient as American storyteller: Demetra Vaka Brown. In Parkin-Gounelas, R. (ed.) *Working Papers in Linguistics and Literature*. Thessaloniki: Aristotle University Press.

Keddie, N.R. (1991) Introduction: Deciphering Middle Eastern women's history. In Keddie, N.R. and Baron, B. (eds) *Women in Middle Eastern History: Shifting Boundaries in Sex and Gender*. New Haven: Yale University Press.

Lefebvre, H. (1991) *The Production of Space*, trans. Donald Nicholson-Smith. Oxford: Blackwell.

Lewis, R. (1999a) Cross-cultural reiterations: Demetra Vaka Brown and the performance of racialised female beauty. In Jones, A. and Stephenson, A. (eds) *Performing the Body/Performing the Text*. London: Routledge.

Lewis, R. (1999b) 'On veiling, vision and visibility: cross cultural dressing and narratives of identity. In *Interventions*, 1(4): 500–20.

Melek Hanoum (1926) How I escaped from the harem and how I became a dressmaker. *The Strand Magazine*, February, pp. 129–138.

Melman, B. (1992) *Women's Orients: English Women and the Middle East, 1718–1918. Sexuality, Religion and Work*. Basingstoke: Macmillan.

Mernissi, F. (1985) *Beyond the Veil: Male–Female Dynamics in Muslim Society*, 2nd edn. London: al Saqi.

Peirce, L. (1993) *The Imperial Harem: Women and Sovereignty in the Ottoman Empire*. Oxford: Oxford University Press.

Quataert, D. (1991) Ottoman women, households, and textile manufacturing 1800–1914. In Keddie N.R. and Baron B. (eds) *Women in Middle Eastern History: Shifting Boundaries in Sex and Gender*. New Haven: Yale University Press.

Shaw, S.J. and Shaw, E.K. (1994) *History of the Ottoman Empire and Modern Turkey, vol. 2. Reform, Revolution and Republic*, 2nd edn. Cambridge: Cambridge University Press.

Vaka Brown, D. (1909) *Some Pages from the Life of Turkish Women*. London: Constable.

Vaka Brown, D. (1915) *A Child of the Orient*. London: John Lane.

Vaka Brown, D. (1923) *The Unveiled Ladies of Stamboul*. Boston: Houghton Mifflin.

Wollen, P. (1987) Fashion/Orientalism/the body. *New Formations* 1, Spring, 5–33.

Zeyneb Hanoum (1913) *A Turkish Woman's European Impressions*, Ellison, G. (ed.). London: Seeley, Service Co.

CHAPTER 9

THROUGH THE LOOKING-GLASS DARKLY: GENDERING THE PRIMITIVE AND THE SIGNIFICANCE OF CONSTRUCTED SPACE IN THE PRACTICE OF THE BRÜCKE[1]

Colin Rhodes

The *Künstlergruppe Brücke* was formed in Dresden in 1905 and dissolved amid much acrimony in Berlin in 1913. Among its key members were Erich Heckel (1883–1970), Ernst Ludwig Kirchner (1880–1938), Otto Mueller (1874–1930), Max Pechstein (1881–1955) and Karl Schmidt-Rottluff (1884–1976). The group is perhaps still best known for its powerful graphic work and primitivistic paintings of bathers in 'nature'. Also important in their collective œuvre, though generally less well known, is a large body of images of human figures in exotic interior settings that began to appear in their work around 1910. While at first sight they seem to be imaginative compositions related to a romantic yearning for some unspecified and fictional primitive arcadia, much in them is in fact the result of picture-making from direct observation. The few extant photographs of Kirchner's studios in Dresden around 1910 (Figure 1) and Berlin two years later (Figure 2) show rooms hung with blankets and batiks painted at first in a vaguely 'oriental' fashion and later in styles clearly derived from Tribal Art. Among the pseudo-exotic patterning – later to become a leitmotiv of Art Deco – could be found erotic scenes which the artists complemented with their own sculpture, furniture and utensils carved in a 'primitive' style.[2] The photographic evidence corresponds closely with elements in paintings and graphic work dating from this time thereby allowing a more comprehensive visualization of these otherwise lost spaces to be attained.

The 'primitive' sources to which the Brücke turned in Germany were comparable with those of the Fauves and Picasso in France, not least because of the common important formative role played by Paul Gauguin in both countries. It is probably partly through their understanding of Gauguin's Tahitian work that the Brücke turned around 1908 to sixth-century Indian Buddhist painting as their first exotic 'primitive' influence,[3] rather than African or Oceanic sculpture, which they did not 'discover' until 1909 – some two or three years after the Fauve painters Maurice Vlaminck, André Derain and Henri Matisse. Like their French counterparts they came to Tribal Art initially mainly through visits to ethnographic museums – in Dresden and Berlin – although unlike them they were not collectors.[4] Significantly,

Figure 1   E.L. Kirchner, Kirchner's Studio in Dresden, Berliner Strasse 65, c. 1910–1911. (Photo: Fotoarchiv Bolliger-Ketterer, Wichtrach/Bern. Copyright by Ingeborg and Dr Wolfgang Henze-Ketterer, Wichtrach/Bern)

Figure 2 E.L. Kirchner, *Kirchner and Erna Schilling in the studio in Berlin-Wilmersdorf, Durlacher Strasse 14, c. 1912.* (Photo: Fotoarchiv Bolliger-Ketterer, Wichtrach/Bern. Copyright by Ingeborg and Dr Wolfgang Henze-Ketterer, Wichtrach/Bern)

the most interesting transformations of 'primitive' sources in their work occur in the context of the studios which they began to decorate probably in late 1909.[5]

THE BRÜCKE STUDIOS

During the Brücke's most important period of activity (c. 1910–1913) the artists' studios were the locus of their practice the crucible into which ideas were poured and artistic transformations wrought. Particularly in the cases of Heckel, Kirchner and Pechstein they served the dual function of both living and working spaces. In this respect, it is important to recognize from the outset that the quasi-primitive furniture and decorative elements were an integral and functional part of complex, bohemian spaces; as much a part of their daily life as the more conventional crockery visible in the photograph of Kirchner and his partner Erna Schilling in Pechstein's Berlin studio.[6] In numerous drawings, especially by Heckel, such as *Nude in a room*, 1912 (Brücke-Museum, Berlin) and *In the studio*, 1913 (Museum Folkwang, Essen), figures often appear among the exotic clutter engaged in mundane domestic activities. Significantly, the figures may be clothed or naked. Either way the viewer is expected to read these as scenes of an easy naturalness.

Two elements are key to understanding the symbolic function of the studio decor in the context of the activities that took place both in the real spaces and within the fictive spaces of Brücke images of interiors, namely, an overt display of sexuality and the presence – in almost every object – of the notionally primitive. Kirchner's own photographs of his Dresden studio reveal murals and drapes depicting naked couples engaged in various sexual acts, in a style related to low relief carvings on house beams from the Palau Islands, Micronesia which the artist had seen in the Dresden Ethnographic Museum, as well as to Javanese shadow puppets which were popular in the music halls frequented by the Brücke artists. Such overtly erotic subject matter refers at least in part to a perceived relationship between artistic creation and the sexual act, related to the artists' reading of Friedrich Nietzsche, whose claim that making art is 'another way of making children'[7] was a common one at the end of the nineteenth century. Kirchner would later describe the Brücke project as a 'naïve attempt to bring art and life into harmony'.[8] Significantly though, his assertion that 'only at home did I have complete freedom in my work'[9] belies the fact that the sexual practices of the artists and the bohemian spaces they inhabited helped to situate the Brücke unequivocally outside 'normal' discourse.

The studio decoration extended to anthropomorphic furniture and utensils carved in a rough style reminiscent of 'primitive' prototypes from Africa, Oceania and European folk carving traditions.[10] The photograph of Kirchner and Erna Schilling shows the decoration augmented by exotic fans and Japanese umbrellas, as well as Kirchner's copy of a painted Buddha from Ajanta, India[11] and these constantly reappear in paintings and graphics. The range of stylistic sources discernible in studio photographs also serves to emphasise the unspecified nature of the 'primitive' in the artists' minds. Characteristically, connections between objects from Africa, Oceania, the Far East, and other places outside Europe are inferred by projecting into them the qualities of a shared eroticism and a spontaneous and emotional use of materials, which the Brücke subsequently carried over into their art.[12] This is especially evident in woodcuts like Heckel's *Couple*, 1910 (Museum Folkwang, Essen), in which the characteristically deliberate rough cutting of the woodblock, without the aid of preliminary drawing, stands as a metaphor for the 'naturalness' of the sexual act depicted.

The decorated studios were also populated with sculptures of the human figure which took their place in the 'life' of the studios beside the figurative murals and the artists' flesh-and-blood models and girlfriends from whom they were almost inevitably derived. The sculptures give few clues as to their function when viewed as isolated *objets d'art*,[13] although something of their place in the Brücke scheme is indicated by photographs of the studios. However, their importance is thrown into sharp relief when paintings and graphic work are read in relation to their constituent parts: for example, the wooden figure in Kirchner's drawing *Two Nudes with Sculpture*, 1911 (Museum Ludwig, Cologne), is not only animated, but occupies something like the same order of existence as the models through the unifying manipulation of the pencil medium.[14] Kirchner goes even further in *Fränzi in Front of a Carved Chair*, 1910 (Thyssen-Bornemisza Collection, Lugano), in which the anthropomorphic backrest of a carved bench[15] is treated in a manner that is, in many respects, more naturalistic than a flesh and blood model in an inversion of his large preparatory chalk drawing (Städtische Galerie im Städelschen Kunstinstitut, Frankfurt).

The formal unification of studio elements and human participants in Brücke studio scenes is further highlighted in Kirchner's *Nude behind a curtain: Fränzi*, 1910/26 (Figure 3). A photograph of Kirchner's studio (Figure 1) taken from an almost identical viewpoint as the painted composition shows that despite its heightened use of colour and rough facture it is a surprisingly faithful rendition of the actual studio space. The accepted title notwithstanding, the model stands in front of a recess, flanked by drapes painted with erotic figures derived from Indian, Javanese and Palau prototypes. The indistinct object in the bottom right-hand corner is, in fact, a roughly carved anthropomorphic stool (visible in the photograph) whose embracing figures are reminiscent of certain Luba headrests from Zaire, and the background pattern relates to a mural containing more erotic figures. The rough, presumably brightly coloured, construction of the actual studio setting is here typically transferred to the nude 'Fränzi' who, in this way, is herself once again implicated in the fictive construction of an alternative reality.[16]

PUBLIC AND PRIVATE SPACES

Heckel, Kirchner and Pechstein, the Brücke artists most committed to avant-garde ideologies, were city dwellers. They lived on the whole in the poorer and industrial quarters of Dresden and Berlin and believed themselves to be living outside, or at least on the periphery, of dominant Wilhelmine society. Accordingly, they chose to construct 'exotic' studios not in the South Seas, as in the case of Gauguin, but physically in the heart of bustling urban centres. The studios provided a self-

Figure 3 *E.L. Kirchner, Nude behind a curtain; Fränzi* (Nacktes Mädchen hinter Vorhang; Fränzi), *1910/26. Oil on canvas, 120 × 90 cm. Stedelijk Museum, Amsterdam. Copyright by Ingeborg and Dr Wolfgang Henze-Ketterer, Wichtrach/Bern*

consciously constructed space *within* the city physically, but *outside* it meta-phorically *and* morally. Yet, despite the fairly rich, though tantalisingly mute, visual evidence of the artists' way of life in Dresden and Berlin accessible today through drawings, graphic work and photographs, for contemporary viewers (except for a few close associates and patrons) knowledge of, and access to, the private spaces that were central to their practice was denied. Before the end of the First World War it was only possible for the public to intuit this private arena through paintings and graphics which were moderated to a certain extent to appeal to a projected middle-class audience whose taste in progressive styles was not necessarily matched by sexually progressive attitudes. For example, although images of naked men and women together in the studios abound in Brücke work in the essentially *private* medium of drawing, they are relatively few in the *public* medium of painting. Where scenes of mixed nudity do occur in paintings it is often in the guise of representations of Europe's others, entirely in keeping with Orien-talist pictorial traditions established in the previous century, as in, for example, Pechstein's *Woman and Indian on a rug*, 1910 (Ketterer Kunst, Munich)

By their very nature, the studio-cum-living spaces provided the Brücke with what Louis Marin has called in another context a 'neutral place', which charac-terizes their essentially utopian base. This is a place 'whose characteristics are semiotically negative, whose specificity consists in being *neither* one *nor* the other, neither this edge nor the other'.[17] They had, on the one side, the city, with its (apparently) clearly defined social, cultural and moral boundaries – its institu-tions speak the 'norm'; its functions are activated by the impersonal desire for a dynamic of progress which nevertheless maintains the status quo. On the other side chaos threatens: we know from published writings and from drawings that artists, as well as models, often went naked, which is symbolic of the 'freedom' to which they aspired and of a break with the hegemony of Wilhelm II's Germany that promised an alternative way of life that was transforming, but (because it was based on individualism above all), remained relatively *unformed*. The conflation of daily life and the fictive existence of their pictures created a precarious reality constantly under threat from the physical proximity of the city and from the tenuousness of an approach to creativity that was driven by a Dionysiac belief in the transforming power of sexuality.

The instability of their urban situation was an important creative element for Heckel, Kirchner and Pechstein and none of them exhibited strong desires to establish a community literally outside the city and thereby beyond the con-ventional and legal constrictions of city life. That they were actively engaged with urban life is shown by the numerous topographical representations of the city that appear alongside other subjects throughout the group's existence. Kirchner's painting, *Dresden-Friedrichstadt*, 1910 (Kunstmuseum Hannover), for example, depicts a smartly dressed couple and three children playing on a wide sweeping road before a group of factory buildings, which is markedly different in feeling to the series of troubled, expressionist Berlin street scenes he began in 1913.

The Brücke's rejection of hegemonic culture was a feature of a bohemianism closer in spirit to elements of the Parisian avant-garde since the mid nineteenth century than the reactionary back-to-nature movements that rejected the modern industrial city out of hand. There was never any question of them joining or attempting to establish one of the rural artists' colonies that were common throughout Europe and the north-eastern seaboard of the USA at the beginning of the twentieth century and among them only Emil Nolde had any formal connection to the famous sanatoria around Dresden, which promised health through nudism, fresh air and sport.[18] Like their Parisian counterparts their bohemianism sheltered a desire to be successful artists with all that that entailed. Thus, many drawings and paintings containing incomers from the city 'outside' the studio space present strangely neutral juxtapositions of naked models, primitivizing studio decoration and fashionably clothed visitors. In the case of Kirchner's *Studio scene*, c. 1910–11 (Nationalgalerie, Berlin), the painter Erich Heckel and Kirchner's girlfriend Doris Grosse (Dodo) provide the sophisticated urban juxtaposition to the nude female model (Marzella), a figurative sculpture and two painted representations of dancing figures.

METAPHORS FOR FREEDOM

The founder members of the Brücke had met as students of architecture at the Dresden Technische Hochschule, during which time it is probable that they became aware of *Jugendstil* or Art Nouveau ideals through the important Belgian architect and artist Henry van de Velde via a number of channels.[19] Kirchner had also brought with him from his studies in Munich at the famous Obrist-Debschitz School the *Jugendstil* belief that art exists in everything one makes; that it is essential to and synonymous with life. He tells us that the Brücke struggled 'with pure problems of art and [placed] its outward life so completely in the service of this struggle that general human considerations perished'.[20] With Heckel, he says, 'we tackled the nature of the girls in my studio and of the men, whom we drew in complete naturalness without posing'.[21] Elsewhere he points out that, 'I never had models in the academic sense' and, precisely because his 'models' consisted of friends, acquaintances and lovers, 'I gained a deeper understanding of human psychology by getting to know my subjects better as human beings'.[22]

Spontaneity and emotionalism are signifiers of a freedom from conventional social strictures to which the Brücke aspired. They are central to their earliest published programme which claimed for their cause 'everyone who with directness and authenticity conveys that which drives him to creation'.[23] Sexual liberation, too, was an important aspect of the quest for authentic experiences and their translation into art. It is, perhaps, not surprising then that Brücke studio decoration not only tends to be highly sexually charged, but that their stylistic sources consist of an amorphous mixture of the art of notionally primitive peoples. Thus, the formal qualities of the figures painted in the roundels of studio hangings and those painted on the walls clearly relate to Palau prototypes, but the overtly erotic subject matter – the pictures depict various acts of sexual intercourse which would certainly have been viewed as deviant by contemporary medical and psychiatric standards – refers to the perceived relationship between artistic creation and the sexual act, which is in this case closely linked to the Brücke artists' interest in oriental erotic writings such as *The Thousand and One Nights* and *The Perfumed Garden*. The unifying factor in all this and, indeed, what raises the overt sexuality of Brücke representations of women above the usual power relationship of domi- nating (male) artistic presence to subjugated (female) model is the gendering of both the spaces and activities undertaken by artist and model alike in the femin- ine. The exoticism inherent in the erotic studio decorations is key to the role played by the studios in Brücke art, for it points to the transformations of complex gendered hegemonic notions of the 'primitive' that operate in their work.

The mirror of artistic primitivism held up to the studio/environments and their occupants by the Brücke relies upon the achievement of a convincing relationship between figures and setting. This occurs mainly in two ways: firstly, by means of a modernist style, which draws upon recent French art as well as notionally 'primitive' forms; and secondly, through the artists' choice of particular *types* of model. In the first place, the various Brücke styles in Dresden and Berlin and, in the case of Kirchner, work made in Switzerland long after the demise of the group, consist of a broad, expressive handling of forms which unify the human figure and its surroundings – so that in the studio works, as I have argued, the rough facture of the actual decoration is transferred to the forms of the models. In addition, the models for these works can (with the occasional, though notable exception of portraits of middle-class patrons like Gustave Schiefler and Rosa Schapire) be identified as 'outsiders' themselves, such as variety artists (including black performers from the *Cirkus Schumann*), dancers, and a number of working-class children.

GENDERED OPPOSITIONS

The appropriation of notionally primitive forms by the Brücke artists was part of a characteristic modernist policy of artistic innovation and cultural opposition and the early redefinition of tribal objects as 'art' in Europe should be viewed in these terms. Interest in the 'primitive' indicates a further questioning of the validity of assumptions about the superiority of Western viewpoints by valuing precisely those people previously held up by the West as culturally, technologically and sometimes even mentally deficient. It is the challenge to dominant Western view- points that interests me here. But I am also interested in the paradox that the Brücke had recourse only to *Western* formulations about its others. Thus, the artists' attack was conducted through inversion and their vitalist battleground was fraught with unresolved and, for them, unresolvable issues of gender, race and sexuality.

Representations of women in the art of Brücke are crucially important here because the *generic* Woman is the link to ideas about the nature of the primitive in late nineteenth-century medico-scientific discourse and thereby the path to sub- version in the practice of Brücke.[24] That women were commonly defined nega- tively in terms of their difference to men at this time is underscored by the arguments of Social Darwinists like Herbert Spencer and Ernst Haeckel. Ideas about the supposed proximity to nature and to the 'primitive' of women in general were utilized throughout scientific writing and literature in the Victorian age in order to theorize both their essentially passive and reactionary character and, by extension, the essentially 'feminine' character of 'primitive' society. For example, writing in 1864, the early anthropologist Carl Vogt remarked upon what he saw as the comparatively small degree of specialization in the social function of the sexes in 'primitive' societies while, 'among the civilised nations, there is a division both in physical and mental labour', with man taking the lion's share of the burden in the latter case. Because of this, he reasoned, 'woman' has maintained her fundamental conservatism, so that, 'just as, in respect of morals, woman is the conservator of old customs [and] usages, of traditions, legends, and religion; so in the material world she preserves primitive forms'.[25]

There is a common tendency in Western art from this period which attempts to deal with questions of otherness to conflate notions about the value of direct creation in art, the physiological and psychological status of modern European women, and the supposedly 'primitive' nature of tribal peoples. Similarly with the projection of feminization in these ideas. Gauguin's experience in Tahiti is a case in point. Despite the obvious hardship endured by him in the South Seas, the paintings he sent home to France were almost without exception images of noble savages living in harmony with a fertile and bountiful Nature. In pictures like *Tahitian Women Bathing*, 1892 (Metropolitan Museum of Art, New York), he transformed the traditional painted subject of the female nude for his Parisian audience into a doubly powerful image of a generalized exotic 'Woman' and a world fully feminized. In a crude piece of evolutionist reasoning Gauguin extended this feminization to the Tahitian males, referring to the 'androgynous aspect of the savage' of both sexes owing to their presumed underdeveloped state of physiological specialization. This accounts for the similarity of the male and female figures in *The Man with the Axe*, 1891 (private collection), and serves as the artist's justification to himself for the homosexual fantasy he related in his Tahitian 'journal' *Noa Noa*.[26] In the art of Heckel and Kirchner, too, there is a progressive collapsing of the physiological distinction between male and female figures in the years leading up to the First World War which results not so much in the 'feminization' of males as to a marked tendency to a common androgyny – though this is at its most pronounced in outdoor bathing pictures, rather than studio scenes.

In the present context it is important to add that in addition to the generally 'primitive' nature assigned to 'civilized' women in the West, the sexualized Western female was generally regarded in terms of the disease model as a *degenerate type* and therefore doubly 'primitive'.[27] Though the prostitute – that stereotype of the sexualized Western female at the end of the nineteenth century – appears in a series of nocturnal street scenes painted by Kirchner between 1913 and 1915 in which a terrible atavistic beauty is indeed implied in the women's gothic frames and mask-like faces, she is generally relatively absent as a subject in the output of the Brücke. Instead we find images of sexually liberated women, offered in a matter-of-fact way, whose cultural and social specificity is difficult to identify. However, their siting in the quasi-primitive decorated studios and their implied active sexuality place them at the periphery of contemporary bourgeois society and

Figure 4 *E.L. Kirchner, Nude couple on a sofa (Nacktes Paar auf einem Kanapee), 1909. Woodcut, 65.5 × 47.7 cm (image). Private collection. Copyright by Ingeborg and Dr Wolfgang Henze-Ketterer, Wichtrach/Bern*

unintentionally allows for the possibility of the early twentieth-century viewer to draw parallels between their conduct and the morality of the prostitute.

Brücke depictions of women usually function antagonistically, as images of 'pathological', primitivized female types *transformed* and *normalized* through the representation. Active female sexuality is a central theme in Brücke images and accordingly, these women tend to be situated outside the normalizing confines of the bourgeois home and, significantly, they fulfil roles that are inconsistent with those expected by and acceptable to bourgeois moral and social codes. Moreover, they are often joined by men, who have 'descended' to a state of primitiveness to take their place also in that feminized world, as in Kirchner's woodcut *Nude couple on a sofa*, 1909 (Figure 4). Erotic subject matter pervades Brücke drawings especially, but the overwhelming feeling communicated by these works is of human beings flouting convention and attempting to lead a sensual existence. In many of them we find evidence of a pleasure in the senses that owes little to Nietzsche's misogyny and much to the American poet Walt Whitman, whose *Leaves of Grass* offered the artists (in particular Kirchner) a less complicated, more idealistic vision of the world based in the present, and one that pledged both the essential beauty of the sexual act and equality between the sexes.

PHYSIOLOGICAL TRANSFORMATIONS

Formal distortions in representations of the human figure by the Brücke should not be equated unequivocally with the idiosyncrasies of a modernist pictorial style. There is much in the artists' rendition of the human form, particularly in the work of Kirchner, and to some extent Heckel and Schmidt-Rottluff, that relates Expressionist distortion to attempts to incorporate specific physiological signs of otherness as markers of an assertion of their own (and their models') difference within Wilhelmine culture. Many Brücke works, in common with other early modernist examples, bring into play conventional early twentieth-century beliefs about the fundamental difference between the features of primitive and civilized peoples as an integral part of the representation. This extends much further than differences in skin colour or hair types to facial and other body features, notably those relating to primary and secondary sex characteristics in both men and women. Thus, the bodies of white Europeans are often rendered strange in their work not only by employing an anti-academic, modernist style, but also through the use of bodily features specific to notionally primitive 'types'. In this way conventional ideas about the primitive are used as a means of challenging Europe's image of itself.

Emerging anthropological interest in an ethnic basis for differing ideals of (inevitably feminine) 'beauty' was widespread at the beginning of the twentieth century – in Germany, Ploss and Bartels' *Das Weib* (first published in 1885, but substantially revised and expanded over the next two decades) devoted a whole section to a comparative survey of 'beauty in racial types'. The information gathered in such texts was almost invariably interpreted in ways that supported assertions of European superiority (and in the case of *Das Weib* northern European superiority). In these dominant discourses Third World bodies were typed as 'primitive' and displeasing to 'civilized' sensibility; inferiority was theorized through physiognomy. This is characterized by the practice of publicly displaying the 'primitive' body in exhibitions and zoos from the end of the eighteenth century.

The assertion of difference through incorporation of 'primitive' characteristics appears strongly, though briefly, in Heckel's and Kirchner's interest in sixteenth-century Buddhist paintings from Ajanta, India, which resulted in images such as Kirchner's *Five Women Bathers*, 1911 (Brücke-Museum, Berlin), where the forms of the 'primitive' prototype are transposed in idealized depictions of European models. The most strident transformations of Western notions of beauty, though, occur as a result of the artists' dialogue with the arts of Africa and Oceania and the idea of the black body itself. The Brücke's experience of actual extra-European peoples occurred in a European context – in exhibitions, the variety theatre, the circus, popular published sources, and from their acquaintance with a number of performers who appear in studio works like Pechstein's *Woman and Indian on a rug* and Kirchner's Gauguinesque, *Milli sleeping*, 1911 (Kunsthalle, Bremen). In common with most Europeans, the Brücke artists made little distinction between tribal peoples and blacks of the diaspora. Thus, in studio pictures the black body often functions as an additional marker of the primitive irrespective of the national and cultural identity of the model, while in images of black dancers and musicians exoticism is emphasized to the point of denying the context of the German theatres in which they took place.

Heckel, Kirchner and Pechstein depicted the black circus performers Sam, Nelly and Milli in the studio many times in all media. Yet nowhere among the extant paintings and graphics are we presented either with images that emphasize the primary markers of 'primitive' sexuality, namely the women's genitalia, or with more active demonstrations through representations of the sexual act. On the contrary, there are two closely related images by Kirchner and Heckel respectively, painted from life in Heckel's Dresden studio,[28] that show Nelly, a friend of Heckel's future wife, the dancer Siddi Riha. In the picture she is portrayed not as a hired model, but as a guest in the artist's studio. Like so many other female visitors depicted by Heckel and Kirchner in the studio she is wearing fashionable European dress. Any real sense of her otherness lies not so much in the colour of her skin, but in her positioning within the bohemian space of the Brücke studio and in the self-conscious modernism of the artists' styles, which relate these images directly to other studio scenes. Nevertheless, pictures of white models produced by Heckel and Kirchner around the same time as their representations of these particular blacks are often possessed of unashamedly sexually explicit iconographies. The woman in Heckel's *Nude*, 1910 (private collection), for example, who is a white European, displays unself-consciously her genital region. And in one of Kirchner's last images of his Dresden girlfriend Doris Grosse, *Nude with Black Hat*, 1912 (private collection), the artist goes as far as to represent in almost medical detail a hypertrophy of the labia – a sign of 'primitive' hypersexuality and pathology in early twentieth-century medico-scientific discourse.

However, the clearest indication of Kirchner's utilization of the primary markers of hypersexuality can be found in a series of six lithographs depicting a couple in various acts of sexual intercourse (Figure 5).[29] They are set in the Dresden studio, but their apparent status as 'matter-of-fact' life drawings is betrayed by Kirchner's tendency to manipulate the shape of the studio decoration so that it corresponds to the shapes of the figures' genitals.[30] The continued underlying power of the image of the hypersexual black in Western culture is emphasized by the fact that the series has since been consistently identified by art historians, apparently on no evidence whatsoever, as depicting Sam and Milli. Yet, when one compares the physiognomies of the figures in this series with known depictions of the pair and other comparable works in which European models are used, it becomes clear that the *Lovers* series depicts a different couple who are, moreover, almost certainly white Europeans.

Kirchner's primitivism is made more subtly manifest in his pictorial use of a physiological condition that had come to be seen as a specific sign for the primitive sexuality of the African woman, namely *steatopygia* (protruding buttocks), a

Figure 5 *E.L. Kirchner, Lovers VI (Liebespaar VI), 1911. Lithograph, 16.8 × 21 cm (image). Private collection. Copyright by Ingeborg and Dr Wolfgang Henze-Ketterer, Wichtrach/Bern. (The present author's original intention of displaying Libespaar IV which demonstrates clearly the visual point discussed in the text alongside VI has unfortunately not proved possible in practice)*

condition most common in the 'Hottentots' of southern Africa and much reproduced in early twentieth-century photographs in popular as well as scientific
literature.[31] The British psychologist Havelock Ellis argued in his *The Psychology
of Sex* (1897) that steatopygia was actually a biological caprice – 'a kind of
naturally fatty tumour' – designed to compensate for the 'primitive' pelvis of the
black as against the beauty of the broad sacrum of 'The white race'.[32] Through his
use of language he placed the Hottentot physiognomy firmly within the category of
the abnormal and the pathological. This is confirmed by Ploss and Bartels in *Das
Weib*, where a full section is devoted to steatopygia, mainly concerning the peoples
of southern Africa, though they point to European cases in which 'gluteal development [is] so pronounced that they are almost steatopygous'.[33] The two women in
their example are of Latin extraction and, moreover, prostitutes, which is significant in a German text that typically saw not only fundamental evolutionary
distance between Europe and its others, but which also subscribed to the notion
(common deep into the twentieth century in popular culture) of significant difference between southern and northern European 'racial' types. Their identification
as prostitutes serves only to confirm for Ploss and Bartels the 'primitive' sexuality
already signified by their bodies.

In Kirchner's pictures of Milli and Nelly, the supposed hypersexuality of the
women can be inferred not by the sexual act, but by the shape of their bodies sited
in the gendered space of the studio. He characteristically emphasizes the proportions of thighs and buttocks in images of black women with the implication that
they have an intrinsically sexual identity. More significantly, insofar as I have
argued that representations of figures in the studio setting perform an essentially

utopian act, at the same time Kirchner often extended this device to his European models in pictures where an apparent steatopygia is actually much more exaggerated. It is clearly visible, for example, in paintings such as *Nude in Bathtub*, 1911 (Kunsthalle, Kiel) or *Bather between rocks*, 1912 (private collection). Kirchner's utilization of such signs for the 'primitive' in these works should be read in the context of his perception of the women's own relative liberation from the constraints placed on the display of sexuality by contemporary German cultural and legal mores. In *Nude in Bathtub* the 'africanization' of the European bather is brought into sharp focus by means of her juxtaposition with a 'primitive' anthropomorphic stool or table. Carved by the artist in a vaguely African style, the piece of furniture serves further to emphasize the conflation of the black body and the forms of African and Oceanic sculpture that often occurs in the work of European artists at this time. There are also a number of related pictures of Kirchner's partner Erna Schilling which exhibit a clever utilization of stereotypes of African physiognomy. In the painting *Seated Woman with Wood Sculpture*, 1912 (Virginia Museum of Fine Arts), for example, the active sexuality of the fully clothed woman is sublimated in the pseudo-primitive sculpture at her side.

CONCLUSION

I have argued that the Brücke studios are characteristically sites that are saturated by gendered notions of primitive authenticity and directness – in life as in sexuality. Also, that they are spaces in which a hypothesized existential equality between men and women is played out. In this respect the studios seem to contain utopian aspirations for that community of individuals meeting briefly and taking their leave of each other without a sense of loss or regret conjured up by Whitman in 'I Sing the Body Electric':

> I have perceiv'd that to be with those I like is enough,
> To stop in company with the rest at evening is enough,
> To be surrounded by beautiful, curious, breathing, laughing flesh is enough,
> To pass among them or touch any one, or rest my arm ever slightly round his
>   or her neck for a moment, what is this then?
> I do not ask any more delight, I swim in it as in a sea
>
> There is something in staying close to men and women and looking on them,
>   and in the contact and odor of them, that pleases the soul well,
> All things please the soul, but these please the soul well

These are, however, environments that are gendered in the 'feminine', where issues of (cultural) control are problematized, but not resolved. While it is not surprising, therefore, that there are many images in which men and women occupy the same spaces in Brücke studio scenes, the majority do depict females only. In the case of the latter, another presence is implied in the form of the viewer – who may be hypothesized as a single individual or a group of people. This imaginary viewer does not simply fulfil the role of the (controlling) artistic gaze and is by no means necessarily gendered as 'masculine'. This is one of the reasons why these representations often are not easy to 'consume'. Images like Kirchner's *Girl Under a Japanese Umbrella*, 1909 (Kunstsammlung Nordrhein-Westfalen, Düsseldorf), or Heckel's coloured woodcut *Standing Child* (1910) are problematical (perhaps unsettling) not because they offer an image of the subjugating male gaze, but because the viewer is hypothesized within the picture space as a *participating* presence.

In emphasizing the sense of community that the Brücke strove to achieve with their models in the studio pictures, and which is mediated through the 'primitive' studio environment itself, I wish to point to the intimacy of these works. This is surely more productive than conventional readings which simply define the studios as urban extensions of the Moritzburg ponds near Dresden, to which the artists made summer bathing and drawing trips. By the middle of the first decade of the twentieth century there was nothing particularly unusual in such 'retreats' from the city as were practised by the Brücke from at least 1906 onwards. However, the self-conscious bohemianism of their studio life after about 1909 remained strange; essentially different not just to the characteristics of the cities in which they were contained, but more importantly to the typical bourgeois home which represented (perhaps with the exception of Pechstein) the artists' own background, as well as the home environment of almost all their patrons and critics. For the latter, especially, the 'primitive' remains unquestionably exotic – they are merely visitors, who will return afterwards to their 'normal' lives. Yet, for the Brücke themselves – and particularly Kirchner – the studio spaces represented precisely their day-to-day working and social environments. In this respect, the decorated studios should not be read as essays in escapism, but rather as an effective and convenient means of situating the artists in a functioning environment that lies outside (or at least at the periphery of) bourgeois society, whilst allowing for a continued and necessary engagement with that very culture.

In this the painters of the Brücke – particularly Heckel and Kirchner – departed fundamentally from the likes of Matisse, in whose work 'exotic' studio objects were utilized simply as decorative props in much the same manner as academic painters at the end of the nineteenth century. Thus, Matisse's interiors of the 1920s which are ostensibly related to Brücke studio works of the previous decade characteristically distance the practice of making art from that of living a life. The sense of community (in any profound sense) was never very strong among the Brücke painters. The drift apart began as early as 1908 when Pechstein moved to Berlin, and in 1913 the group finally split. Utopian ideals based on apolitical, single-minded individualism might, it could be argued, be bound to fail, but the remnants of the fragile edifice erected around the Brücke studios were in any case wiped away emphatically in 1914 by that most impersonal and absurd engine of the state, war.

NOTES

1. This essay has developed over a number of years. Its content has been explored in different forms in lectures delivered at the Association of Art Historians Conference in Newcastle (1996) and at the Wellcome Institute, London (1997). Parts of the discussion

have appeared in similar form in Dutch in my 'Fauvisme en expressionisme' (in A. Martis and M. Rijnders, (ed.), *Expressionisme en primitivisme*, (Heerlen, 1998, pp. 47–100)). I would like to thank all those people who have made critical contributions to the project, but especially most latterly Mieke Rijnders for her help and friendly encouragement.

2. In fact very little of this decoration was actually tribal in origin. The highly-finished Cameroon Leopard Stool visible in a photograph of Kirchner's Berlin studio (see Nationalgalerie Berlin, *Ernst Ludwig Kirchner 1880–1938*. Exh. cat. Berlin, 1979, p. 19) and Heckel's *Girl with Pineapple*, 1910 (whereabouts unknown) is a notable exception.

3. The artists' knowledge of this imagery was gleaned not from the originals, but from John Griffiths' book *The Paintings in the Buddhist Cave-Temples of Ajanta, Khandesh, India* (London, 1896–1897) (see D.E. Gordon, 'Kirchner in Dresden', *The Art Bulletin* 48 (1966) 357ff).

4. Emil Nolde (only briefly a member of Brücke, in 1907) is an exception. Heckel, Pechstein and Schmidt-Rottluff began acquiring Tribal Art only later, Kirchner not at all.

5. Much work has been done by numerous scholars since Donald Gordon's groundbreaking research in the 1960s in attempting to establish a chronology for the successive studio decorations. The accumulated material is collected and discussed in J. Lloyd, *German Expressionism: Primitivism and Modernity* (New Haven and London, 1991), pp. 21–48.

6. Heckel, Kirchner, Pechstein and Mueller appear to have maintained highly decorated studio/living spaces into the First World War, though only Kirchner continued to develop this in its bohemian conception (in self-imposed exile in Switzerland) after the war.

7. Nietzsche, *The Will to Power*. Translated by W. Kaufmann and R.J. Hollingdale, New York, 1968, p. 421. In another aphorism concerning the viewer, he tells us: 'The demand for art and beauty is an indirect demand for the ecstasies of sexuality communicated to the brain' (p. 424).

8. Diary, 6 March 1923 (in L. Grisebach (ed.), *E.L. Kirchners Davoser Tagebuch* (Cologne, 1968), p. 78).

9. Diary, 1 March 1923 (ibid., p. 74).

10. There are precedents in the European context of which the Brücke artists were almost certainly aware, for example, in decorated furniture and utensils made by Gauguin and the School of Pont-Aven which relied heavily on Breton folk art traditions. The Dresden artists may have become familiarized with similar north European folk practices through Nolde and the Finnish painter Axel Gallen Kallela, both members of the Brücke for a time.

11. The studios are all now destroyed and very little remains of their contents. Exceptions include two anthropomorphic wooden bowls by Kirchner (1910–1911; private collection and c. 1912; Kirchner-Haus Davos) and his copy of the Buddha (c. 1910; Bündner Kunstmuseum, Chur), and Pechstein's batik, *At the Seashore* (c. 1910–1911; Brücke Museum, Berlin).

12. Compare Goethe's early praise in 1772 for what he then saw as the holism at the root of the creativity of tribal peoples: 'Art is formative long before it is beautiful,' he says, 'and so the savage articulates his coconut shell, his feathers, his body with fantastical lines, hideous forms and gaudy colours. And even if this making visibly expressive is made up of the most arbitrary forms, they will still harmonize without any obvious relationship between them, for a single feeling has created a characteristic whole. Now this characteristic art is the only true art.' (in J. Gage, *Goethe on Art* (London, 1980)).

13. I make this point because Brücke sculpture, though not originally produced to be viewed as single pieces of art, but as a functioning part of the studio, is now inevitably shown in a decontextualized state. On the importance of Brücke sculpture, see W. Henze, 'Genèse de la sculpture expressioniste' (in Musée d'art moderne de la ville de Paris, *Figures du moderne: L'Expressionisme en Allemagne 1905–1914*, Exh. cat., Paris, 1992, pp. 69–74).

14. For a different and in many ways contrasting interpretation of the relationship between sculptures and models in Kirchner's work see Lloyd, *German Expressionism*, pp. 119–20. The continued importance of sculpture as an animate presence in the studio for Kirchner's later Swiss work is nowhere more clearly evident than in his 1920 *Studio*

scene (Staatliche Museen, Nationalgalerie Berlin), which depicts a room populated only by sculpted figures and in which even the presence of the artist and his partner is alluded to by their carved effigies as the backrest of the so-called 'Adam and Eve Chair' (since destroyed).

15. The linden bench, painted pink and black, was reputedly Kirchner's first carving influenced by Cameroon objects (see Gordon, 'Kirchner in Dresden', p. 354). Now destroyed, it can be seen more clearly in a photograph in the Kirchner estate of a lost painting, *Nude Fränzi in Profile*.

16. As in the previous example the model in Kirchner's gouache sketch for the subject (Museum Folkwang, Essen) is treated in more lifelike colours.

17. L. Marin, 'The Frontiers of Utopia' in S. Bann (ed.), *Utopias and the Millennium* (London, 1993), p. 10.

18. See P. Reece, 'Edith Buckley, Ada Nolde and *Die Brücke*: Bathing, Health and Art in Dresden 1906–1911' in B.K. Smith (ed.), *German Expressionism in the United Kingdom and Ireland* (Bristol, 1985), pp. 22–7.

19. Namely, his German lectures (published in 1902); his participation in the Dresden Exhibition of Applied Arts (1897 and 1906); and his interior decorations for Karl Ernst Osthaus' Folkwang Museum in Hagen (1900–1902).

20. Grisebach, *E.L. Kirchners Davoser Tagebuch*, p. 77.

21. Ibid., p. 74.

22. As quoted in V. Miesel (ed.), *Voices of German Expressionism* (New York, 1970), p. 18.

23. *Programme die Brücke*, Dresden, 1906; as quoted in Selz, *German Expressionist Painting* (Berkeley, 1957), p. 95. Compare Nietzsche's assertion that, 'Artists should see nothing as it is, but fuller, simpler, stronger: to that end, their lives must contain a kind of youth and spring, a kind of habitual intoxication' (*The Will to Power*, p. 421).

24. While it is true that by 1910 many of the scientific assumptions described here and in the ensuing discussion were being questioned by pioneers in the fields of medicine, anthropology and sociology, it must be remembered that the Brücke artists were not specialists in any of these areas. Their understanding (with the exception of certain areas of anthropology) was gained, on the whole, through popular sources which tended to reproduce 'old' knowledge.

25. Vogt, *Lectures on Man*, as quoted in B. Dijkstra, *Idols of Perversity* (Oxford, 1986), pp. 171–2.

26. Gauguin describes a male Tahitian youth in terms of his apparent androgyny: 'From this friendship so well cemented by the mutual attraction between simple and composite, love took power to blossom in me.' Ironically, as Nicholas Wadley points out, 'When Gauguin first arrived in Tahiti, he was dubbed *taata vahine* (man-woman) by the natives, because of his picturesque hat and the shoulder length of his salt-and-pepper hair' P. Gaugin, *Noa Noa*, edited and introduced by N. Wadley (Oxford, 1985, pp. 25, 74).

27. J.-J. Rousseau (*Émile, or Education*, trans. Barbara Foxley. London, n.d.) is no less prey to this assumption than scientists writing a century later. In the final part of *Émile* (Book V) he seems at first to argue that women and men occupy positions of biological equality: 'But for her sex, a woman is a man; she has the same organs, the same needs, the same faculties' (p. 321). However, it quickly becomes clear that he considers that the 'nature' of the two sexes is fundamentally different: 'The man should be strong and active; the woman should be weak and passive' (p. 322); and 'The mutual duties of the two sexes are not, and cannot be, equally binding on both . . . [E]very faithless husband who robs his wife of the sole reward of the stern duties of her sex, is cruel and unjust; but the faithless wife is worse; she destroys the family and breaks the bonds of nature; when she gives her husband children who are not his own . . . her crime is not infidelity but treason' (pp. 324–5).

28. Kirchner, *Portrait of a woman*, 1911 (Albright-Knox Art Gallery, Buffalo) and Heckel, *Nelly (Dresden)*, 1911 (whereabouts unknown, reproduced in Rhodes, 'Fauvisme en expressionisme', p. 81).

29. *Liebspaar I–VI*, 1911. Series of six lithographs, each 17 × 21 cm. See Dube, Annemarie and Wolf-Dieter, *E.L. Kirchner. Das graphische Werke*, 2 vols (Munich: Prestel, 1967), cat. 185–190.

30. This is particularly apparent in cat. 188.

31. I am indebted to Sander Gilman for first bringing my attention to this phenomenon in the context of nineteenth-century French art in his *Difference and Pathology* (Ithaca, 1985).

32. H. Ellis, *Studies in the Psychology of Sex*, 2 vols., (New York: Random House, 1942), vol. 1, part 3, p. 165.

33. Ploss and Bartels, *Woman. An Historical, Gynaecological and Anthropological Compendium*, trans. by Eric Dingwall (London: Heinemann, 1935), p. 304.

NOTES ON CONTRIBUTORS

Christy Anderson held a Research Fellowship at Worcester College, Oxford, and is currently Assistant Professor at Yale University. Her books, *Inigo Jones: Books and Buildings in the English Renaissance*, and *European Architecture 1400–1600*, are currently in press.

Esther de Costa Meyer is Assistant Professor in the Department of Art and Archaeology at Princeton University. She is the author of *The Work of Antonio Sant'Elia: Retreat into the Future*; her articles have appeared in *Assemblage*, *Modernism/Modernity* and *New German Critique*.

Louise Durning is Senior Lecturer in the Department of History of Art at Oxford Brookes University. Her *Gender Perspectives in Architectural History: a Working Bibliography* (Humanities Research Centre, Oxford Brookes University) appeared in 1995. Her article in the current volume forms part of a larger project on 'Gender and Space in English Collegiate Architecture'.

Helen Hills is Lecturer in Art History at Manchester University. She is the author of *Invenzione ed Identità: Marmi Mischi Siciliani* (Archivio Storico Messinese Scholarly Monograph Series, 1999). She is preparing *Constructing Devotion: Architectural Patronage of Female Convents in Southern Italy* for publication with Oxford University Press. Her article for the present volume was written while she held a J. Paul Getty Postdoctoral Fellowship in the History of Art and the Humanities.

Tanis Hinchcliffe is Senior Lecturer in the School of the Built Environment at the University of Westminster. Her publications include *North Oxford* (Yale University Press, 1992), and articles on eighteenth-century French architectural theory, nineteenth-century English suburbs, and twentieth-century housing history.

Reina Lewis is Senior Lecturer in the Department of Cultural Studies at the University of East London. She is the author of *Gendering Orientalism: Race, Femininity, and Representation* (Routledge: London, 1996), and co-editor, with Peter Horne, of *Outlooks: Lesbian and Gay Sexualities and Visual Culture* (Routledge: London, 1996).

Joanne Mosley's doctoral thesis was 'A Critical Edition of Arnaud Sorbin's *Vie de Charles IX* (1574)' (Oxford Brookes University).

Jane Rendell is an architect and architectural historian, and is Lecturer at the University of Nottingham. Her book *The Pursuit of Pleasure* is to be published by Athlone Press. She has co-edited *Strangely Familiar* (Routledge: London, 1995),

Gender, Space, Architecture (Routledge: London, 1999), and the forthcoming volume, *Intersections: Architectural History and Critical Theory* (Athlone Press: London).

Colin Rhodes is Reader in Art History and Theory at Loughborough University. His publications include *Primitivism and Modern Art* (Thames & Hudson, 1994), Outsider Art: Spontaneous Alternatives (Thames & Hudson, 2000) monographs on the contemporary British sculptor Dave Morris and artist Ian Breakwell, and a film on expressionism for the Dutch Open University.

Richard Wrigley is Principal Lecturer in the Department of History of Art at Oxford Brookes University. He is the author of *The Origins of French Art Criticism: from the Ancien Regime to the Restoration* (Oxford: Oxford University Press, 1993), and has published on aspects of the visual culture of the French Revolution, and medical aspects of Italian travel. He is currently preparing a monograph on *The Politics of Appearances: the Symbolism and Representation of Dress in Revolutionary France* for publication.

ACKNOWLEDGEMENTS

We would like to thank all those who attended and helped organize the conference on *Gender and Architecture*, held at the Humanities Research Centre, Oxford Brookes University, which led, ultimately, to this volume. Tristram Palmer made a positive editorial contribution to the early stages of the project. We wish to acknowledge the kind co-operation of the British Library in the provision of illustrations for Reina Lewis's chapter. Esther da Costa Meyer's chapter is, in slightly revised form reprinted from *Assemblage*, with the permission of Massachussetts Institute of Technology Press. We have made every effort to obtain copyright permissions where relevant. We are especially grateful to Karen Knorr for allowing us to use one of her photographs for the cover (and to Christy Anderson for help in setting this up). We are extremely grateful to those owners of copyright who have generously chosen to waive fees. We are also very grateful to Erica Davies of the Freud Museum, London, for her timely help. Many thanks to Louise Portsmouth, Maggie Toy and Lewis Derrick at John Wiley for their help in seeing the text to press. Finally, and most importantly, we are lucky to have had such an efficient, encouraging and above all patient group of authors to work with.

Oxford and Shepherds Bush
February 2000

Index

(Page numbers in *italics* refer to *figures*).

Index compiled by George Curzon, Indexing Specialists, Hove, UK